Pressures on the Press

HILLIER KRIEGHBAUM

Pressures on the Press

THOMAS Y. CROWELL COMPANY
NEW YORK   ESTABLISHED 1834

Other Books by Hillier Krieghbaum

American Newspaper Reporting of Science News

Facts in Perspective

When Doctors Meet Reporters

Science, the News and the Public

The Student Journalist: A Handbook for Staff and Adviser (with Edmund C. Arnold)

Science and the Mass Media

To Improve Secondary School Science and Mathematics Teaching (with Hugh Rawson)

An Investment in Knowledge (with Hugh Rawson)

Designed by Abigail Moseley

Manufactured in the United States of America

L.C. Card 78-182809
ISBN 0-690-65459-6

1 2 3 4 5 6 7 8 9 10

For Kay and Kay-K

Contents

1   "Without an Informed and Free Press" / *1*

2   The Accelerating Caterwaul of Criticism / *7*

3   The Nixon Administration and the Media / *24*

4   Freedom—and Responsibility—for Media / *45*

5   The Rules of "Thou Shalt" and "Thou Shalt Not" / *58*

6   Pressure Points for Managing the News / *78*

7   Breaking Out of the Straitjackets
of Journalistic Practices / *98*

8   Cluttering Up the News Picture / *119*

9   Mass Media as Big Business / *141*

10   The Threat of One-Newspaper Towns—and All That / *155*

11   The Impact of Pressure Groups: Real and Synthetic / *170*

12   The Right to Privacy Versus Publicity for Profit / *191*

13   Who's to Keep the Media's Conscience? / *217*

   For Further Reading / *239*

   Index / *240*

1. "Without an Informed and Free Press"

The mass media have many roles assigned to them but one that seems to be increasingly frequent is to receive the criticisms of political figures, social commentators, and various members of the general public that they serve.

An adversary relationship with government figures goes back as far as print has been a common channel for public information, but the infighting has escalated significantly in degree and in kind during the past decade, and especially during the Nixon Administration. The press (which I use to include both print and broadcasting) now is blamed routinely for sins both real and synthetic. Others with a special stake in the *status quo* have joined in. Readers, listeners, and viewers—some for good reasons and some for little more than emotional scapegoating—have poured vitriol on media performances.

If our democratic society is to survive under the vast tensions to which it is currently subjected, then the American people have not only the right, but the overwhelming need, to know the facts. As news coverage is spreading into new fields, the gathering and disseminating of information to the mass audiences becomes more and more demanding. Thus, the people must understand some of the real pressures on the press—beyond those articulated by politicians and other self-serving critics. This book seeks to illuminate these various areas so that news as printed and as broadcast will have more significance for its "consumers" and less bias and prejudice.

Among its various roles as an essential social institution, the press has the centuries-old assignment to serve as watchdog of government. In fact, until the twentieth century, that seemed to be its most important task. But now, in addition to the job of exposing what officials are doing, both well and badly, newsmen have to keep their audiences abreast of the world's happenings, so that they have the information they need not only for decision-making in a democratic society but sometimes for every-day living, as well as for sheer enjoyment and fun.

In the manipulative processes of trying to create a favorable public opinion or, as it has been called recently, "image making," public officials have collided often with reporters seeking news items. Inevitably, there have been conflicts. If there were no frictions between newsmen and politicians, it would indicate either a breakdown in the media's long-time role as watchdog or the widespread selection of angels for jobs in both groups. In these contests, one conventional reaction was to find somebody or some institution with whom to share—or even unload all—the blame. Both government and media have tried this procedure. Yet the media's duty is clear, as Justice Potter Stewart wrote in his concurring opinion in *New York Times Co. v. United States* (1971):

> In the absence of the governmental checks and balances present in other areas of our national life, the only effective restraint upon executive policy and power in the area of national defense and international affairs may lie in an enlightened citizenry—in an informed and critical public opinion which alone can here protect the values of democratic government. For this reason, it is perhaps here that a press that is alert, aware, and free most vitally serves the basic purpose of the First Amendment. For without an informed and free press there cannot be an enlightened people.

While contests and competitions between politicians and reporters have occurred since George Washington's day, many observers of media and most newsmen feel that the struggles during the past decade and especially during the administration of Richard M. Nixon have been far more sophisticated and, from the press's standpoint, almost Machiavellian and mischievous. No longer is there the polite bow before combat, and brass knuckles occasionally are visible. No one can claim that either politics or media performance is above criticism. They definitely are not. However, they are both part of the mortar that keeps contemporary society —any modern societal organization—together. Thus those who attack may be wrenching the social fabric. All of which is not a plea to be silent but a request to count the consequences.

★ John S. Knight, editorial chairman of the newspaper group that bears his name, said during a 1970 talk to the International Mailers Union convention at Akron:

> The government, which has long suffered from a credibility gap of its own, is now attempting under the Nixon administration to destroy the credibility of what you read and hear.

★ Jules Witcover, veteran Washington correspondent now with the *Los Angeles Times* bureau there, wrote this evaluation in the *Columbia Journalism Review* (Spring, 1970):

> He [Herbert Klein, President Nixon's Director of Communications for the Executive Branch of the Federal Government] has installed the most imaginative and effective system yet seen in Washington for putting an Administration's best foot forward on a continuing basis. The operation is much more astute than diabolical. It takes advantage of opportunities that earlier government public relations chiefs have ignored, and it undoubtedly increases public knowledge of what the Administration is saying. But it is an exercise in propaganda, and the same hand that pushes open doors wraps Administration ideas and men in the most appealing packages.

★ Rep. Ogden R. Reid, Republican from Westchester County, N.Y., and former president and editor of the *New York Herald Tribune,* made this comment immediately after the Supreme Court had upheld *The New York Times'* right to publish the Pentagon Papers in mid-1971:

> At least two Administrations, if not three, believed that they were not accountable to the Congress and the American people for watershed decisions taken about Indochina.
>
> The present Administration has gone even further and launched the most serious attack on the press in our history: subpoenaing reporters' notes, threatening reprisals against television and radio stations under the power to license, and, for the first time nationally, invoking prior restraint against the right to publish.

★ Ben H. Bagdikian, *Washington Post* assistant managing editor for national news, wrote in *Columbia Journalism Review* (September/October, 1971):

> Government antagonism to the press is not new or bad. The press shouldn't expect to be loved. . . . But this Administration has a special attitude toward the working press that is ideological and cultural, it has a political stake in spreading hatred of the metropolitan press, and unlike other administrations that fought with the press this one has an itch for the jugular.

★ James Reston, associate editor and columnist of *The New York Times,* wrote:

> This conflict between the Government and the press is only a symbol of a much larger and more serious problem. There has always been a certain amount of deception between the executive and legislative branches, but it has been much worse under Presidents Johnson and Nixon and suspicion grows on itself. For years now, we have not had that feeling of honest differences openly faced and plainly discussed which is essential even in adversary proceedings. Almost everybody in Washington is looking for the other motive or the dirty trick.

★ Fred Powledge reported in a study for the American Civil Liberties Union in late 1971 that he found the Nixon Administration engaging in "the engineering of restraint" in its public information policies. Government–press relations almost always had been adversary, he wrote, but then he continued:

> In recent years, though, that relationship has deteriorated. The federal government has sought to change the rules of the old game. Attacks on the press by officers of government have become so widespread and all-pervasive that they constitute a massive federal-level attempt to subvert the letter and the spirit of the First Amendment. . . .
> The most significant result of the attacks, so far, has not been a series of court and administrative rulings permanently restraining the freedom of the press; for, although the administration is attempting to obtain such restraints, it has, in one sense, so far failed. Rather, it has been the subtle tendency—almost impossible to document or measure—of the press itself to pull back; to consider the controversial-

ity of its actions before it takes them, and then, in some cases, not to take those actions—to engage in self-censorship.

The Washington News Committee of the Associated Press Managing Editors told its annual convention in October 1971, "No President in modern times has so consciously isolated himself from the press." The committee report also said that Mr. Nixon had "found a way to raise questions on the credibility of the press" in responses at most of his recent press conferences.

These and similar comments certainly can not all be dismissed as "essentially knee-jerk reaction," the phrase used by Franklin B. Smith in the *Burlington* (Vt.) *Free Press* to characterize his fellow newspapermen's support of the right of *The New York Times* and other papers to publish the classified Pentagon Papers.

Just what is the background to this fervent criticism?

Vice-President Spiro T. Agnew in a speech at Des Moines, Iowa, on Nov. 13, 1969, pointed out the capacity of the "privileged men" of television—the news announcers and commentators—to influence U.S. public opinion and called upon his nationwide audience of listeners to "let the networks know that they want their news straight and objective." The response was so resounding that news programing has not been quite the same since that speech. Later that same month, the Vice-President expanded his attacks to include print, naming *The New York Times* and the *Washington Post* for what he considered journalistic derelictions in performance.

More than a year and a half later, after most of the 2,500,000 words of the Pentagon Papers had been "leaked," as it were, to a number of daily newspapers, the Department of Justice went into court to halt publication of news stories and analyses based on these still "top secret" documents about how the United States became involved in the Southeast Asian war. In record time, the case rocketed to decision by the U.S. Supreme Court after special sessions for arguments. In a short "per curiam," a majority of six justices held that the government had not persuasively established a right for prior restraint on publication. However, so diverse was the legal support and dissent to this conclusion that each of the nine justices wrote his own opinion to state his rationale.

Also before the courts and Congress during the late 1960's and early 1970's was the privilege of either print and broadcast reporters to refuse to turn over notes, film, and recordings of news sources. Eventually a case involving the refusal of Earl Caldwell, a black newsman for *The New York Times,* to hand over notes and tapes of his interviews with Black Panther leaders reached the Ninth Circuit Court of Appeals. The judges held that a newsman could be ordered to provide such information only when "a compelling and overriding national interest" could be served by no other alternative means. Newsgatherers, it was held, could not lightly be converted into Department of Justice investigators.

Congress faced much the same issue when the Columbia Broadcasting System refused to turn over untelevised materials from the production of its controversial program, "The Selling of the Pentagon." In July 1971, the House of Representatives declined to hold CBS and its president, Dr. Frank Stanton, in contempt of Congress by a vote of 226 to 181.

Attacks on the media as social institutions, needless subpoenas, and court injunctions to prevent publication may generate two reactions that could effectively change the role of print and broadcasting in the United States: (1) They could downgrade the generally high status that media have enjoyed until fairly recently and (2) they could instill fear in the minds of news sources upon whom reporters depend to obtain information. Opinion polls in the past have shown a public approval of media performance far higher than that of churchmen, law enforcement officers, and politicians, either local or national. Now a ferment seems to be at work and the media face mounting public disapproval and a serious weakening of their ability to function. Nixon Administration spokesmen insist that the Vice-President and Attorney General were not seeking to install some sort of news censorship but simply that they wanted to promote better news dissemination in a democratic society.

Probably the critical (and, at times, predictably caustic) comments and condemnation of contemporary press performances have not yet reached a crescendo. And one should always remember that there is no sound reason why media should be exempt from such evaluative observations and remarks as editorial writers and commentators often shower on other social institutions. However, a more useful exchange may take place if certain background and guidelines are kept in focus. As Persian generals knew, it is easy to have the bearer of bad tidings killed; but that would not solve the problems that confront the United States today.

2. The Accelerating Caterwaul of Criticism

During the early days of this country, partisan attacks on politicians and their journalistic supporters were commonplace and the uninhibited style of that period makes contemporary criticisms sound almost like mild compliments. The modern day comments, however, have had massive impact because the remarks touched a responsive feeling of vague disenchantment with all the media among much of the public and because they followed a long era when journalists, especially those of the print media, assumed a lofty position of being above the battle concerning possible misconduct by their fellows. Editors and commentators repeatedly told the world's and nation's leaders how to run their provinces, suggested improvements in business conduct and general professional ethics, advised on social reforms and new legislation, and told the public how to vote and what to think, but they wrote hardly a line on what their colleagues might be doing, particularly if they disapproved. The silence had something of the smell of a conspiracy, albeit a tacit one. Into this easy and particularly sanctified atmosphere came the criticisms of recent years, notably with the speeches by Vice-President Spiro T. Agnew, followed by the issuance of subpoenas for newsmen to appear before grand juries, and the Department of Justice's injunctions to stop publication of the Pentagon Papers.

There are subtle but observable differences between the flamboyant name-calling of the post-Revolutionary editors (and even the individualized attacks of the late Senator Joseph McCarthy of Wisconsin in the 1950's) and the blunderbuss broadsides that hit media as an institution in modern society. For instance, when the Vice-President cited television's "tiny enclosed fraternity of privileged men," instead of enumerating commentators by name, he indulged in sweeping generalizations—inherently difficult to refute completely. In his second speech, concerning print, Mr. Agnew was much more specific and cited *The New York Times, Washington Post,* and their communications affiliates.

To illustrate the early rambunctiousness, Benjamin Franklin Bache, who was nicknamed "Lightning Rod Junior" in honor of his famous grandparent, struck out at Noah Webster, editor of a rival Federalist paper, as a "jackall of the British faction." Then he added, "If ever a man prostituted the little sense that he had, to serve the purposes of a monarchic and aristocratic junto, Noah Webster, Esq., must be the man." Two days after John Adams' inauguration to succeed George Washington as U.S. president, Bache printed, "If ever there was a period of rejoicing this is the moment—every heart, in unison with the freedom and happiness of the people ought to beat high with exultation, that the name of WASHINGTON from this day ceases to give currency to political iniquity, and to legalize corruption. . . . Such however are the facts, and with these staring us in the face, this day ought to be a JUBILEE in the United States." William Cobbett, a Federalist editor, called Bache's paper a "vehicle of lies and sedition."

George Washington was not only the first U.S. president but also the first to manage the news for his administration's advantage. For instance, his annoyance with most press coverage and his desire to ensure a favorable response for his Farewell Address led him to provide a copy of the document to a friendly publisher who he knew would give it prominent display. His successors have been using varying, but equally effective, techniques ever since.

When Thomas Jefferson wanted to present his viewpoints without interference from hostile critics, especially in the press, he and his associates founded newspapers in the various states that were edited and controlled by party faithful. Andrew Jackson had Amos Kendall, his own news advisor and a key member of the presidential "Kitchen Cabinet," put on the federal payroll as a junior official in the Treasury Department. Of Kendall, formerly a Kentucky editor, a congressman of the time said, "He was the President's *thinking* machine, and his *writing* machine—ay, and his *lying* machine!" Despite the demands on his time during the Civil War, Abraham Lincoln wrote a reply to an editorial page argument by Horace Greeley of the *New York Tribune* so promptly that Greeley apologized for taking up the President's time and attention. Lincoln also would give his confidants news tips and items with instructions to pass them along "for use or guidance of the *Tribune*." Henry J. Raymond, founder of *The New York Times* and generally a Lincoln supporter, was a frequent White House visitor during those crowded war years.

Throughout much of the nineteenth century, newspaper editors were concerned primarily with how to gather news and how to influence opinions toward the politics they favored and supported. In return, there were few attacks on the conduct of the press; always there was a chance for eventual conversion and editorial endorsements in the future.

There were two conspicuous exceptions when dailies explored new depths of sensationalism. James Gordon Bennett, Sr., and later William Randolph Hearst were denounced by religious leaders and others who felt that they had to keep the public conscience alert to new vulgarities. Both told more about illicit sex relations in high society and sordid police court news than their conservative journalistic rivals, who took broad swipes at the new styles in reporting. In no cases did these comments turn the general public against the media.

Not until the twentieth century did newsmen have regular access to a U.S. president and thus obtain some chance of learning what was on his mind. This closer contact brought a chance of incurring an executive's personal displeasure. Presidents were never completely happy with their press relations. Theodore Roosevelt picked out favorite reporters and met them informally at the White House, sometimes while he was shaving. He used the newsmen to launch "trial balloons"; if the public rejected the ideas so advanced, the President disowned them, much to the distress of reporters.

Woodrow Wilson, the professor and college president from Princeton, held the first regular, formal presidential press conferences. Author of a series of books on government and how it should operate, he worked hard to put across his ideas, preparing, he said later, "as carefully as for any lecture." Wilson launched the off-the-record remark during his White House years and would preface such a comment with "Now this is just for background." However, his assessment of the Washington news corps was not flattering: "Some men of brilliant ability were in the group, but I soon discovered that the interest of the majority was in the personal and trivial rather than in principles and policies."

Franklin D. Roosevelt established the pattern for news conferences which has continued into the 1970's with some modifications in specific details but not in major concepts. Roosevelt abolished written questions in advance and took the reporters' queries as they were asked orally. The New Deal President so delighted capital correspondents at his first session with them that they applauded him and the newly announced ground rules, a completely unprecedented gesture of approval. Yet before he completed his total of 998 news conferences, he had long been unhappy with the media's performances. For instance, he was so outraged during the early war years at one negative dispatch which he thought hurt recruiting women for the U.S. Army that he attempted to award a Nazi Iron Cross to its author. However, the writer failed to show up that day at the White House news conference.

An early ripple in what seems to be becoming a tidal wave of modern criticism about U.S. media came with a speech by Adlai Stevenson, then the Democratic candidate for president, on Sept. 8, 1952, in Portland, Oregon. Stevenson was concerned about the "one-party press," as he called it, and its potential dangers. The almost monolithic support of Republican presidential hopefuls for the right to live in 1600 Pennsylvania Avenue had been bothering newspaper professionals for years but the Democratic presidential candidate brought this shop talk to public attention when he made these comments after some formal bows to the press' impact:

> I am in favor of a two-party system in politics. And I think we have a pretty healthy two-party system at this moment. But I am in favor of a two-party system in our press too. And I am, frankly, considerably concerned when I see the extent to which we are developing a one-party press in a two-party country. . . .
>
> But, as an ex-newspaper man and as a citizen, I am gravely concerned about the implications of this one-party system for our American press and our free society.
>
> A free society means a society based on free competition and there is no more important competition than competition in ideas, competition in opinion. This form of competition is essential to the preservation of a free press. Indeed, I think the press should set an example to the nation in increasing opposition to uniformity.

I think you will agree that we cannot risk complacency. We need to be rededicated every day to the unfinished task of keeping our free press truly free. We need to work harder for the time when all editors will honor their profession, when all publishers will have a sense of responsibility equal to their power and thus regain their power, if I may put it that way.

It's not honest convictions honestly stated that concern me. Rather it is the tendency of many papers, and I include columnists, commentators, analysts, feature writers and so on, to argue editorially from the personal objective, rather than from the whole truth.

As the old jury lawyer said: "And these, gentlemen, are the conclusions on which I base my facts."

In short, it seems to me that facts, truth, should be just as sacred in the editorial column as the news column. And, as I have said, happily most papers, but by no means all, do struggle with sincerity for accuracy in the news. Coming from Chicago, of course, I am not unfamiliar with the phenomenon of an editorial in every news column!

During that same decade of the 1950's, the late Senator McCarthy turned his investigating eyes toward the media, citing specific persons that he suspected might have been Communists or associates of such groups. As one who lived by publicity, he curbed much of his oratory in relation to the media as an institution. He had much to lose if he antagonized those controlling the main streams of communication.

However, McCarthy did, over the years, force the managers of media to reexamine their own standards of performance and to begin facing up to some of the blatant weaknesses of their own professional techniques. Eventually, many of them came to realize that it was not enough just to report accurately what an individual said, regardless of whether what he said was true or false. It was, in a way, a nose-to-nose confrontation with the realistic requirements of objectivity and fairness. Previously journalists had done a lot of talking, some of it rather loosely, but now they had to face up to the reality that a prominent individual, with senatorial privilege, could make virtually any statement that he wanted to. What did the reporter do if a senator's facts were in doubt—or obviously wrong? Rapidly, it dawned on an increasing number of people that just playing back what an individual said might not be the sole requirement of fair and honest journalism. As Elmer Davis, broadcaster and commentator, said at the time, this kind of playback journalism—"so and so said it, and if he's lying in his teeth it isn't my business to say so"—could salve a newsman's conscience as well as his devotion to objectivity. "But what about his loyalty to the reader?" Some newsmen, even in the 1970's, were still working out their answers to these questions, unfortunately for the readers and listeners.

The assassination of President John F. Kennedy in Dallas and the "live" shooting of Lee Harvey Oswald on television two days later had profound consequences on journalistic practices. At best, print and broadcast performances left something to be desired, as hundreds of newsmen arrived in Dallas. Their conduct provided critics of media with specific illustrations to document what they thought was wrong with media. Now millions of Americans had seen at least some of the press' actions on television and heard or read volumes of comments, much of them critical.

The presidential commission headed by the then Chief Justice Earl Warren complained, bitterly many journalists thought, about the newsmen's conduct during that tragic weekend. Reporters in Dallas faced intense competition to obtain news from any source and by almost any means. With the world spotlight on them, Dallas police and law enforcement officers often needed scant prodding before they yielded information for media dissemination. Certainly it is true that if the press men and broadcasters had not provided news, some of which turned out to be erroneous, wilder rumors undoubtedly would have filled the gaps. To the press' credit, the Warren Commission, with nearly a year to do its investigating —as compared with the hours or, at most, days for the news media— turned up no spectacular finding that had eluded the newsmen in Dallas during the week following the shootings.

However, with real validity, the Warren Commission did cite the legal implications of such massive press coverage. Among the comments in the Commission's report were these:

> . . . the right of the public to know does not give the press license to interfere with the efficient operation of law enforcement agencies. . . .

> It was therefore proper and desirable that the public know which agencies were participating in the investigation and the rate at which their work was progressing. The public was also entitled to know that Lee Harvey Oswald had been apprehended and that the State had gathered sufficient evidence to arraign him for the murders of the President and Patrolman Tippit, that he was being held pending action of the grand jury, that the investigation was continuing, and that the law enforcement agencies had discovered no evidence which tended to show that any other person was involved in either slaying.

However, neither the press nor the public had a right to be contemporaneously informed by the police or prosecuting authorities of the details of the evidence being accumulated against Oswald. Undoubtedly the public was interested in these disclosures, but its curiosity should not have been satisfied at the expense of the accused's right to a trial by an impartial jury. The courtroom, not the newspaper or television screen, is the appropriate forum in our system for the trial of a man accused of a crime. . . .

The general disorder in the Police and Courts Building during November 22-24 reveals a regrettable lack of self-discipline by the newsmen. The Commission believes that the news media, as well as the police authorities, who failed to impose conditions more in keeping with the orderly process of justice, must share responsibility for the failure of law enforcement which occurred in connection with the death of Oswald. . . .

The experience in Dallas during November 22-24 is a dramatic affirmation of the need for steps to bring about a proper balance between the right of the public to be informed and the right of the individual to a fair and impartial trial.

In the vernacular, "It takes two to tango," and if officials want to safeguard the rights of an accused, they should restrain themselves. The bulk of the blame for such threats to justice belongs with lawyers and law enforcers, not newsmen.

Properly the Warren Commission report put a considerable portion of blame for the press' activities with the Dallas police and law enforcement officers. One should never forget that a cooperating news source among officialdom will almost inevitably be the first sought by any experienced reporter. This is one of the prevailing practices of the business of news gathering. A noncompliant news source may not dry up the supply of information for long but he certainly can put the operation on another level of difficulty.

After a year-long investigation, the Press-Bar Committee of the American Society of Newspaper Editors reported in the spring of 1965 that it could not accept many of the Warren Commission's major conclusions about the media's performance after the Dallas shootings. The press-oriented group said that the newsmen acted, not as instigators, but as reporters of what actually took place. False reports, it was claimed, originated with the official sources and were not created by press and broadcast representatives.

Although it was, in a major sense, an anticlimax, the trial of Jack Ruby on the charge of slaying Oswald focused attention again on media performances, which again left something to be desired for many individuals concerned with fair trial and press professionalism. John Kaplan and Jon R. Waltz in *The Trial of Jack Ruby* (Macmillan, 1965) relate this incident about Alice Nichols, Ruby's ex-girl friend, after she had testified at his trial:

> Just as she left the courtroom, the flashbulbs began exploding in her face, and this additional stress was enough to destroy her brittle composure. She broke into tears and struggled to get away from the pursuing photographers. She ran out of the courthouse and down the steps, followed by a shouting mob of some twenty photographers snapping pictures all the way. They had been told to get a picture of Ruby's girl friend and this they intended to do. Finally, about a half a block from the courthouse, the strange procession ended when Miss Nichols, out of breath, permitted herself to be surrounded by her pursuers, who snapped picture after picture as she sobbed and shouted incoherently.

As a result of all these criticisms, the media became a convenient scapegoat for those who were unhappy or discontented with coverage that they, their friends, their favorite causes, and their own institutions and professions had received. Seeds for much of the disenchantment with the mass media were sown during the months and years following the assassination of President Kennedy and the shooting of Lee Harvey Oswald despite the fact that the fair trial–free press controversy had been around, to a lesser extent, since the trial and conviction of Bruno Richard Hauptmann for the kidnapping death of Charles A. Lindbergh, Jr.

Just how deep the antimedia feelings ran was demonstrated when former President Dwight D. Eisenhower received an unexpected (to him, at least) ovation at the Republican convention in San Francisco in 1964 when he said:

> . . . let us particularly scorn the divisive efforts of those outside our [Republican] family, including the sensation-seeking columnists and commentators, because, my friends, I assure you they couldn't care less about the good of our party.

In the demonstration following these remarks, some of the convention delegates shook their fists at the newsmen sitting in the nearby sections reserved for media.

Two responses grew out of the Warren Commission's findings: (1) Renewed interest in a second petition to the U.S. Supreme Court by Dr. Sam Sheppard that his constitutional right to a fair trial had been prejudiced by the press coverage prior to and during his 1954 conviction for slaying his wife, Marilyn, and (2) formation of an Advisory Committee on Fair Trial and Free Press by the American Bar Association under Associate Justice Paul C. Reardon of the Supreme Judicial Court of Massachusetts.

The Supreme Court had denied Dr. Sheppard a writ of certiorari on Nov. 13, 1956, and thus refused to review his case. When a second petition reached the justices on Nov. 15, 1965, almost exactly two years after the Kennedy and Oswald shootings, they readily agreed to review the Sheppard conviction.

The Supreme Court's majority opinion cited approvingly this quotation from the findings of Judge James F. Bell's opinion for the Ohio Supreme Court:

> Murder and mystery, society, sex and suspense were combined in this case in such a manner as to intrigue and captivate the public fancy to a degree perhaps unparalleled in recent annals. Throughout the preindictment investigation, the subsequent legal skirmishes and the nine-week trial, circulation-conscious editors catered to the insatiable interest of the American public in the bizarre. . . . In this atmosphere of a "Roman holiday" for the news media, Sam Sheppard stood trial for his life.

Dr. Sheppard's case had virtually all of the lures of sensational journalism and much of the media did not resist them. For instance, the majority court opinion cited publication of much material "never heard from the witness stand," some of which undoubtedly reached at least some of the jurors, including "a front-page picture of Mrs. Sheppard's blood-stained pillow [which] was published after being 'doctored' to show more clearly an alleged imprint of a surgical instrument," and repeated front-page headlines such as "Quit Stalling—Bring Him In," "Why Isn't Sam Sheppard in Jail?" and "But Who Will Speak for Marilyn?"

The opinion commented:

> The fact is that bedlam reigned at the courthouse during the trial and newsmen took over practically the entire courtroom, hounding most of the participants in the trial, especially Sheppard.
>
> . . . every court that has considered this case, save the court

that tried it, has deplored the manner in which the news media inflamed and prejudiced the public. . . .

The carnival atmosphere at trial could easily have been avoided since the courtroom and courtroom premises are subject to the control of the court. . . .

The fact that many of the prejudicial news items can be traced to the prosecution, as well as the defense, aggravates the judge's failure to take any action. Effective control of these sources—concededly within the court's power—might well have prevented the divulgence of inaccurate information, rumors, and accusations that made up much of the inflammatory publicity, at least after Sheppard's indictment. . . .

Due process requires that the accused receive a trial by an impartial jury free from outside influences. Given the pervasiveness of modern communications and the difficulty of effacing prejudicial publicity from the minds of jurors, the trial courts must take strong measures to ensure that the balance is never weighed against the accused. . . . Of course, there is nothing that proscribes the press from reporting events that transpire in the courtroom. But where there is a reasonable likelihood that prejudicial news prior to trial will prevent a fair trial, the judge should continue the case until the threat abates or transfer it to another county not so permeated with publicity. . . . If publicity during the proceedings threatens the fairness of the trial, a new trial should be ordered. But we must remember that reversals are but palliatives; the cure lies in those remedial measures that will prevent the prejudice at its inception.

Dr. Sheppard was ordered to a second trial, at which he was acquitted. Although there was no mistaking the thrust for trial judges to manage their own courtrooms, Justice Tom Clark, who wrote the Supreme Court's majority opinion, insisted in interviews that there was "no collision whatsoever" between a fair trial and the press arising from his decision. But many attorneys were not so sure that it did not provide a potential precedent for curtailing coverage of criminal court sessions or possibly even for closed hearings—if media coverage might jeopardize a defendant's right to a fair trial.

In December 1966, after more than a year's work, the ABA fair trial–free press group released its tentative draft of standards for legal and journalistic practices. After discussions by both attorneys and journalists, a "Proposed Final Draft" was released in December 1967, and it was approved two months later by the ABA House of Delegates. Most lawyers and some journalists praised ABA efforts to arrange its own business by imposing restraints on statements to the media by police and other law and court officials but practically all news professionals feared the use of contempt powers against errant press and broadcast procedures. A week after the ABA House of Delegates' approval of the "Proposed Final Draft," the Judicial Conference of the United States, an administrative branch of the federal judiciary, rejected any direct curbs on the media as unwise and posing serious constitutional questions in connection with the First Amendment guarantee of freedom to the press and also refused to approve proposals to bar reporters from portions of pretrial hearings and from criminal trials.

Thus the free press–fair trial discussions moved from the national level to the local scene where judges, bar associations, journalists, and media groups contemplate the havoc they may create by their own misconduct and attempt to do something about it. Some cases that seemed to border on Star Chamber proceedings were reported and when these got into higher courts, frequently in actions initiated by publishers and broadcasters, the judges often turned to the dicta stated in the U.S. Supreme Court decision in *Craig v. Harney* (1947): "A trial is a public event. What transpires in the court room is public property."

During the trial of Sirhan B. Sirhan for the shooting of Senator Robert F. Kennedy in Los Angeles, Judge Herbert V. Walker admitted that "the court cannot suppress anything from the press if they want to get it." He pointed out any danger for the defendant was lessened since the jurors were sequestered "in the tightest security" and their reading matter was censored and broadcast programs to which they listened were monitored. As one associated with Sirhan's defense staff wrote later, "Now Judge Walker was saying that the time had come to tell the world. It was another frank admission from Walker that the trial was being played to world opinion as much as, perhaps even more than, to the jury." Reporting of celebrated murder trials, it was obvious, might be used for building audience interest in broadcasts and news dispatches but it also could be used to influence world opinion—or possibly voters the next time the judge or prosecuting attorney was running for reelection. These nonjournalistic aspects were not always mentioned prominently by lawyers when they spoke or wrote on the topic of fair trial and free press.

Press conference statements by Mayor Samuel Yorty of Los Angeles after the death of Senator Kennedy in June 1968 illustrated how a public official may contribute far more than the media to potential damage to a defendant's rights to a fair trial. Sirhan B. Sirhan was detained at the scene of the shooting by Kennedy bodyguards and onlookers and then held under rigorous security guard. The Los Angeles police chief, Thomas Reddin, with due regard for protecting Sirhan's legal rights, refused to answer newsmen's questions. But Mayor Yorty told reporters about two notebooks found at the suspect's home which read, "Kennedy must be assassinated before June 5, 68," the anniversary of the beginning of the Arab-Israeli "six day" war. At another news conference, Yorty released further entries from Sirhan's diary and said that it disclosed the suspect's definite "Communist inclinations."

In talking with newsmen in early August 1970, President Richard M. Nixon remarked that Charles Manson was "guilty, directly or indirectly," while the hippie cultist was on trial in Los Angeles in connection with eight slayings, including that of actress Sharon Tate. His comments were made during a briefing at the Federal Court Building in Denver just before he met more than a hundred federal and state officials attending a conference on crime control sponsored by the Law Enforcement Assistance Administration. The President said the media had a role in maintaining respect for law and justice and then added:

> I noted, for example, the coverage of the Charles Manson case when I was in Los Angeles, front page every day in the papers. It usually got a couple of minutes in the evening news. Here is a man who was guilty, directly or indirectly, of eight murders without reason.

Later the presidential press secretary issued a statement for Mr. Nixon which included:

> My remarks were in the context of my expression of a tendency on the part of some to glamorize those identified with a crime.
>
> The last thing I would do is prejudice the legal rights of any person in any circumstances.
>
> To set the record straight, I do not know and did not intend to speculate as to whether the Tate defendants are guilty, in fact, or not. All of the facts in the case have not yet been presented. The defendants should be presumed to be innocent at this stage of the trial.

While attorneys and journalists were arguing about their respective rights and responsibilities, newsmen covering the escalating war in Vietnam were involved in a far noisier confrontation between inquiring reporters and reluctant government (especially military) officials. It was a collision between individuals who claimed they supported the people's right to know and those who argued for curtailments in the name of national or military security.

Coverage of the Southeast Asia war developed, eventually, into a contest between officials in Washington, in Saigon, and at the fighting fronts who sought to put the most optimistic interpretations on what was happening because they had a vested interest in success, and war correspondents and Pentagon reporters who believed that their chief responsibility was to tell what they saw. It wasn't often a case of either deliberate repression (although there was some of that) or conscious exaggeration (although as it came out in the United States there was some of that, too). The military argued that some of the information sent out from Vietnam served no national objectives as they saw them and possibly harmed the United States "image." Newsmen said that they simply held the mirror up to events and if the pictures came out badly for their country it was the government, not they, who should do something about it. Name-calling reached its peak under the Johnson presidency as the war escalated until more than half a million U.S. troops were in the field.

Starting in 1962, while John F. Kennedy was still president, a cadre of newsmen in Saigon began reporting Vietnamese developments that were far less optimistic than those cited in the official documents and public statements from Saigon or Washington. (Incidentally, when the Pentagon Papers were published in 1971, they revealed that even private government reports supported the gloomy view of the correspondents.) Shortly a real credibility gap developed and as the fighting mounted, so did the differences as to what was the truth. Among the correspondents who were denounced by officials as little short of unpatriotic and not members of "the team" were Homer Bigart and David Halberstam of *The New York Times;* Malcolm W. Browne and Peter Arnett of the Associated Press; Neil Sheehan of United Press International; Charles Mohr and Mert Perry of *Time,* both of whom quit when their New York office queried the accuracy of their dispatches; and Francois Sully of *Newsweek,* who was suspected of being anti-American because of his French background. Some attempts were made by officials, including those in the White House staff in at least one case, to have such critical correspondents as Halberstam, for instance, transferred away from Saigon but the efforts were in vain. As the war dragged on and on, and especially after the Tet offensive in 1968, the validity of the news stories was tragically confirmed. It became increasingly clear that the military's predictions of speedy approach toward success in Vietnam were glaringly in error.

An illustration of the dangers from an information policy of less than complete candor was the impact of Harrison E. Salisbury's reporting from behind enemy lines in *The New York Times* during December 1966 and January 1967. A considerable part of the tremendous reaction to Salisbury's articles arose because of a Pentagon-generated impression (possibly not deliberately intended) that U.S. bombs were not hitting nonmilitary targets. If the American public had been informed that bombs did not distinguish between the military and nearby civilians—information obviously available to the U.S. military—then these stories from Hanoi probably would have raised far less immediate concern. But the U.S. information officers had not opted to make clear this background and thus the dispatches aided the rising protest movement against the bombing of North Vietnam. Eventually that protest sentiment prompted President Johnson to curtail that aspect of the war and to withdraw as a 1968 presidential candidate.

If the government uses "the right to lie," a privilege that Assistant Defense Secretary Arthur Sylvester asserted it had, then who is to tell the people the truth? Are the media supposed to abdicate their traditional function as watchdog of the government? But if they choose to go a path opposite to that favored by their government, then who is to decide who is right and who is wrong? The public? Only if it has the facts, and even when the reporters seek to uncover the full story, there well may be information that is not discovered and printed. And is there never an occasion when disclosure is in fact a menace to survival, as in events that might end in nuclear disaster?

William J. Barnds, Senior Research Fellow at the Council on Foreign Relations, in a special study on "The Right to Know, to Withhold & to Lie" for the Council on Religion and International Affairs (1969), pointed out the opposing arguments when he wrote:

> The right of the executive office to withhold from its citizens a large part of the raw information it possesses is only one part of a complicated picture, however, and when public officials place an undue emphasis on such withholding they do so at their ultimate peril. The executive also has the obligation of keeping its citizens informed of its general purposes in the area of foreign policy, and this

responsibility arises from the requirements of practical politics as well as from democratic principles.

Reporting of the My Lai incident in the American mass media illustrates how easy, initially, it was for the unpleasant aspects of that event to be varnished over. Stories of the loss of Vietnamese lives at the village were reported in the U.S. press within days after the alleged slayings took place. For instance, the following news item appeared on page one of *The New York Times* on March 17, 1968:

G.I.'s, in Pincer Move, Kill 128 in a Daylong Battle

Special to The New York Times

SAIGON, South Vietnam, Sunday, March 17—American troops caught a North Vietnamese force in a pincer movement on the central coastal plain yesterday, killing 128 enemy soldiers in daylong fighting.

Two American soldiers were killed and 10 wounded, according to an American spokesman.

The fighting erupted six miles northeast of Quangngai in an area of sand dunes and scrub brush between Highway 1 and the South China Sea.

At the same time, South Vietnamese rangers backed by a company of United States armor from the 11th Armored Cavalry Regiment were reported to have killed 95 of the enemy in a six-and-a-half-hour fight 16 miles northwest of Saigon.

The American headquarters said there were no United States casualties. South Vietnamese casualties were described as light.

The action was part of a vast operation under way in five provinces around Saigon to eliminate the enemy threat against the capital.

In the fighting near Quang-

Statistics were on the smallish side but the gigantic hole in the dispatch was the omission of the facts about the virtual massacre of the village's inhabitants. No deaths of civilians were mentioned. Later when enterprising newsmen, especially in Seymour M. Hersh's stories for Dispatch News Service and an interview on CBS-TV News with a former soldier who had been there, brought out the bloody details, most of the American media (but not all) tried to redeem their previous deficiencies by massive coverage of the breaking news developments. Much of this belated reporting was to the press' credit but criticism came from two fronts: (1) Those who felt the war correspondents should have detected the scent of massacre (especially since a few foreign newsmen reported some particulars of the killings long before their American colleagues did), and (2) those who believed the U.S. "image" should be protected from such damaging details.

A floodtide of adverse criticism, however, broke over media, especially broadcast, for their coverage of the 1968 Democratic convention in Chicago. To what extent did they help to increase the obvious tensions in the Windy City and did some reporters, in efforts to obtain violent confrontations for the sake of news impact, tip off demonstrators and stage events? Few categories of misconduct were not laid at the doorsteps of newsmen by at least some critics. For instance, among those seriously investigated by a special subcommittee of the House Committee on Interstate and Foreign Commerce and reported in a staff paper made public on July 23, 1969, were the following: (1) Animosity and bias on the part of television news organizations, (2) prejudicial selection of film, (3) prejudicial editing, (4) staging of events, (5) cooperation between news media and demonstrators, (6) unfair juxtaposition and intercutting of live and taped material, (7) noncooperation with police, and (8) electronic eavesdropping.

While the hard core documentation is absent in most of the alleged instances of bias and prejudice, often there are enough concrete particulars to feed at least some of the often-held resentments against the media. Part of the adverse reaction rested on a belief that the messenger who brought the bad news in some way could have done better if he had not told all the facts. And part arose because one man's bias and prejudice may be another's objectivity. Subjective processes, as many news decisions are, cannot always be measured as neatly as a chemical analysis or a mathematic computation.

Reflecting some of these sentiments, the essence of the subcommittee's conclusions are embodied in this quotation:

> The investigation to date has not disclosed any instances where the broadcasters could clearly be shown to have violated existing law. At the same time, it should be pointed out that the existing law in this area is quite imprecise. . . .
>
> In general, there seems to be substantial evidence of animosity by members of the television news organizations against the Democratic Party, or at least against certain of its prominent members, and the administration of the city of Chicago. This seems to have been

reflected in the slanting of the reporting of events as they took place. The staff has reviewed the television news coverage, both broadcast and outtakes, and has spoken with people who were witnesses to the disturbances in downtown Chicago. It does seem in retrospect that the picture presented over the networks did not place sufficient evidence before the public as to the nature and motives of the demonstrators. . . .

Because of the inability to definitely establish such a general charge as bias, and the slanting of news, it is difficult to see what action the subcommittee could take in this area. While these abuses may be real, they would seem to be part of the price that must be paid for a completely independent press.

A subcommittee staff report did suggest that better identification of instances of film editing and electronic intercutting was needed so that the viewers and probably the interviewees would be informed. It also proposed some sort of "workable and fair" code of cooperation between television camera crews and the police. As in the case of a similar suggestion by the Warren Commission earlier, a key unresolved question was who was to adjudicate areas of dispute between the two groups when such differences arose. Certainly newsmen would not surrender to any governmental arbiter (or probably even to any professional attorney) their perceived rights to represent the public and carry forward its "right to know."

Professional discussions of media's actions during convention week in Chicago filled many, many pages in journals that the general public does not regularly see. For instance, a *Broadcasting* editorial (Sept. 19, 1968) claimed that "too little was reported of provocations by the demonstrators" and that "a more comprehensive story of cause and effect would have been desirable." Moreover, a considerable wave of criticism came from the viewers, too.

Thus a crop of antimedia sentiments had grown up during much of the 1960's and was awaiting harvesting. Vice-President Spiro T. Agnew got a bumper yield from his twin attacks on the media—at Des Moines, Iowa, and at Montgomery, Ala. And the field has not been left idle since then, with some members of Congress trying to get in on the action through their unsuccessful efforts to charge contempt of Congress against the Columbia Broadcasting System and its president, Dr. Frank Stanton.

3. The Nixon Administration and the Media

The Nixon Administration's first widely publicized antimedia sentiments came in a talk by Vice-President Spiro T. Agnew before the Midwestern Regional Republican Committee meeting in Des Moines, Iowa, on Nov. 13, 1969. There the Vice-President launched his attacks on how the public got its news. The date was not without significance because two days later antiwar demonstrations were scheduled for many communities, including Washington, D.C.

Using President Nixon's Vietnam war report of earlier that same month, Mr. Agnew said that the Chief Executive's television audience of an estimated 70,000,000 viewers was inherited by "a small band of network commentators and self-appointed analysts, the majority of whom expressed, in one way or another, their hostility of what he had to say." The President's views, the Vice-President said, were thus subjected to "instant analysis and querulous criticism."

The Des Moines audience of Republicans applauded and millions of nighttime television viewers listened to him instead of their usual programing. Mr. Agnew commented:

Now how is this [regular evening] network news determined? A small group of men, numbering perhaps not more than a dozen anchor-men, commentators and executive producers, settle upon the twenty minutes or so of film and commentary that's to reach the public.

He said these men could create national issues overnight, could reward some politicians with national exposure and ignore others. He philosophized that television had portrayed the horrors of war as no other medium had been able to do. These "privileged men" had power not only to select the events that appeared but to put them in a special frame of reference.

A raised eyebrow, an inflection of the voice, a caustic remark dropped in the middle of a broadcast can raise doubts in a million minds about the veracity of a public official or the wisdom of a government policy.

Then the Vice-President questioned the commentators' and announcers' power:

Is it not fair and relevant to question its concentration in the hands of a tiny, enclosed fraternity of privileged men elected by no one and enjoying a monopoly sanctioned and licensed by Government?

The views of the majority of this fraternity do not—and I repeat, not—represent the views of America.

. . . perhaps it is time that the networks were made more responsive to the views of the nation and more responsive to the people they serve.

Turning to television's concentration on the dramatic and the controversial, he said:

Now the upshot of all this controversy is that a narrow and distorted picture of America often emerges from the television news. A single dramatic piece of the mosaic becomes, in the minds of millions, the whole picture. And the American who relies upon television for his news might conclude that the majority of American students are embittered radicals; that the majority of black Americans feel no regard for their country; that violence and lawlessness are the rule, rather than the exception, on American campuses. We know that none of these conclusions is true. Perhaps the place to start looking for a credibility gap is not in the offices of the government in Washington but in the studios of the networks in New York.

Mr. Agnew said that he was not asking for censorship of any kind but queried if there already might not be some "by a handful of men responsible only to their corporate employers" and where news "is filtered through a handful of commentators who admit to their own set of biases."

The answers, the Vice-President told his audience, could come from (1) the media men, whom he "challenged to turn their critical powers on themselves, to direct their energy, their talent and their conviction toward improving the quality and objectivity of their news presentation" and (2) the American people, who should "let the networks know that they want their news straight and objective." He said the listeners "can register their complaints on bias through mail to networks and phone calls to local stations." The instructions were specific, indeed.

Responses were immediate and loud. Viewers followed the Vice-President's instructions and mail bags accumulated in network offices and telephone calls nearly swamped local station switchboards. Network officials and television commentators defended themselves, their staffs, and their integrity. Television executives' memoranda told staff members to be unintimidated, yet none associated with the medium could forget that they were being observed more critically than ever before.

What was the net result on television?

Many watchers felt that some of the "bite" disappeared from political commentaries. Richard Salant, president of CBS News, admitted, "We're off balance." NBC News President Reuben Frank said, "There has been a sensitization."

The Alfred I. duPont–Columbia University 1969-70 Survey of Broadcast Journalism reported, "Broadcasters were watching themselves, and being watched, as never before." A content analysis of ninety before and after news broadcasts from the three networks found "the almost complete lack of judgment sentences, either favorable or unfavorable, toward the Administration," but despite this Dennis T. Lowry, wrote in *Journalism Quarterly* (Summer, 1971) that he had to give an affirmative response to the question: "Can an administration which has no *de jure* control over news content succeed in using *de facto* pressure to significantly influence network TV news treatment of itself?"

Prof. M. L. Stein of the New York University Department of Journalism wrote in *The Nation* (Sept. 7, 1970), "The first round has gone to Agnew. TV executives, although claiming a business-as-usual policy, are depressed and embittered. Nothing in television has been the same since Agnew's Des Moines speech."

Many broadcast executives properly pointed out that the local stations, not the networks, were the ones licensed by the Federal Communications Commission. Yet few who understand the economics and mechanics of broadcasting were unaware that community protests against the local stations eventually might change network programing. Fred W. Friendly, former CBS News president and now with the Columbia Graduate School of Journalism, commented that meeting with affiliate managers was "like talking to 182 Agnews."

The Sigma Delta Chi Advancement of Freedom of Information Committee reported as follows to the 1970 convention of that professional journalism society:

> It is difficult to answer the frequently recurring question: "What has the impact of Agnew been?" One result of the Vice President's attacks has been to make television critics out of vast numbers of persons who never thought they were before. Many view the output of the networks and see things that they hadn't before. Though there is little concrete evidence of change in the pattern of network on-air broadcasts, some see subtle signs of intimidation by Agnew. Fully as many others, if one is to judge by the mail, see just the opposite and are critical because the networks continue their "excesses." Many journalists, primarily newspapermen, are convinced that there is a new, cautious, fearful atmosphere in network reporting. Others, primarily broadcasters, see no signs of this and ask, "Where is the evidence?"

Certainly one of the more widely quoted comments on the reactions to the speech was attributed to the President's daughter, Tricia, who told a United Press International reporter who asked about the impact of the Agnew attacks, "I'm a close watcher of newspapers and TV. I think they've taken a second look. You can't underestimate the power of fear."

A week after his Des Moines talk, Vice-President Agnew went to Montgomery, Ala., to address the Alabama Chamber of Commerce on Nov. 20 and there he broadened his criticism to include such newspapers as *The New York Times* and *Washington Post*. He said:

> I'm opposed to censorship of television, of the press in any form. I don't care whether censorship is imposed by government or whether it results from management in the choice and presentation of the news by a little fraternity having similar social and political views. I'm against, I repeat, I'm against media censorship in all forms.

After repeating the Des Moines criticism of television news, he went on:

And the American people should be aware of the trend toward the monopolization of the great public information vehicles and the concentration of more and more power in fewer and fewer hands. . . .

But a single company, in the nation's capital, holds control of the largest newspaper in Washington, D.C., and one of the four major television stations, and an all-news radio station, and one of the three major national news magazines—all grinding out the same editorial line—and this is not a subject that you've seen debated on the editorial pages of The Washington Post or The New York Times. . . .

Many, many strong, independent voices have been stilled in this country in recent years. And lacking the vigor of competition, some of those who have survived have—let's face it—grown fat and irresponsible.

Mr. Agnew cited specifics of his reactions against the *Post* and *The Times* and warned:

The day when the network commentators and even the gentlemen of The New York Times enjoyed a form of diplomatic immunity from comment and criticism of what they said is over. Yes, gentlemen, the day is passed.

Just as a politician's words—wise and foolish—are dutifully recorded by press and television to be thrown up at him at the appropriate time, so their words should be likewise recorded and likewise recalled.

When they go beyond fair comment and criticism they will be called upon to defend their statements and their positions just as we must defend ours. And when their criticism becomes excessive or unjust, we shall invite them down from their ivory towers to enjoy the rough and tumble of public debate.

I don't seek to intimidate the press, or the networks or anyone else from speaking out. But the time for blind acceptance of their opinions is past. And the time for naive belief in their neutrality is gone.

Most commentators on Mr. Agnew's Montgomery remarks conceded there were hazards from news monopoly, points that had been discussed in professional media circles since at least World War II. Some of them cited omissions from the Vice-President's talk, such as (1) that one of the biggest communications combinations was the *Chicago Tribune* and New York *Daily News* and their broadcast subsidiaries, which had supported candidates Nixon and Agnew in 1968; (2) that the two local daily newspapers in Montgomery were owned by a single conglomerate corporation although they maintained competing news staffs; and (3) that there were only two U.S. international news-gathering associations.

Both publishers Arthur Ochs Sulzberger of *The New York Times* and Mrs. Katharine Graham of the *Washington Post* replied to what they thought were factual errors. Sulzberger denied that *The Times* had "ever sought or enjoyed immunity from comment and criticism" but asked that such comments rest on accurate information. Mrs. Graham denied that media of the Washington Post Company ground out "the same editorial line" but rather reflected "a maximum of freedom" and "journalism of a high caliber that is notable for a diversity of voices on a wide range of public issues."

Norman Isaacs, then president of the American Society of Newspaper Editors, said, "It is an attack not merely on our mistakes of judgment—and which many of us admit—but on the basic principle of free speech."

Right along with the Vice-President's two talks came a request from Federal Communications Commission Chairman Dean Burch, recently appointed by President Nixon to his job, for certain network tapes of comments following the President's Vietnam war speech. The harshness of the Agnew speeches plus the implied coercive aspects of the FCC request seemed, at least to some, to have potentially sinister implications despite the Vice-President's denials of any censorship threat. Certainly to substitute any group of politicians in place of a "tiny, enclosed fraternity of privileged men" in print or broadcasting would be an extraordinarily poor replacement. Even with such biases and prejudices as now exist, most journalists possess a sense of professionalism that would be largely absent in any other group. Even in the most irresponsible newsman, there is a gnawing feeling of guilt—whether he will admit it in public or not. And the range of vested interests and profit lures almost certainly is less among newsmen than it would be for ambitious politicians or corporate publicists who might manage the news.

At about the same time as the Agnew speeches, what the *Columbia Journalism Review* called "the subpoena epidemic" was shaping up. For decades, reporters have on occasion worked with law enforcement agencies on a voluntary basis. Swapping such information paid off in news stories for media and missing evidence for police, FBI agents, and others. Until the disorders at the time of the Chicago Democratic convention, formal requests by subpoena were rare indeed. Late in 1968 and during 1969, however, prosecutors, defendants, grand juries, and a presidential commission all requested photographs, film, and videotapes —by subpoena. According to one trade report, the National Broadcasting Company spent approximately $150,000 to reproduce film and videotape to comply with such demands. No media organizations were reimbursed for either time or materials, it was reported.

Under Attorney General John Mitchell, subpoenas were served for notes, unpublished photographs, or untelevised film taken in covering the Weathermen demonstrations. Requests went to the four Chicago daily papers, *Time, Newsweek, Life* and NBC. CBS-TV and Earl Caldwell, black newsman on *The New York Times,* were requested to turn over materials dealing with the Black Panthers. After some compliances and some protests, Mitchell promised in February 1970 to take "steps to insure that, in the future, no subpoenas will be issued to the press without a good-faith attempt by the Department of Justice to reach a compromise acceptable to both parties prior to the issuance of a subpoena." Before the spring was gone, additional subpoenas had gone to CBS-TV newsmen for "outtakes" of a filmed interview in Algiers with Eldridge Cleaver, Black Panther leader, and to *Times* reporter Caldwell.

American newsmen can not refuse all subpoenas, obviously, but can any U.S. law enforcement agency enlist independent newsmen as "investigative collaborators," as one commentator put it? Among the developments bothering newsmen and their bosses was, for example, the comment of a Wisconsin state judge that "something has to give" in a clash between law enforcement and a free press and the added remark: "What has to give is the First Amendment privilege in the interest of justice."

On the other hand, the refusal of Earl Caldwell to produce tapes and notes of his interviews with Black Panther leaders, as requested, eventually reached the Ninth Circuit Court of Appeals in November 1970. That court declared that federal officials had to make a "clear showing of a compelling and overriding national interest that cannot be served by any alternative means" before reporters could be subpoenaed. The judges wrote:

The need for an untrammeled press takes a special urgency in times of widespread protest and dissent. In such times the First Amendment protections exist to maintain communication with dissenting groups and to provide the public with a wide range of information about the nature of protest and heterodoxy. . . .

To convert newsgatherers into Department of Justice investigators is to invade the autonomy of the press by imposing a governmental function upon them. To do so where the result is to diminish their future capacity as newsgatherers is destructive of their public function.

Although reluctant to label the ruling a "landmark," Stanford University law professor Anthony Amsterdam, Caldwell's attorney, pointed out that the action was the first appellate-court decision recognizing a newsman's right not to appear at all before a grand jury. Moreover, a *Times* representative earlier had warned, "To testify about or produce unpublished material given in confidence would have what the Supreme Court has called a 'chilling effect' on the rights guaranteed by the First Amendment."

In April 1971 a congressional subcommittee asked the Columbia Broadcasting System for all its televised and untelevised materials after a controversy arose from the network's showing of "The Selling of the Pentagon." The request was not entirely unexpected since a *New York Times* reviewer the morning after the broadcast predicted that the Pentagon "seems certain to wince under the expose" and, "inevitably, there may be screaming from sincere patriots." Dr. Frank Stanton, CBS president, and his associates agreed to provide such films and text as were broadcast but declined to yield other requested materials such as untelevised film, statements or disbursements of money to individuals on the program, and copies or descriptions of any contracts and agreements with participants. In May, the documentary won an Emmy Award, one of the industry's highest recognitions, from the National Academy of Television Arts and Sciences. In July, the House Commerce Committee voted to ask contempt of Congress charges against CBS and its president, Dr. Stanton. However, the House voted, 226 to 181, to recommit the proposed citation, thus in effect killing a move that might have tested the federal government power to investigate in-house details of broadcast journalism decision-making.

During the eighteen days between the following front page headlines in *The New York Times,* some of the most historic legal history concerning the print media went from initial publication to final decision by the U.S. Supreme Court:

SUPREME COURT, 6-3, UPHOLDS NEWSPAPERS
ON PUBLICATION OF THE PENTAGON REPORT;
TIMES RESUMES ITS SERIES, HALTED 15 DAYS   Sunday, June 13, 1971

Vietnam Archive: Pentagon Study Traces
3 Decades of Growing U. S. Involvement   Thursday, July 1, 1971

Little wonder that a *Times* commentator called it "one of the most frenzied court battles in history" and Chief Justice Warren E. Burger, in his dissenting opinion, complained, "No member of this Court knows all the facts" because the cases were conducted in such "unseemly haste."

After the first three installments of the Pentagon Papers series had been published, the government, at the direction of Attorney General Mitchell, sought to suspend publication. In rapid sequence, the *Washington Post, Boston Globe, Chicago Sun-Times, St. Louis Post-Dispatch,* Knight newspaper group, *Los Angeles Times,* and *Christian Science Monitor* in Boston, all launched their own versions of commentaries from the 7,000 pages in the Pentagon Papers—1,500,000 words in historical narratives plus another million words of appended documents. The government obtained injunctions against some (but not all) of these papers, in an effort to stop the increasing leaks in the informational dike.

After halting the series so that he could hear arguments, a U.S. District judge on Saturday, June 19, refused to further suspend *The Times'* series but the effect of his decision was short-lived when a U.S. Court of Appeals judge continued the embargo. District Judge Murray I. Gurfein said in part:

> If there be some embarrassment to the Government in security aspects as remote as the general embarrassment that flows from any security break we must learn to live with it. The security of the Nation is not at the ramparts alone. Security also lies in the value of our free institutions. A cantankerous press, an obstinate press, a ubiquitous press must be suffered by those in authority in order to preserve the even greater values of freedom of expression and the right of the people to know. . . . Yet in the last analysis it is not merely the opinion of the editorial writer, or of the columnist, which is protected by the First Amendment. It is the free flow of

information so that the public will be informed about the Government and its actions.

Within a week, *The New York Times* and *Washington Post* cases were before the U.S. Supreme Court for an extraordinary special session on Saturday, June 26. Associate Justice William O. Douglas flew back to Washington from the Pacific Coast to listen to the arguments.

Erwin N. Griswold, Solicitor General from the Department of Justice, argued that there was no constitutional rule that there could never be prior restraint on the press. He said:

> There cannot be the slightest doubt, it seems to me, no matter what the motive, no matter what the justification, that both The New York Times and The Washington Post are here consciously and intentionally participating in a breach of trust. They know that this material is not theirs. They do not own it. I am not talking about the pieces of paper which they may have acquired. I am talking about the literary property, the concatenation of words, which is protected by the law of literary property.

Under questioning by Justice Potter Stewart, Griswold said the documents had been classified under executive orders approved by Congress and had "obviously" been "improperly acquired."

> Justice Stewart: That may have a great deal to do with the question of whether or not somebody is guilty of a criminal offense, but I submit it has very little to do with the basic First Amendment issue before this Court in this case.

> Griswold: All right, Mr. Justice, I repeat, unless we can show that this will have grave, and I think I would like to amend it—I know the Court's order had said "immediate," but I think it really ought to be "irreparable harm to the security of the United States."

In response to Justice John Marshall Harlan, Griswold replied:

> . . . I also think the heart of our case is that the publication of the materials specified in my closed brief will, as I have tried to argue here, materially affect the security of the United States. It will affect lives. It will affect the process of the termination of the war. It will affect the process of recovering prisoners of war. I cannot say that the termination of the war or recovering prisoners of war is something which has an immediate effect on the security of the United States. I say that it has such an effect on the security of the United States that it ought to be the basis of an injunction in this case.

Prof. Alexander M. Bickel, Yale Law School faculty member, argued for *The New York Times* that "we have all along in this case conceded for purposes of argument, that the prohibition against prior restraint, like so much else in the Constitution, is not an absolute." But then he added, "If the criminal statute 'chills' speech, prior restraint 'freezes' it."

Justice Stewart asked, "Your standard is that it has to be an extremely grave event to the nation and it has to be directly proximately caused by the publication."

Bickel replied, "That is exactly correct."

William R. Glendon, for the *Washington Post,* said that the "proper test" for injunctive prohibition was when "the publication of the material would so prejudice the defense interests of the United States or result in such irreparable injury to the United States as to justify the extraordinary relief that was asked, to wit, a prior restraint."

Questioned by Chief Justice Burger how one could be sure of the consequences of disclosures, Glendon replied:

> Your Honor, I think if we are to place possibilities or conjecture against suspension or abridgement of the First Amendment, the answer is obvious. The fact, the possibility, the conjecture or the hypothesis that diplomatic negotiations would be made more difficult or embarrassed does not justify, and this is what we have in this case, I think, and is all we have, does not justify suspending the First Amendment. Yet this is what has happened here. Conjecture can be piled upon surmise. Judge Gurfein used the words up in New York, and I am sure used it respectfully, but he said when there is a security breach, people get the jitters. I think maybe the Government has a case of the jitters here. But that, I submit, does not warrant the stopping the press on this matter, in the absence of a showing.

Discussing the classification system later, the *Post* attorney elaborated:

> On other occasions, the Government engages itself in leaks, because some official will feel that in the public interest it is well for the public to know, and that overrides any particular judgment of security or classification.
>
> The record, Your Honors will find, is replete with instances

where leaks of confidential, secret and top-secret materials have been given to the press, or the press has found them out and published them, and of course nothing has happened. I think that is significant because here this is the sort of thing we feel we are talking about. As far as classification itself is concerned, and you will remember the documents that we are talking about are a mixed bag.

Justice Byron R. White: Mr. Glendon, wouldn't you be making the same argument if your client had stolen the papers?

Glendon: I don't think the source of how we obtained them features in this case.

Justice White: Then it would not make any difference? The leak aspect has no relevance to the case, either.

Glendon: I think it is relevant as background.

The lawyer called allegations of grave damage "a case of broad claims and narrow proof." He said that the single document produced by government attorneys during private hearings to "let us look at what we are talking about, instead of dealing just with abstractions and conjectures" was one which "any high school boy would have no difficulty in either putting together himself or readily understanding."

Glendon argued that the government had not produced a single document from the forty-seven volumes in the Pentagon's "top secret" history that would justify suspending publication under the First Amendment guarantees.

Your Honor, the Government came into court. They suspended the First Amendment; they stopped us from printing, and they said they were going to prove this. This is an injunction proceeding. . . . I say, Your Honor, in our system, as I understand it, when you bring a case, you are supposed to prove it, and when you come in claiming irreparable injury, particularly in this area of the First Amendment, you have a very, very heavy burden.

. . . but you are weighing here an abridgement of the First Amendment, the people's right to know. That may be an abstraction, but it is one that has made this country great for some 200 years. You are being asked to approve something that the Government has never done before. We were told by the Attorney General to stop publishing this news. We did not obey that order, and we were brought into court. We ended up being enjoined.

During oral argument in rebuttal, Solicitor General Griswold was questioned by Justice Thurgood Marshall about possible restraints on future studies:

Griswold: I think if properly classified materials were improperly acquired, and that it can be shown that they do have an immediate or current impact on the security of the United States, that there ought to be an injunction. I think it is relevant, at this point—

Justice Marshall: Wouldn't we then—the Federal courts—be a censorship board, as to whether this does—

Griswold: That is a pejorative way to put it, Mr. Justice. I do not know what the alternative is.

Justice Marshall: The First Amendment might do.

Griswold: Yes, Mr. Justice, and we are, of course, fully supporting the First Amendment. We do not claim or suggest any exception to the First Amendment. . . . The problem in this case is the construction of the First Amendment.

This further exchange took place between Justice Stewart and Griswold:

Griswold: Everything about this case has been frantic. That seems to me to be most unfortunate. I would like to point out that The New York Times—

Justice Stewart: No. The reason is, of course, as you know, Mr. Solicitor General, that unless the constitutional law, as it now exists, is changed, a prior restraint of publication by a newspaper is presumptively unconstitutional.

Griswold: It is a very serious matter. There is no doubt about it, and so is the security of the United States a very serious matter. We have two important Constitutional objectives here which have to be weighed and balanced and made as harmonious as they can be. But it is well known that The Times had this material for three months. It is only after The Times had had an opportunity to digest it, and it took them three months to digest it, that it suddenly becomes necessary to be frantic about it.

The following Wednesday, the Supreme Court gave its 6-3 decision, with each justice writing his own separate opinion, none attracting concurrence of more than three men. The flood of opinions ran to 11,000 words. The majority agreed on a short "per curiam" which said the government had not met the "heavy presumption against its constitutional validity" which faces any system of prior restraints on expression. The nine justices divided into four discernible groups. Justices Hugo L. Black, Douglas, and William J. Brennan, Jr., held that the First Amendment stood as "an absolute bar" to prior restraints in circumstances such as presented. Justice Marshall said that Congress had never enacted legislation for such restraints as proposed, and thus the Supreme Court should not condone what legislators never enacted into law. The three dissenters believed the President's authority to conduct foreign affairs gave him powers to define what were secrets of state. The other two justices sought, largely without great success, to define circumstances that might justify "national security" restraint on publication.

Justice Black, with Justice Douglas joining, bluntly stated:

I believe that every moment's continuance of the injunctions against these newspapers amounts to a flagrant, indefensible and continuing violation of the First Amendment. . . .

Now, for the first time in the 182 years since the founding of the Republic, the Federal courts are asked to hold that the First Amendment does not mean what it says, but rather means that the Government can halt the publication of current news of vital importance to the people of this country. . . .

Both the history and language of the First Amendment support the view that the press must be left free to publish the news, whatever the source, without censorship, injunctions or prior restraints. . . .

The press was to serve the governed, not the governors. The Government's power to censor the press was abolished so that the press would remain forever free to censure the Government. The press was protected so that it could bare the secrets of government and inform the people. Only a free and unrestrained press can effectively expose deception in government. And paramount among the responsibilities of a free press is the duty to prevent any part of the Government from deceiving the people and sending them off to distant lands to die of foreign fevers and foreign shot and shell.

In my view, quite far from deserving condemnation for their courageous reporting, The New York Times, The Washington Post and other newspapers should be commended for serving the purpose that the Founding Fathers saw so clearly. In revealing the workings of government that led to the Vietnam war, the newspapers nobly did precisely that which the founders hoped and trusted they would do.

Justice Douglas, with whom Justice Black joined, wrote:

The dominant purpose of the First Amendment was to prohibit the widespread practice of governmental suppression of embarrassing information. . . .

Secrecy in government is fundamentally antidemocratic, perpetuating bureaucratic errors. Open debate and discussion of public issues are vital to our national health. On public questions there should be "open and robust debate." . . .

The stays in these cases that have been in effect for more than a week constitute a flouting of the principles of the First Amendment . . .

In his concurring opinion, Justice Brennan wrote:

To begin with, there has now been ample time for reflection and judgment; whatever values there may be in the preservation of novel questions for appellate review may not support any restraints in the future. More important, the First Amendment stands as an absolute bar to the imposition of judicial restraints in circumstances of the kind presented by these cases.

The error which has pervaded these cases from the outset was the granting of any injunctive relief whatsoever, interim or otherwise. The entire thrust of the Government's claim throughout these cases has been that publication of the material sought to be enjoined "could," or "might" or "may" prejudice the national interest in various ways. But the First Amendment tolerates absolutely no prior judicial restraints of the press predicated upon surmise or conjecture that untoward consequences may result. Our cases, it is true, have indicated that there is a simple, extremely narrow class of cases in which the First Amendment's ban on prior judicial restraint may be overridden. Our cases have thus far indicated that such cases may arise only when the nation "is at war." . . . Unless and until the Government has clearly made out its case, the First Amendment commands that no injunction may issue.

Justice Marshall argued:

The issue is whether this Court or the Congress has the power to make law. . . .

It would, however, be utterly inconsistent with the concept of separation of power for this Court to use its power of contempt to prevent behavior that Congress has specifically declined to prohibit. . . . It [the Constitution] did not provide for government by injunction, in which the courts and the executive can "make law" without regard to the action of Congress. It may be more convenient for the executive if it need only convince a judge to prohibit conduct rather than to ask the Congress to pass a law, and it may be more convenient to enforce a contempt order than seek a criminal conviction in a jury trial. . . .

It is not for this Court to fling itself into every breach perceived by some Government official, nor is it for this Court to take on itself the burden of enacting law, especially law that Congress has refused to pass.

In his dissenting opinion, Chief Justice Burger held:

In this case, the imperative of a free and unfettered press comes into collision with another imperative, the effective functioning of a complex modern government, and specifically the effective exercise of certain constitutional powers of the executive. Only those who view the First Amendment as an absolute in all circumstance—a view I respect, but reject—can find such a case as this to be simple and easy. . . .

It is not disputed that The Times has had unauthorized possession of the documents for three to four months, during which it has had its expert analysts studying them, presumably digesting them and preparing the material for publication. During all of this time, The Times, presumably in its capacity as trustee of the public's "right to know," has held up publication for purposes it considered proper and thus public knowledge was delayed. No doubt this was for a good reason . . .

But why should the United States Government, from whom this information was illegally acquired by someone, along with all the counsel, trial judges, and appellate judges be placed under needless pressure? After these months of deferral, the alleged right to know has somehow and suddenly become a right that must be vindicated instanter.

. . . To me it is hardly believable that a newspaper long regarded as a great institution in American life would fail to perform one of the basic and simple duties of every citizen with respect to the discovery or possession of stolen property or secret Government documents. That duty, I had thought—perhaps naively—was to report forthwith, to responsible public officers. This duty rests on taxi drivers, justices and The New York Times. . . .

The consequences of all this melancholy series of events is that we literally do not know what we are acting on.

Justice Harlan, with the Chief Justice and Justice Harry A. Blackmun joining, wrote:

The time which has been available to us, to the lower courts and to the parties has been wholly inadequate for giving these cases the kind of consideration they deserve. It is a reflection on the stability of the judicial process that these great issues—as important as any that have arisen during my time on the Court—should have been decided under the pressures engendered by the torrent of publicity that has attended these litigations from their inception. . . .

I cannot believe that the doctrine prohibiting prior restraints reaches to the point of preventing courts from maintaining the status quo long enough to act responsibly in matters of such national importance as those involved here.

The third dissenter, Justice Blackmun, said:

What is needed here is a weighing, upon properly developed standards, of the broad right of the press to print and of the very narrow right of the Government to prevent. Such standards are not yet developed. The parties here are in disagreement as to what those standards should be. But even the newspapers concede that there are situations where restraint is in order and is constitutional. . . .

I strongly urge, and sincerely hope, that these two newspapers will be fully aware of their ultimate responsibilities to the United States of America. . . . I hope that damage already has not been done.

If, however, damage has been done and if, with the Court's action today, these newspapers proceed to publish the critical documents and there results therefrom "the death of soldiers, the destruction of alliances, the greatly increased difficulty of negotiation with our enemies, the inability of our diplomats to negotiate," to which list I might add the factors of prolongation of the war and of further delay in the freeing of United States prisoners, then the nation's people will know where the responsibility for these sad consequences rests.

Justices Stewart and White both wrote concurring opinions with which the other joined, thus presenting a twin impact for the middle-ground positions.

Justice Stewart's opinion included his remarks on "an informed and free press" as a prerequisite for an enlightened people but then he added:

Yet it is elementary that the successful conduct of international diplomacy and the maintenance of an effective national defense require both confidentiality and secrecy. Other nations can hardly deal with this nation in an atmosphere of mutual trust unless they can be assured that their confidences will be kept. . . . In the area of basic national defense the frequent need for absolute secrecy is, of course, self-evident.

. . . I should suppose that moral, political and practical con- siderations would dictate that a very first principle of that wisdom would be an insistence upon avoiding secrecy for its own sake.

For when everything is classified, then nothing is classified, and the system becomes one to be disregarded by the cynical or the careless, and to be manipulated by those intent on self-protection or self-promotion. I should suppose in short, that the hallmark of a truly effective international security system would be the maximum possible disclosure, recognizing that secrecy can best be preserved only when credibility is truly maintained. . . .

Undoubtedly Congress has the power to enact specific and appropriate criminal laws to protect Government property and pre- serve Government secrets. . . . Moreover, if Congress should pass a specific law authorizing civil proceedings in this field, the courts would likewise have the duty to decide the constitutionality of such a law as well as its applicability to the facts proved.

But in the cases before us we are asked neither to construe specific regulations nor to apply specific laws. We are asked, instead, to perform a function that the Constitution gave to the executive, not the judiciary. We are asked, quite simply, to prevent the publication by two newspapers of material that the executive branch insists should not, in the national interest, be published. I am convinced that the executive is correct with respect to some of the documents involved. But I cannot say that disclosure of any of them will surely result in direct, immediate and irreparable damage to our nation or its people. That being so, there can under the First Amendment be but one judicial resolution of the issues before us.

I join the judgments of the court.

Justice White mentioned "the circumstances by which the newspaper came into possession of the information" but his arguments included:

I do not say that in no circumstances would the First Amendment permit an injunction against publishing information about Government plans or operations. . . . Indeed, I am confident that their disclosure will have that [damaging] result. But I nevertheless agree that the United States has not satisfied the very heavy burden which it must meet to warrant an injunction against publication in these cases, at least in the absence of express and appropriately limited Congressional authorization for prior restraints in circumstances such as these.

. . . because the material poses substantial dangers to national interests and because of the hazards of criminal sanctions, a responsible press may choose never to publish the more sensitive materials. To sustain the Government in these cases would start the courts down a long and hazardous road that I am not willing to travel, at least without Congressional guidance and direction. . . .

Prior restraints require an unusually heavy justification under the First Amendment; but failure by the Government to justify prior restraints does not measure its constitutional entitlement to a conviction for criminal publication. That the Government mistakenly chose to proceed by injunction does not mean that it could not successfully proceed in another way. . . .

The Criminal Code contains numerous provisions potentially relevant to these cases. . . . If any of the material here at issue is of this nature, the newspapers are presumably now on full notice of the position of the United States and must face the consequences if they publish. I would have no difficulty in sustaining convictions under these sections on facts that would not justify the intervention of equity and the imposition of a prior restraint.

How does it all add up?

A majority of six judges held that in these specific cases the First Amendment guarantees allowed *The New York Times* and the *Washington Post* to run the presses and pay the piper, if at all, after the news was out. This was no new concept, having been expressed by Chief Justice Charles E. Hughes in *Near v. Minnesota* (1931). Yet three of those who joined the majority were gravely disturbed about two points:

(1) that classified documents had come to the papers through far-from-normal channels, at least someone had "purloined" them, as it was phrased, and (2) that diplomacy and defense seemingly could not always operate in a goldfish bowl environment.

James J. Kilpatrick, an ardent defender of the press, wrote in his syndicated column:

> Well, it wasn't a glorious triumph. Our side won, but didn't win much. . . . A close reading of the individual opinions reveals that six of the nine justices, given a sharper set of facts and a stronger statutory law, might very well go along with the despotism we so abhor.

A Louis Harris poll of 1,493 households questioned face-to-face during July 10-16, 1971, a week after the Supreme Court verdict, showed 41 percent agreed that "the papers which printed secret documents about the war" in the Pentagon Papers cases were "more right than the federal government which said printing the papers was harmful to the national interest." Thirty-five percent supported the government and 24 percent was undecided. An outright majority of the sample (54 percent) felt "it's about time the public was given the truth about how we got into the war." Like the justices themselves, a majority of those questioned felt it was all right to abridge the freedom to publish if it had been clearly proven that national security interests were being jeopardized; nearly two-thirds felt the press, when it obtained "top secret" documents, should first try to get the government's consent to print them.

The New York Times in its "The Week in Review" on the Sunday after the decision put it this way:

> Their decision . . . was by no means the end of the affair of the Pentagon papers. Some of the repercussions were clearly evident, but most were still the subject of widespread speculation.

The remark was so correct. A news release from the Department of Justice pointed out that "all avenues of criminal prosecution remained open" and that the department was "continuing its investigation and will prosecute all those who have violated Federal criminal laws in connection with this matter." Obviously, this was a proper posture for the government's law enforcement agency but will editors and reporters face prosecution for their roles in the affair? Media watchers will focus on this aspect of the Nixon Administration's relations with those who cover the news for some time.

It is of more than passing interest that *The New York Times* during the past fifteen years opted both ways—sometimes to publish, sometimes to suppress—when issues of "national security" were purportedly involved in items about to be printed. When its reporters found out about nuclear testing hundreds of miles above the earth's atmosphere, *The Times* published the news on Project Argus in March 1959, giving the White House and Pentagon several hours' advance notice that a story would be in the next day's edition. However, during the Bay of Pigs and Cuban missile crisis, the publisher and editors decided to accede to White House requests to delete specific details in their coverage. Earlier, when Secretary of State John Foster Dulles wanted the top secret Yalta Papers published in *The New York Times,* he personally declassified them and gave them to James Reston of the paper's Washington bureau.

4. Freedom — and Responsibility — for Media

The phrase "freedom of the press" is one of the most beloved by journalists—and rightly so, in its true meaning. But increasingly a wide range of questions has arisen in recent years about what it really signifies. Freedom to whom? Freedom from what? Freedom for what purposes, if any?

Two centuries or more ago, it meant almost exclusively freedom from governmental controls—first from licensing and then from oppressive royal regulations, including before the American Revolution a stamp tax on newsprint from overseas. Yet one should not forget that the Founding Fathers did not guarantee press freedom in the original document. Libertarians among them forced freedom of the press into the First Amendment of a ten-part Bill of Rights. It reads:

> *Congress shall make no law* respecting an establishment of religion, or prohibiting the free exercise thereof; or *abridging the freedom of speech, or of the press;* or the right of the people peaceably to assemble, and to petition the government for a redress of grievances. [Italics supplied.]

Under the libertarian theory, if the press had untrammeled freedom to pursue the truth, men would use their reason and intellect to winnow out falsehoods. For, as John Milton said, ". . . who ever knew Truth put to the worse, in a free and open encounter?" Idealistically the "open marketplace" concept of truth's ultimate victory was sound but, in the monopolistic phase of an intensely commercial and technological society, could the people be sure that it would work that way? During much of the twentieth century, the owners of media—publishers and later station and network proprietors—developed what Prof. Theodore Peterson of the University of Illinois and his associates called "the social-responsibility theory." Under this, it was not enough to make a profit and pay high dividends to operate successfully. One had to be a good citizen, too. Peterson, Jay W. Jensen, and William L. Rivers wrote in *The Mass Media and Modern Society* (Holt, Rinehart & Winston, 1965):

> Today, especially in their public appearances, publishers and broadcasters commonly speak of "the public's right to know" and "the responsibility of the press." What this amounts to is a shift in the theoretical foundation of freedom of the press from the individual to society. What was once looked on as a universal, personal right to free expression is now described in terms of public access, of the right to know.

Thus an idea of fairness, which definitely was not included in the Founding Fathers' philosophy, was added as part of an already rather large assignment. The shift in emphasis from individual expression to public access was not unpredictable since a shirt-tail printer with several hundred dollars of type and a press could start a daily paper in New York City 140 years ago compared with a contemporary cost running into tens of millions. Also, broadcasting stations may sell for millions of dollars when the most valuable item comprises Federal Communications Commission permission to use the air waves.

Just what is the role of mass media in contemporary society? A wide spread of replies have been advanced by various critics and commentators but most of them center on these key roles:

★ Town crier messages. Media should provide a report of the world's news that is true, reasonably complete, and meaningful for the audience toward which it is aimed. The channels of print and broadcasting serve as the circulatory system of a modern society, providing the informational nutrient that keeps it alive and well. Without an input of news that keeps people aware of what is happening, the ties from community to community and from nation to nation would unravel and the societal fabric would fray badly, if not rip. Beyond this, the media as town crier may entertain and amuse; everything reported need not be serious and bleak.

★ Cracker barrel discussions. Some forum for opinions and exchange of attitudes is a necessary part of community intercourse. The mass media allow various groups to discuss their social goals and how they hope to reach them. At best, this introduces new ideas that may improve general well-being; even at worst, it allows a safety valve for potential hostility to escape without damage to the social structure. This embraces Milton's requirement of an "open marketplace" in which truth may compete.

★ Teacher's lessons. By the nature of the news on which they concentrate and the values they stress, media serve as transmission belts for the cultural heritage. Sometimes, this aspect of communications alienates segments of the audiences and, if this becomes too pervasive, there may be few people left to serve.

Few, indeed, are the news dispatches and broadcasts that combine all three functions, but each of the media, over a long period, contributes at all of these levels. Again, it is a dangerous oversimplification to talk about "the media" as if a network television documentary were comparable in the scales of performance evaluation with a brief death notice in a small Montana weekly. And since the whole topic concerns human beings under the stress of deadlines and their subjective actions in picking what events to report, one should remember that perfection is a goal rather than a frequent achievement.

How well are these three assignments being carried out?

Technological advances in communications satellites and facsimile transmissions make it possible to cover the world better than newsmen used to be able to report their own home community. For a scheduled event, such as a coronation, Olympic games, or international convention, "live" television may take the viewer to the scene as it is occurring. Now the audience can join astronauts for rides on the moon. In contrast, the first Atlantic cables linked the United States with Europe little more than a century ago; before that, news had to come by ship and it took a week or more. Yet the benefits may be blunted—as far as public enlightenment is concerned—if this huge machinery is used primarily to report the birth of a premature baby to a noted motion picture actress or an unusual contest to chase bulls through the streets of a medieval town. There is nothing inherently wrong with reporting the exotic but use of the communications process chiefly for that type of news may contribute little to the decision-making of a democratic society. News should be both interesting and important.

Just as the news agencies have to pick and choose what they will distribute, so the publications and stations that they serve have a massive surplus from which selections must be made. To illustrate, a large metropolitan daily such as *The New York Times, Chicago Tribune,* or *Los Angeles Times* prints little more than one-tenth of all the words that speed into its plant during twenty-four hours. Substantially the same choice is provided broadcasters. Deciding what is news involves subjective judgments and that is where the press is vulnerable to most telling thrusts of criticism, rather than in deficiencies in the machinery.

Some of the news media have earned demerits for concentrating on the dramatic highlights of an event. An assignment editor picks those happenings that he believes are unusual and exciting or significant and important. Reporter and cameraman concentrate on what they consider the exciting and unusual—or most important—aspects of what happens. Then the editor or television producer may again re-edit the copy or film to cut out the less dramatic. In simplified form, this procedure is an escalating spiral for insuring that the unusual, the exciting, the dramatic get to public attention—generally guaranteeing that the more sober, somber, but highly informative parts of a story get lost in the battle for mass audience attention.

Until the late 1960's, the majority of American dailies and television programs had not yet discovered the nation's minority groups, except during outbursts of violence. The Report of the National Advisory Commission on Civil Disorders in 1968 documented media activities in a rather uncomplimentary chapter on coverage of the ghettos. Some improvement has taken place but many observers consider it little better than marginal, on the whole, in view of what is required if the country is to survive its current racial discords.

To illustrate what one critic was thinking, Miss Jean Fairfax, chairman of legal information and community services of the Legal Defense and Educational Fund, warned a joint session of the International Radio and Television Society and the National Academy of Television Arts and Sciences in 1970 that many broadcasters were "too reluctant, timid or frightened" to produce the programs that blacks increasingly were demanding. She also said that, even now, the broadcast industry did not regard blacks as "serious, intelligent citizens with broad civil concerns."

Failure of media to report *all* of the social scene undoubtedly con-

effect of press on society ↓

tributed to alienation of many of those who live among the unreported audiences, whether they be underprivileged blacks or whites, those concerned with intellectual pursuits, or those college trained who despise monumental trivia. Even some of Middle America was disenchanted with what it saw—or thought it saw—as witness the mail that poured into television stations and networks after Vice-President Spiro T. Agnew's remarks in Des Moines, Iowa. Other signs of discontent have not been absent. In recent years, for instance, expanding circulation for the "underground" press showed unhappiness and disappointment with conventional Establishment papers by a sizeable part of the mass audience.

Journalistic sins which some excused in the name of "freedom of the press" clutter the record. For instance:

★ Particularly biased publishers and editors have deleted any mention of individuals or groups with whom they had a personal vendetta—in effect, treating these non-persons as if they had departed from the globe when the feud began. The Soviets omit news of their non-persons that way but it has happened in Chicago, Philadelphia, and smaller United States cities where there were no competing papers to which readers could turn.

★ Reporters have accepted favors and gifts from corporations, professional sports teams, and politicians at Christmas time and free trips to exotic places. They seldom told their audience of their indebtedness.

★ Regular advertisers, be they motion picture, real estate, or new shopping center, have obtained supposed news space for favorable comments on their activities when news managers failed to draw a firm line on what was legitimate coverage and what was plug.

★ "Confession"-type magazines published, uninhibitedly it would seem, a flood of stories about imagined romances of the late President John F. Kennedy's widow, or of Hollywood stars.

★ Many journalists intruded with notebook and open microphone to record the reactions of an essentially private figure in times of deepest tragedy for a curious, sensation-seeking public. The newsmen claimed the people had a right to know.

★ Photographers for both print and broadcasting have pointed their cameras into the faces of survivors of a major disaster and taken pictures so that all could see their grief, fatigue, and anguish.

Even when they have not lived up to their own professional standards, both print and broadcast journalists have had some measure for judging their own actions. Their codes of conduct told them what, ideally, they should do. Some expressed qualms about their deficiencies in private, if not publicly.

At best, "freedom of the press" has provided a responsible reporter and editor with a maximum facility for gathering, writing, and disseminating news and information to the American public. "Freedom of information," to use the phrase from legislation passed in the late 1960's, was as good a key as any to open doors to government and corporate officials and to other public figures. The majority decisions in the cases involving the Pentagon Papers (quoted in Chapter Three) supported the media's right to print and pay the price—if that was the way it had to be.

Few knowledgeable individuals would argue that other countries have found a better system for spreading news. Complaints center around American newsmen not living up to their idealized potential, not that others have developed a better way. Certainly, on the basis of any track records to date in their own professions, volunteer politicians or lawyers do not offer much hope for the media's salvation, an assignment some in both groups have indicated they would undertake if given a chance.

An essential point that apparently gets lost in almost all of these discussions of media is that journalists, being human, should have the right to make mistakes if their intentions are honorable. A corollary is that news judgments, being subjective, may appear as either pluses or minuses, depending on the news consumer's viewpoint. Part of the package of freedom is the right to be wrong. One can only hope that mistakes are not too often made.

If the First Amendment freedoms were to be applied only to the approved and the popular, there would be little need for such constitutional protection. The weight of public opinion would safeguard them. Legal restraints become especially meaningful when they uphold the weak, the dissident, and the ill-protected. The rich and powerful have their own guardians by right of their money and positions.

However, few individuals, except the late Supreme Court Justice Hugo L. Black and his hardy band of purists, argued that First Amendment guarantees are absolute. (Few things in contemporary life are that clean cut.) Newsmen have repeatedly embargoed news about ship and troop movements in wartime without feeling themselves unduly deprived of their freedom. Even more classic is Justice Oliver Wendell Holmes' example from the unanimous decision in *Schenck v. United States* (1919): "The most stringent protection of free speech would not protect a man in falsely shouting fire in a theatre and causing a panic." Complexities arise when the time comes to place a marker where freedom ends. Here the courts, frequently the U.S. Supreme Court, play the decisive role.

In the twentieth century, the Supreme Court has been a bulwark against attempts to bypass the First Amendment freedoms. With the highest court deciding the constitutionality of state laws as well as national, the justices determined the limits for legislative and judicial actions that could be taken regarding the press. In making these decisions, a majority held that there could be no prior restraints or censorship of publication (a point reinforced in 1971 regarding the Pentagon Papers); that no special punitive taxes could be imposed; and that these rights were not absolute, thus setting legal limits for any "clear and present danger."

In decisions upholding conviction of the Communist Party leadership under the Alien Registration (Smith) Act, passed in 1940, both concurring and dissenting opinions in *Dennis et al. v. United States* (1951) discussed the importance of free expression and the limitations upon it.

Justice Felix Frankfurter, concurring with the affirmation of the lower court's conviction, said in part:

> The language of the First Amendment is to be read not as barren words found in a dictionary but as symbols of historic experience illumined by the presuppositions of those who employed them. Not what words did Madison and Hamilton use, but what was in their minds which they conveyed? Free speech is subject to prohibition of those abuses of expression which a civilized society may forbid. As in the case of every other provision of the Constitution that is not crystallized by the nature of its technical concepts, the fact that the First Amendment is not self-defining and self-enforcing neither impairs its usefulness nor compels its paralysis as a living instrument. . . .
>
> Freedom of expression is the well-spring of our civilization—the civilization we seek to maintain and further by recognizing the right of Congress to put some limitation upon expression. Such are the paradoxes of life. For social development of trial and error, the fullest possible opportunity for the free play of the human mind is an indispensable prerequisite. The history of civilization is in considerable measure the displacement of error which once held sway as official truth by beliefs which in turn have yielded to

other truths. Therefore the liberty of man to search for truth ought not be fettered, no matter what orthodoxies he may challenge. Liberty of thought soon shrivels without freedom of expression. Nor can truth be pursued in an atmosphere hostile to the endeavor or under dangers which are hazarded only by heroes.

In a dissenting opinion in the same case, Justice William O. Douglas wrote:

Free speech has occupied an exalted position because of the high service it has given our society. Its protection is essential to the very existence of a democracy. The airing of ideas releases pressures which otherwise might become destructive. When ideas compete in the market for acceptance, full and free discussion exposes the false and they gain few adherents. Full and free discussion even of ideas we hate encourages the testing of our own prejudices and preconceptions. Full and free discussion keeps a society from becoming stagnant and unprepared for the stresses and strains that work to tear all civilizations apart.

Full and free discussion has indeed been the first article of our faith. We have founded our political system on it. It has been the safeguard of every religious, political, philosophical, economic, and racial group amongst us. We have counted on it to keep us from embracing what is cheap and false; we have trusted the common sense of our people to choose the doctrine true to our genius and to reject the rest. This has been the one single outstanding tenet that has made our institutions the symbol of freedom and equality. We have deemed it more costly to liberty to suppress a despised minority than to let them vent their spleen. We have above all else feared the political censor. We have wanted a land where our people can be exposed to all the diverse creeds and cultures of the world.

There comes a time when even speech loses its constitutional immunity. Speech innocuous one year may at another time fan such destructive flames that it must be halted in the interests of the safety of the Republic. That is the meaning of the clear and present danger test. When conditions are so critical that there will be no time to avoid the evil that the speech threatens, it is time to call a halt. Otherwise, free speech which is the strength of the Nation will be the cause of its destruction.

. . . But the command of the First Amendment is so clear that we should not allow Congress to call a halt to free speech except in the extreme case of peril from the speech itself. The First Amendment makes confidence in the common sense of our people and in their maturity of judgment the great postulate of our democracy. Its philosophy is that violence is rarely, if ever, stopped by denying civil liberties to those advocating resort to force.

Just what may be a "clear and present danger"? Justice Holmes pointed out some aspects of such a threat in *Schenck v. United States* (1919):

> The question in every case is whether the words used are used in such circumstances and are of such a nature as to create a clear and present danger that they bring about the substantive evils that Congress has a right to prevent. It is a question of proximity and degree.

Much of the judicial rhetoric is impressive and exhortatory but what the decisions will be in the last quarter of the twentieth century must depend, quite frankly, on how the Supreme Court justices interpret these precedents in the light of forthcoming cases. What direction they may take few men would be bold enough to forecast. As was correctly stated by Justice Frankfurter, judges "unconsciously are too apt to be moved by the deep undercurrents of public feeling" and the recently expressed lack of public confidence in the First Amendment freedoms is not a hopeful omen.

Support for much of the Bill of Rights has turned demonstrably negative during the past generation. This is especially true if the possible curbs concerned freedoms involving "the other fellow" rather than the self. A public opinion poll cited on a 1970 Columbia Broadcasting System "60 Minutes" program indicated that the First Amendment guarantees probably could not gain majority support in the 1970's. Disagreeing with the Bill of Rights provision, 55 percent of 1,136 adults in a national random telephone sample would deny newspapers, radio, and television in peacetime "the right to report any story . . . if the government feels that it's harmful to our national interest." Note the phrase "national interest" rather than the more narrowly defined national security. A *Newsweek* magazine survey showed 47 percent thought national security more important than press freedom, which got 34 percent, but only 33 percent approved of the government trying to stop publication of the Pentagon Papers. Forty-eight percent disapproved that effort. At a Gridiron Club Dinner in Washington during the winter of 1970, there was a joke that if the country rescinded the First Amendment, it still would have twenty-five left. Not very funny, some Americans thought, when they heard the story repeated. Marquis Childs, syndicated columnist and long-time newsman, claimed the average American's concern with the First Amendment can be "measured in an eye-dropper."

Beyond the possibilities of adverse court rulings and the popular disenchantment looms an even greater danger—within the media themselves. When American journalists used their freedoms and rights to harm individuals and to do serious damage to society, they hurt their own cause by their lapses into irresponsibility. But these exceptional cases are more than overbalanced by examples of public service that year after year are considered for Pulitzer Prizes and other awards. And who is to set limits on freedom and still maintain a free and responsible media? Certainly, the government would be a poor agency to act as a public guardian—even when one's own favorite politicians won the elections.

Some newsmen may not realize the potential dangers to their freedoms. This hazard was made pointedly clear by Barry Bingham, Jr., editor and publisher of the *Courier-Journal* and *Louisville Times,* during these comments in a 1970 Sigma Delta Chi Foundation lecture at the University of Wisconsin:

> We journalists have long been lulled into a false sense of security by the First Amendment to the Constitution. We fancy that because a free press is guaranteed to the American people, then we as journalists must be guaranteed the privilege of operating newspapers as we think best for the public welfare.
>
> The American people could soon put a stop to any such foolish assumption, if they should decide that the press simply is not operating in their best interest.

As the "people's right to know" has been a rallying cry during the past decade or longer, professional journalistic organizations have pushed hard to obtain legislation to force reluctant government officials to disgorge secrets that did not imperil the security of the state. Part of the difficulties in these discussions (or "battles" as they sometimes were accurately called in news dispatches) was that what officials often thought of as deepest confidences were considered simply skeletons of official mismanagement by the reporters. Hardly a single newsman wanted to jeopardize the lives of Americans in military uniform but they did not feel that political survival necessarily merited the same cozy treatment in news control. "Credibility gap" and "managed news" are terms frequently heard in this connection, but lawyers for the newspapers and most justices accepted the implications of some restrictions on the right to publish during the proceedings on the Pentagon Papers.

After a long campaign by reporters, especially Sigma Delta Chi, professional journalism society, a Freedom of Information Act became effective on July 4, 1967. In its report later that year, the SDX Advancement of Freedom of Information Committee called the legislation "a breakthrough, a clear change that leaves the parties [government and the news media] in redefined positions" and claimed that 1967 could be marked down as "a historic turning point." In a memorandum to guide all government agencies under the new law, Ramsey Clark, then attorney general, included these comments:

> If government is to be truly of, by and for the people, the people must know in detail the activities of government. Nothing so diminishes democracy as secrecy. . . . Never was it more important than in our times of mass society, when government affects each individual in so many ways, that the right of the people to know the actions of their government be secure. . . .

After several years of operation, enchantment and hopes for better flow of information under the Freedom of Information Act wilted. Among the most critical of comments was a twenty-page report by Ralph Nader, consumer advocate, and one hundred of his college-student "raiders" after a three-month study during the summer of 1969. Nader concluded, "The Freedom of Information act which came in on a wave of liberating rhetoric is being undermined by a riptide of bureaucratic ingenuity." For example, the "raiders" cited one official in the Pesticide Regulation Division of the Department of Agriculture who ordered material removed from a public departmental library when he learned they were examining it. The Federal Water Pollution Control Administration declined to release data on the sewage from domestic military bases because the Department of Defense was "finicky," it was said, about releasing figures under the claim that publication might be a matter of national security.

The Nader report enumerated specific tactics as follows:

★ Delay. "The typical tactic is to delay replying for several weeks and then state that the request for information was not specific enough. . . . The citizen is exposed to a charge of non-specificity. The more knowledgeable and fraternally received lobbyists, on the other hand, have no such problems."

★ Misclassification. Facts and documents are classified as "under investigation" or "internal communication" or "for official use only" to prevent disclosure. None of the agencies studied by Nader and the college students was concerned directly with military or foreign affairs.

★ High charges. Nader reported that some agencies charged as much as $1 a paper to copy information from their files. When a Cleveland *Plain Dealer* reporter, for instance, asked the Justice Department for the record of all federal pardons in 1967, he got the information from the master records in a 900-page volume. His paper got a bill for $245, which it paid.

★ Complicated appeals. Sometimes it took "weeks or months" to meander through the multiple layers of appeals that the information requests had to follow.

★ Inconsistent interpretations. Kinds of information available and procedures for appeals varied widely from agency to agency.

In summary, Nader's report said:

> These violations have come so regularly and with such cynicism that they seriously block citizen understanding and participation in government. There is prevailing an official belief that these federal agencies will not stand for searching inquiries, or even routine inquiries that appear searching because of their rarity, from citizens.

Nader's "raiders" were seeking information for consumers but their difficulties were not much different from some of those encountered by newsmen. The 1969 SDX Advancement of Freedom of Information Committee report faulted some reporters for not being as aggressive as they might have been. It said:

> Some affirmative steps were taken to open up government information channels in some departments, but the performance remains spotty. Part of the blame could be placed upon the press for not organizing a consistent planned assault upon the obvious misinterpretations of the Freedom of Information law by political appointees as well as by career bureaucrats.

Nader went further and blamed media for not "systematically following through to the courts on denials of agency information." The cost for filing such a suit in the District of Columbia is only $10 and since major news organizations already have legal counsel little, if any, additional costs would be involved. Yet the SDX report cited only two Washington correspondents—Clark R. Mollenhoff and Helene C. Monberg, Western Papers' Washington correspondent—for effective use of the

Freedom of Information law during 1969. Later that year Mollenhoff left his job as a long-time, prize-winning Washington correspondent with a talent for crusading journalism to become deputy counsel on the White House staff, a job he left within eighteen months.

So it is that some anticipated benefits for "the people's right to know" have been frittered away because correspondents were not eager enough to dig out what really was taking place behind the scenes so the public would be truly and fully informed. Media's audiences—in whose name much of the arguments for a free press are made—should be aware of the subtle pressures to manage the news. With the obvious advantages to not rocking the boat, it is probably surprising that there is as much crusading and exposé in American media as there is. Usually it requires guts and courage to buck the status quo and these characteristics are not in universal supply among journalists—or any other group, for that matter.

5. The Rules of "Thou Shalt" and "Thou Shalt Not"

What bothered the media most about Vice-President Spiro T. Agnew's criticism in 1969 was not that he didn't like them and their performances during the Nixon Administration. They had suffered brickbats previously and, despite some occasional peevishness about being spanked in public, had reacted with considerable decorum. It was not what Agnew said but the behind-the-scene implications that disturbed them.

Government agencies, under either Democratic or Republican presidents, set the rules for "Thou shalt" and "Thou shalt not" of many aspects of news dissemination operations—and that was what upset media representatives most about the Agnew speeches. For instance, the Federal Communications Commission allocates broadcast licenses to the air waves, without which no station may operate. The Federal Trade Commission decides what advertising is unfair competition and thus illegal. Along with Congress, the Post Office Department has much to do with which and under what circumstances publications may be sent under special postal rates. During the 1950's and 1960's, the Department of State determined who had permission for legal visits to such off-limits countries as Communist China, Cuba, North Vietnam, and Albania. And the judiciary branch of the government may affect press activities through a wide variety of means, including contempt proceedings and rules for cameras in the courtrooms.

Because of these and other controls by government the media saw a potential threat that the Nixon Administration would use such agency clout as it possessed to punish those whose performances it did not approve. Agnew, his administration associates, and their public information officers protested that such possible actions had never been contemplated. Yet media representatives were not so sure. They know that any president's influence on government agencies is real although it usually is a slow-motion process. In most cases, only a single appointment to a specific agency comes up to be filled in any calendar year but this provides a chance to eliminate those who oppose his philosophies when their terms expire. If a chief executive successfully screens the new appointees' thinking on matters in which the administration has a special interest, his viewpoint eventually prevails. An over-eager manipulation through choices that run against the prevailing mores of the U.S. Senate could encounter difficulties there in confirmation but, by and large, presidential appointments are approved. All of this might seem quite sinister but it really isn't despite the fact that most presidents eventually have imposed their thinking on federal agencies when they sought to do so. They just had to be satisfied to do it at snail's pace. The game is applied politics.

Now let's look at the governmental controls over various media and how they have been used in recent years.

The physical fact that the number of wave lengths available for media, either radio or television, is limited has loomed large in the rationale for government regulation of electronic journalism. To start a new daily newspaper in any of the nation's metropolitan areas requires primarily an "angel" with a multimillion-dollar bank account or credits. To launch a new radio or television station in any of these areas requires not only the funds but also a U.S. license before the first program goes on the air. This factor has dominated broadcasting ever since, in the time when Herbert Hoover was Secretary of Commerce, so many broadcasters took to the air waves that they got into each other's way; that is, with no rules on what frequencies to use, they succeeded in jamming each other's programs, producing utter chaos. A 1969 U.S. Supreme Court decision described the preregulation period as "the cacophony of competing voices, none of which could be clearly and predictably heard."

Federal Circuit Judge Warren Burger, before he became Chief Justice of the United States, told of the need for government regulation of the air waves in this 1966 decision:

> A broadcaster has much in common with a newspaper publisher, but he is not in the same category in terms of public obligations imposed by law. A broadcaster seeks and is granted the free and exclusive use of a limited and valuable part of the public domain; when he accepts that franchise, it is burdened by enforceable obligations. A newspaper can be operated at the whim or caprice of its owners; a broadcasting station cannot. After nearly five decades of operation, the broadcasting industry does not seem to have grasped the simple fact that a broadcasting license is a public trust subject to termination for breach of duty.

Broadcast regulations, now set up under the Communications Act of 1934, are extensive and the Federal Communications Commission, which it established, has augmented the legislation with its own interpretations. One of the act's most important provisions is that licenses are to be given if "the public convenience, interest, or necessity will be served thereby." Such licenses are granted for not more than three years and then subject to renewal "if the Commission finds that public interest, convenience, and necessity would be served thereby." Why "public interest" was ranked first for renewals but not in the language discussing original licenses has not been clarified. Does it mean the scales for renewal are different than for the first time around?

In a 1943 case challenging the FCC's authority, then concerned with radio, the U.S. Supreme Court upheld the act and added:

> Unlike other modes of expression, radio inherently is not available to all. That is its unique characteristic, and that is why, unlike other modes of expression, it is subject to government regulations. Because it cannot be used by all, some who wish to use it must be denied. . . . The licensing system established by Congress in the Communications Act of 1934 was a proper exercise of its power over commerce. The standard it provided for the licensing of stations was the "public interest, convenience, or necessity." Denial of a station license on that ground, if valid under the Act, is not a denial of free speech.

With the legal base thus established, the FCC has had to interpret, in recent years, just what the "public interest, convenience, or necessity" involved. Admittedly, many of these decisions have been subjective judgments and, especially in the late 1960's as the FCC firmed up some of its licensing requirements, they have resulted in a barrage of legal contests between the government agency and the broadcasting industry.

Although the FCC has been most reluctant to tell broadcasters just what specific programs they should put on the air, situations have arisen in which the agency had to decide if a station's defects were so grievous that it could no longer be said to be operating in the public interest. Attempting to set some guidelines that could be applied consistently, the FCC proposed that station programs be allocated toward some sort of balance between public service programing and the ever-popular entertainment and sports broadcasts. Commission members have focused especially on two areas when renewal times arrived: (1) The percentages of time allocated to such basic categories as religion, education, public affairs, news, and discussion programs and (2) the amount of time devoted to local self-expression, service to minority groups, political broadcasting, and children's programs. Certainly these deserve attention when licenses are up for review but, as a 1963 *Harvard Law Review* article stated, statistics were not a perfect measure:

> Critics contend that a category analysis is too uncertain a means of evaluating the nature and quality of program content. Nevertheless, by working with percentages and broad categories, the Commission may maintain at least a minimal degree of program control while avoiding the difficult value judgments involved in closer qualitative content regulation. Since "what seems to be trash may have for others fleeting or even enduring values," it would probably not be administratively feasible for the FCC to weigh qualitatively the merits of individual programs. However, a refinement of certain of the broad program categories—notably entertainment—would be practical. A narrower breakdown of programs into drama, light comedy, variety, classical music, and popular music, for example, might make the data on program balance more meaningful than they are now.

In 1965, FCC commissioners developed a "Policy Statement on Comparative Broadcast Hearings" and thus paved the way for questioning the procedures which Commissioner Nicholas Johnson called, "a blind reaffirmation of the present license holder" at renewal time. Up until then, practically all a station owner had to do to have his license renewed was keep his record reasonably untarnished by a large number of complaints of bias or other deficiencies and to file the necessary papers. Now it was to be somewhat different, apparently because in America's eleven largest cities not a single one of the lucrative Very High Frequency (VHF) television stations affiliated with a network was truly locally owned and independently managed. All of these thirty-three network-affiliated stations belonged to the networks, multiple station owners, or major local newspapers. According to a study released in early 1970, 256 daily newspapers had corporate ties with broadcast license holders in their cities. So, while the First Amendment freedoms protected newspaper owners in their primary investments from considerable government regulation, their broadcast subsidiaries provided much more vulnerable hostages for any administration that wished to push its agency powers to the limit.

A key illustration of how the revised policies might work for stations was shown in withdrawal of the license for Station WHDH in Boston, in which the Herald-Traveler Corporation had substantial holdings. Broadcasters were far less than enchanted at what they saw and they moved to protect their investments through the political route.

The license for WHDH, granted originally in 1957, had been before the FCC and then appealed to the courts during the 1960's. The death in late 1963 of Robert B. Choate, who had been president of both the Boston Herald-Traveler Corporation and WHDH, Inc., brought reopening of the whole record and continued arguments about the station's license renewal. Finally, in January 1969, a majority of FCC commissioners found that "the public interest, convenience, and necessity will be best served . . . by denial of the renewal application of WHDH, Inc." and gave approval for a new license to a competing local group, Boston Broadcasters, Inc. Since the issue was still in the courts, no date was set for the transfer.

In this landmark case, the Commission denied the application of an established and presently operating station for license renewal. The majority was concerned over (1) the "unauthorized transfers of control" after two WHDH presidents, in succession, died and were replaced; (2) failure to provide programs on controversial issues of local public importance; and (3) the *Herald-Traveler*'s failure to share a Massachusetts Crime Commission draft report with its sister station because "such news broadcast would have adversely affected the 'scoop' value of the story" in the Boston daily. As the majority explained, "In this instance, the joint ownership of newspaper and broadcast interest inured to the disadvantage of the broadcast stations and their listeners."

In support of their decision to support a different station management, the FCC majority argued:

As noted in the *Policy Statement,* diversification is a factor of first significance since it constitutes a primary objective in the Commission's licensing scheme. . . . When compared with Charles River and BBI [two competing rivals], WHDH manifestly ranks a poor third because of its ownership of a powerful standard broadcast station, an FM station, and a newspaper in the city of Boston itself. . . . A new voice would be brought to the Boston community as compared with continuing the service of WHDH-TV. We believe that the widest possible dissemination of information from diverse and antagonistic sources is in the public interest, and this principle would be significantly advanced by a grant of either the Charles River or the BBI application.

Commissioner Robert E. Lee dissented from the majority view, holding that "the renewal applicant's existing track record" was a most persuasive argument and that it certainly was entitled to more consideration than his colleagues seemed to give it. Then he added:

To hold otherwise would permit a new applicant to submit a "blue sky" proposal tailor-made to secure every comparative advantage while the existing licensee must reap the demerits of hand-to-hand combat in the business world, and the community it serves, in which it is virtually impossible to operate without error or complaint, if for no other reasons than there are insufficient hours in the broadcast day with which to satisfy all the desires of the public.

The issue of whether a licensee operated in the "public interest, convenience, and necessity" was even more sharply defined in the battle over Channel 11, the New York City WPIX station owned by the *Daily News.* On May 22, 1969, a competing application for the WPIX channel was filed by Forum Communications, a group which included Lawrence K. Grossman, an advertising man, as Forum head; Harry Belafonte, singer; Amalia Betanzos, executive director of the Puerto Rican Community Development project; Mrs. Ronnie Eldridge, aide to Mayor John Lindsay; Irwin (Sonny) Fox, one-time television show host; Paul Roebling, actor; and T. George Silcott, director of the Wiltwyck School for Boys.

During lengthy FCC hearings, some WPIX news staff members charged that old film clips had been misidentified and aired as if they were from current events and that *Daily News* reporters had broadcast without that fact being noted, leaving the impression with some viewers that they were full-time staff members. WPIX, to show its responsiveness to the needs and desires of the local community, cited its programs on education, housing, environment, recreation, religion, sports, and transportation and its special emphasis on news of community action, ghetto coverage, and investigative reporting. Forum countered that, if it received the channel, its main stress would be on local and community developments and it would surpass any other independent or network-owned station in the metropolitan area in the amount of its news coverage. As was pointed out in the WHDH opinions, a station seeking a renewal had to defend its track record while a competitor was free to pick that performance apart and to promise improvements.

Jack Gould, *The New York Times* broadcast commentator, explained repercussions that might follow a WPIX decision when he wrote (July 13, 1971):

> At stake is the equity of billions of dollars belonging to existing broadcasters arrayed against the determination of newcomers, who feel control of the medium should be more widely shared and afford a voice to others than the millionaires who got in on the ground floor 25 years ago.

While the debates were going on over ownership of WHDH and WPIX, license holders in a number of other communities also underwent challenges at renewal time. Among those under attack were Station KFBC-TV, Cheyenne's only television station, owned by the Frontier Broadcasting Company which also ran two radio stations and a cable television system in that city; Station WMAL-TV, operated by the *Washington* (D.C.) *Evening Star;* Station WTOP, controlled by Post-Newsweek Stations, Inc., a subsidiary of the Washington Post, Inc.; and Station KHJ-TV, whose Los Angeles license was held by RKO General Corporation. Among arguments made in these renewal contests were statements that wider ownership, preferably by local groups, would serve the public interest in more diversified programing.

With the FCC giving more attention to performance records at renewal time and with more contests in the offing, Sen. John O. Pastore, Dem., Rhode Island, one of Congress' influential communications specialists, introduced a bill that would prevent new applicants from challenging current station operators unless an existing license had been revoked for failure to serve the public interest. Broadcasters said they needed the legislation to protect their investments but their critics argued that all concerned had known about the three-year license period when they applied, and accepted, grants and renewals. Such legislation could tend to reinstitute the former FCC procedures which were called "a blind reaffirmation of the present license holder."

Under the threat of new restrictive legislation, the commissioners issued a policy-clarifying statement explaining that future challenges would be dismissed if broadcasters demonstrated at renewal time that their programing "substantially" had served the public interest, but the courts were unhappy with this proposed solution.

Discussing license renewals and the FCC clarifying statement that a station's track record definitely would count, Chairman Dean Burch told a National Association of Broadcasters' 1970 convention that, although "the broadcaster doing a good job has nothing to fear at renewal time," the FCC would not "protect the minimal operator against competition." Then he added:

> The reasonable broadcaster is safe; the broadcaster whose only thought is to get by with as little service to the public as possible is in danger.
>
> He must run on his record without upgrading when the competitor appears on the scene, and he must run the risk of losing to a better competitor.

According to news dispatches, the audience did not applaud this latest interpretation of how renewals could be turned down.

That the challenges to television station licenses have been invigorating for programing at the local level can be demonstrated in numerous cities. *Variety,* certainly not unsympathetic to broadcasters' problems, reported that the level of programing "without question" had been raised in most major markets, especially those where potential new owners were waiting to be heard by the FCC. "There is on the whole discernibly more local involvement, more community affairs and educational programing, more news and discussion and more showcasing of minority talent since the license challenges than there were before," the show-business publication said.

What should be kept in mind in these discussions is that keystone set in place when the first governmental controls were established over broadcasting in 1927: that the air ways belong to the people—not the station owners.

Complaints are heard that FCC commissioners, assigned by law to act in the "public interest," are subservient to industry's beck and call and that politicians, including those who name them, are too accommodating. In November 1969, after Vice-President Agnew had launched his attack on television commentators, Commissioner Johnson claimed that two Nixon appointments to the FCC had been cleared with the broadcasting industry. Of the heads of the three large commercial networks, he said in a New York speech, "Never in history have a handful of men had more power over their government than do these men." The language compared with the Vice-President's but they described an entirely different group of network officials. Who watches the watchers? A key question!

Multiple ownership, in and of itself, need not be a diabolical thing but diversity has been accepted in this country as a sign of faith in the democratic process. Statistics are scarce but the whole antitrust concept rests on the assumption of potential or real dangers from monopoly and conglomerate owners. Further, as Commissioner Johnson said, one could hope that in the near future at least one of the thirty-three network-affiliated television stations in the eleven major U.S. metropolises would be truly independently owned and oriented.

First stated in 1929, the FCC's position has been that "public interest requires ample play for the free and fair competition of opposing views." This has become known in broadcasting circles as the "fairness doctrine," the name given to it in the 1949 FCC report, "Editorializing by Broadcast Licensees." The commissioners later promised that they would not substitute their own judgments in assessing complaints about a controversial issue of public importance but, rather, "determine whether the licensee can be said to have acted reasonably and in good faith." They added that there was considerably more discretion here than under the "equal opportunity" requirement for candidates for the same political office. Repeatedly the Commission has referred to its 1949 report and said that broadcasters have an "affirmative duty" to seek out and encourage opposing viewpoints for dissemination over their facilities.

An essential part of the 1949 report said:

> If, as we believe to be the case, the public interest is best served in a democracy through the ability of the people to hear expositions of the various positions taken by responsible groups and individuals on particular topics and to choose between them, it is evident that broadcast licensees have an affirmative duty generally to encourage and implement the broadcast of all sides of controversial public issues

over their facilities, over and beyond their obligation to make available on demand opportunities for the expression of opposing views.

The fairness doctrine was extended to require a station to allow free time to rebut what is considered a personal attack upon an individual. The case which did that was *Red Lion Broadcasting Co., Inc., v. Federal Communications Commission.* The U.S. Supreme Court decided it in 1969. On Nov. 27, 1964, as part of a "Christian Crusade" series broadcast over Pennsylvania Station WGCB, owned by the Red Lion Broadcasting Company, the Rev. Billy James Hargis attacked Fred J. Cook, author of the book, *Goldwater—Extremist on the Right.* Hargis said Cook had been fired from his newspaper job for fabricating false charges against New York City officials, had worked for a Communist-affiliated publication, and had now written a "book to smear and destroy Barry Goldwater." When Cook heard about the broadcast later, he requested free time to reply to what he considered a personal attack. The station declined, sending him its advertising rate schedule and asking if he could find a sponsor to pay for the rebuttal time. Cook was upheld in his right to reply in a Supreme Court decision which argued that a broadcast licensee had no constitutional right "to monopolize a radio frequency to the exclusion of his fellow citizens," adding:

> There is nothing in the First Amendment which prevents the Government from requiring a licensee to share his frequency with others and to conduct himself as a proxy or fiduciary with obligations to present those views and voices which are representative of his community and which would otherwise, by necessity, be barred from the airwaves. . . .
>
> It is the purpose of the First Amendment to preserve an uninhibited marketplace of ideas in which truth will ultimately prevail, rather than to countenance monopolization of that market, whether it be by the Government itself or a private licensee. . . . It is the right of the public to receive suitable access to social, political, esthetic, moral, and other ideas and experiences which is crucial here. That right may not constitutionally be abridged either by Congress or by the FCC.

In the late 1960's, the federal courts held that the fairness doctrine could be applied to broadcast advertising. Thus, prior to the FCC ban on commercials promoting cigarettes after January 1, 1971, such announcements were counterbalanced with others pointing out the hazards of smoking. In August 1971 the U.S. Court of Appeals in Washington ruled, 2 to 1, that broadcasters could no longer refuse to sell advertising time to groups wishing to broadcast controversial messages simply because they might trigger legal demands for free and equal time in which to reply. Judge J. Skelly Wright, for the majority, reasoned that individuals should have the right, under the First Amendment, to buy advertising time if they felt a station was not expressing adequately all viewpoints. Broadcasters had argued that excessive demands for free replies might drive them into bankruptcy.

Aware that the price of free rebuttal could become high but unwilling to allow the stifling of controversial and unconventional programs, the FCC has tried to establish a middle course. Illustrative of this right to provide programs that might offend some listeners has been the renewal of FM licenses to stations of the Pacifica Foundation. Complaints claimed Pacifica's California and New York City stations were "filthy" and Communist-oriented. In granting a renewal in 1964, the FCC admitted that "such provocative programing as here involved may offend some listeners" but the decision to relicense added that "this does not mean that those offended have the right, through the commission's licensing power, to rule such programing off the airwaves."

Much has been heard about broadcasting's equal time or equal opportunity provision for political candidates. Policies to insure this approach began with the first regulations in 1927 and provided that stations had to give equal opportunity to all "legally qualified" opponents if time was provided for any political candidate. Not only must the provision be for an equal amount of time but for comparable opportunity to reach the station's audience. In other words, midmorning time on a Sunday is not a satisfactory offer to one candidate when prime time during the evening hours is available for his opponent. Uninformed politicians or those with special axes to grind have asked for time, for instance, to reply to a U.S. president when neither he nor they were formally announced candidates. Although networks and stations have granted time for a few such requests, this is a misinterpretation of the Communication Act's Section 315 on "equal opportunities," which is the phrase used in the law. In 1959, Congress excluded on-the-spot news coverage, news interviewing, and bona fide news documentaries.

In the spring of 1970, FCC commissioners sought to break what some TV critics called the stranglehold of major networks on prime-time programing. On May 7, the Commission's majority ruled that, effective with the start of the 1971 fall season, stations in the fifty top markets would have to program at least one of their four nightly prime-time hours with independently produced material. These fifty markets include approximately three-quarters of the nation's television sets. Even majority members in the split voting were not sanguine about what would happen to what they called "quality" programing. They argued that the action represented just about the last chance to force diversity through regulation in the hope of breaking into the networks' prime-time domains. Dissenters to the new rule called it "Pollyanna-ish" and predicted it would provide "more of the same," such as game shows, "light entertainment along proven formulas," and "emcee" talk programs. Recent experience would seem to support the latter viewpoint because, with a few exceptions, such as man's first moon walk in July 1969, U.S. viewers have not gotten as excited about news documentaries as they have about prime-time entertainment specials and such features as sports, travel, history, and nature. Of 176 prime-time specials rated by A. C. Nielsen Company from September 1969 to April 1970, only eighteen were news documentaries and eight of these were Apollo flights. None ranked in the top twenty-five more popular programs. A well-reviewed American Broadcasting Company show, "A Matter of Conscience—Ethics in Government" rated in last place. As the Alfred I. duPont–Columbia University 1969-70 broadcast survey commented, ". . . there was little indication that the American viewer was getting more serious in his interests." It seemed a dubious choice of either local diversity with emphasis on the highly rated, popular entertainment-type programing versus network monoliths with some insistence on a quest for quality. Final resolution remains in the future.

Because they are all forms of communication and thus under its purview, the FCC also supervises rate schedules on commercial wire systems, fees for use of the government-chartered Communications Satellite Corporation (Comsat), and rates and other jurisdictional problems of the burgeoning community antenna television systems (CATV). The Commission also sets the guidelines on what may and may not be disseminated about such lotteries as those of New Hampshire and New York state. Stations may provide "legitimate news stories appropriate to broadcasting" but they can't promote lotteries by telling where to buy tickets or by airing live the actual drawings of winners.

Much more indirect than the FCC in its relationship with broadcasting, the Federal Trade Commission helps to determine what gets used and, to some extent, how much money is spent to tell the sellers' message. The FTC deals with those who write or buy advertising space or time. The Commission was created in 1914, to a large degree due to the dramatic journalism of muckrakers in the early twentieth century. The agency was to promote "the preservation of an environment which would foster the liberty to compete" and so over the earlier years false advertising became one of its prime targets. After the passage of the Wheeler-Lea Amendments of 1938, the Commission's concern increasingly shifted from restraint of trade practices to consumer protection. Among notable cases to come before the FTC during the past decade or more have been: the Palmolive Rapid Shave "sandpaper shave" and Geritol's "tired blood."

In 1959, Kyle Rote and Frank Gifford, both then professional football players with heavy beards, appeared in advertisements for Rapid Shave aerosol shaving cream, a product of Colgate-Palmolive Company. Both easily shaved with Rapid Shave on camera. Then the television commercial claimed, "Rapid Shave out-shaves them all" and an announcer said, "To prove Rapid Shave's super-moisturizing power, we put it right from the can onto this tough, dry sandpaper. It was apply . . . soak . . . and off in a stroke." As he spoke a razor cleaned a path removing all abrasive grains in its way. A FTC examiner found that sandpaper of the kind used in the TV commercial had to be soaked approximately eighty minutes before it could be shaved off easily and that the Ted Bates-produced film had used a "mock-up" prop of plexiglas to which sand had been applied. The commissioners issued a cease-and-desist order against Colgate and Bates because the demonstration was "not in fact genuine or accurate" and did not prove the quality or merits of the product. The order set off protracted appeals and the U.S. Supreme Court settled the case. Chief Justice Earl Warren in a 1965 decision wrote:

> We agree with the Commission, therefore, that the undisclosed use of plexiglass in the present commercials was a material deceptive practice, independent and separate from the other misrepresentation found. We find unpersuasive respondents' other objections to this conclusion. Respondents claim that it will be impractical to inform the viewing public that it is not seeing an actual test, experiment or demonstration, but we think it inconceivable that the ingenious advertising world will be unable, if it so desires, to conform to the Commission's insistence that the public be not misinformed. If, however, it becomes impossible or impractical to show simulated demonstrations on television in a truthful manner, this indicates that

television is not a medium that lends itself to this type of commercial, not that the commercial must survive at all costs.

So it would seem that the Court's decision still permitted, as it said, "the ingenious advertising world" considerable territory in which its clients could garner sales dollars.

The Geritol "tired blood" case began in April 1959, when the FTC staff launched an investigation. Three and a half years later, the Commission issued a complaint. On Sept. 28, 1965, a cease-and-desist order was unanimously issued and twenty-three months later upheld, in substance, by the Sixth Circuit Court. A revised order, which became final Dec. 31, 1967, required the company to specify that "the great majority of tired people don't feel that way because of iron-poor blood and Geritol won't help them." When the company started a new television series, however, the FTC believed that it, like the earlier ads, violated the cease-and-desist order and held protracted discussions with the manufacturer. Almost a year after Ralph Nader's "raiders" had cited the Geritol case as illustrating how lax FTC was in enforcement, the Commission requested the Department of Justice to sue the makers of Geritol for deceptive advertising. The government filed a million dollar suit in April 1970, half against the manufacturing concern and half against its advertising firm. So more than a decade after the FTC staff first began its investigation, the case again moved into the judicial mainstream for court action.

Although the two cited cases involved broadcasting commercials, FTC does have authority to take action against individuals and firms that it considers may have violated fair practices in their print advertising or made misleading statements. For instance, the FTC in mid-1971 asked seven automobile manufacturers to substantiate several dozen advertising claims, such as "over 700 percent quieter" and "109 advantages to keep it from getting old before its time." Motor companies were given sixty days to submit sworn statements verifying the accuracy of their advertising.

Newspapers and magazines face heavy and direct restraints from the U.S. Postal Service. The postmaster general and his associates interpret the law that establishes second class mailing privileges. This is extremely important because, as the U.S. Supreme Court said in *Hannegan v. Esquire* (1946), "The second-class privilege is a form of subsidy." It involves the amount of money to be paid by publishers for postal distribution of their wares and thus has a business office impact, which sometimes can be quite great. While second class postal rates have mounted under inflationary pressures during recent years, loss of such privileges to a publication easily could mean the difference between profits and a possible loss on its balance sheet. When *Life* magazine inadvertently violated a base requirement for second class mailing rights for one issue by inserting special size advertising brochures, it was estimated that approximately $2,000,000 was riding on the outcome of negotiations between the publishing firm and the government. And that was just a single week's issue of one nationally circulated magazine.

The Founding Fathers' concept for special postal rights for publications rested on the Miltonian idea of stimulating a free marketplace for ideas. For the general public to receive and thus evaluate all possible ideas was worth a price—reduced mailing costs for newspapers and magazines at public subsidy. The practice continues today.

To obtain second class mailing privileges, newspapers and periodicals must be issued regularly, at least four times a year, must not be printed primarily for advertising purposes, must print a notice of entry as second class matter at a specific post office, and must have a "legitimate list of subscribers." The purpose of the publication must be "dissemination of information of a public character, or devoted to literature, the sciences, arts, or some special industry." Pornographic materials, including papers, magazines, and books, are not entitled to the First Amendment privileges and sending that kind of material through the mails is punishable with prison sentences. One difficulty in the 1970's has been to determine what, if anything, judges would consider obscene.

The Customs Bureau also exercises some curbs on the mass media. For instance, when three U.S. photographers returned from North Vietnam in August 1969, the Customs Bureau seized twelve thousand feet of undeveloped film that they had shot in Hanoi and its environs. The cameramen charged harassment and intimidation. Customs representatives said a federal statute prohibited importation of printed matter or pictures that advocated or urged treason or insurrection against this country and that, until they developed the film, they did not know what had been photographed. The developed pictures were returned approximately a week later.

Mail from Communist countries that is considered propaganda also may be seized but, in recent years, that addressed to media and learned societies has moved through fairly promptly.

The Passport Office of the Department of State has imposed a slightly inhibiting role upon newsmen since the tenure of the late Secretary of

State John Foster Dulles. He denied permission for reporters to visit Communist China and Albania as part of his cold war arsenal but the Chinese learned the lesson so rapidly that they, too, raised bars to U.S. newsmen by declining to grant them visas. Cuba and North Vietnam later were added to the list. In the late 1960's and 1970's, the embargo dam broke with more and more reporters going to Hanoi and Peking with both passports and visas in order.

Government agencies having little to do with communications sometimes make requests to which the media listen and sometimes pay attention. For instance, the Federal Aviation Administration during the summer of 1971 asked some five hundred television broadcasting stations not to rerun "The Doomsday Flight," a 1966 film which apparently was triggering telephoned bomb threats to airlines. The FAA wrote stations that they could make "the highest possible contribution to the safety of more than 160 million passengers" by not showing the film. In Canada the film was run on July 26 and within a week a British Overseas Airways Corporation Boeing 747 with 379 persons aboard had to be diverted to Denver from a Montreal-London flight because a telephone call said a bomb would explode if the plane flew below 5,000 feet. The caller asked $250,000 ransom to tell where the bomb was hidden but search of the aircraft at the mile-high Denver airport disclosed none was aboard. Although only twenty U.S. stations replied to the FAA within six weeks, an agency spokesman said he knew of no stations running the film after the letters were mailed. The film's distributor expected to remove the film from packets already sold for broadcast.

That the First Amendment guarantees did not exempt news organizations from regulatory legislation passed by Congress for application to all U.S. industries was brought out in a historic 1937 case involving the Associated Press. Upon appeal of a National Labor Relations Board decision, the U.S. Supreme Court held the right to organize by reporters was the same as the right of automobile workers, miners, and salesmen: "The business of the Associated Press is not immune from regulation because it is an agency of the press. The publisher of a newspaper has no special immunity from the application of general laws."

An earlier case established another limit: that legislatures could not enact special laws aimed at controlling or curbing the press. After the more widely circulated Louisiana dailies opposed him politically, Senator Huey Long, Dem., Louisiana, former governor and state political boss, got state legislators to pass an act which taxed papers with the larger circulations in that state. The targets were specific and the legislation was carefully drafted to eliminate all the smaller journals that supported the Senator and his machine. The U.S. Supreme Court held in *Grosjean v. American Press Company* (1936):

> The tax here involved is bad not because it takes money from the pockets of the appellees. If that were all, a wholly different question would be presented. It is bad because, in the light of its history and of its present setting, it is seen to be a deliberate and calculated device in the guise of a tax to limit the circulation of information to which the public is entitled in virtue of constitutional guaranties. A free press stands as one of the great interpreters between the government and the people. To allow it to be fettered is to fetter ourselves.

The ideal solutions to the multifarious problems arising from government regulations require the avoidance of dangers from overweening subservience to industry's most rampant commercial aspirations, on the one hand, and of ruthless exploitation by politicians, on the other. To serve the "public interest," as the FCC commissioners are charged directly and as others are charged by implication, demands an eternal vigilance that unfortunately is not found in every appointee to a federal agency. Thus it is that pressures often build up to a point where the media make some decision because of the possible reaction—and, to some observers, punitive action—by a majority in a government regulatory group.

Just as the Congress through legislation and the president and his administration through federal agencies may influence media action, the courts make decisions that affect various segments of the press. In recent years, these have been chiefly through (1) contempt procedures and (2) restrictions on the use of cameras, still or TV, in a courtroom as they might interfere with efforts to preserve the dual constitutional guarantees of a free press and a fair trial.

Most journalists and practically all lawyers agree that some sort of courtroom decorum has to be established for suspected individuals to have a fair trial. Practically all journalists and most lawyers also agree that a free press is necessary to a free society. Yet the two professions get into disagreements, sometimes exacerbative and more emotional than rational, over how to interpret just what constitutes a "clear and present danger" to trial procedures. When contempt cases finally have reached the U.S.

Supreme Court, it has consistently upheld media's freedom to report judicial proceedings, but in cases involving pretrial publicity the justices have said unkind words about media performances, especially in those of the local newspaper stories and editorials about Dr. Sam Sheppard (see Chapter Two) and the television broadcasts of the Billie Sol Estes hearings.

In *Pennekamp v. Florida* (1946), the U.S. Supreme Court carefully delineated the responsibilities of judges and newsmen and these guidelines remain, in principle, for today. The case involved a contempt citation after the *Miami Herald* printed a series of editorials and a cartoon which the Florida courts said created a "clear and present danger" to justice. Key parts of the decision, to which there was no dissent, follow:

> Without a free press there can be no free society. Freedom of the press, however, is not an end in itself but a means to the end of a free society. The scope and nature of the constitutional protection of freedom of speech must be viewed in that light and in that light applied. The independence of the judiciary is no less a means to the end of a free society, and the proper functioning of an independent judiciary puts the freedom of the press in its proper perspective. For the judiciary cannot function properly if what the press does is reasonably calculated to disturb the judicial judgment in its duty and capacity to act solely on the basis of what is before the court. A judiciary is not independent unless courts of justice are enabled to administer law by absence of pressure from without, whether exerted through the blandishments of reward or the menace of disfavor. . . . A free press is not to be preferred to an independent judiciary, nor an independent judiciary to a free press. Neither has primacy over the other; both are indispensable to a free society. The freedom of the press in itself presupposes an independent judiciary through which that freedom may, if necessary, be vindicated. And one of the potent means for assuring judges their independence is a free press. . . .
>
> Weak characters ought not to be judges, and the scope allowed to the press for society's sake may assume that they are not. No judge fit to be one is likely to be influenced consciously except by what he sees and hears in court and by what is judicially appropriate for his deliberations. However, judges are also human, and we know better than did our forebears how powerful is the pull of the

unconscious and how treacherous the rational process. While the ramparts of reason have been found to be more fragile than the Age of Enlightenment had supposed, the means for arousing passion and confusing judgment have been reinforced. And since judges, however stalwart, are human, the delicate task of administering justice ought not to be made unduly difficult by irresponsible print. . . .

If men, including judges and journalists, were angels, there would be no problems of contempt of court. Angelic judges would be undisturbed by extraneous influences and angelic journalists would not seek to influence them. The power to punish for contempt, as a means of safeguarding judges in deciding on behalf of the community as impartially as is given to the lot of men to decide, is not a privilege accorded to judges. The power to punish for contempt of court is a safeguard not for judges as persons but for the function which they exercise. It is a condition of the function—indispensable for a free society—that in a particular controversy pending before a court and awaiting judgment, human beings, however strong, should not be torn from their mooring of impartiality by the undertow of extraneous influence. In securing freedom of speech, the Constitution hardly meant to create the right to influence judges or juries. That is no more freedom of speech than stuffing a ballot box is an exercise of the right to vote.

American judges have been strict in curbing—or, as most do, banning —cameras in the courtroom. When Estes had a preliminary hearing and trial in Texas on swindling charges during 1962, television and still photographers were allowed, virtually without restraint, at the two-day hearing. After his original conviction, Estes appealed to the U.S. Supreme Court and the majority of the judges ordered a new trial. Justice Tom C. Clark, who delivered the majority opinion, said:

A defendant on trial for a specific crime is entitled to his day in court, not in a stadium, or a city or nationwide arena. The heightened public clamor resulting from radio and television coverage will inevitably result in prejudice. Trial by television is, therefore, foreign to our system.

In a strongly worded dissent, Justice Potter Stewart argued that "the introduction of television into a courtroom is, at least in the present state of the art, an extremely unwise policy," but he added that "I am unable to escalate this personal view into a *per se* constitutional rule."

Despite the best efforts of bar associations and journalism societies at local, state, and national levels, it has been demonstrated that neither lawyers nor newsmen were "angels," which was known long before the 1946 court decision. Ideally each side in this argument could police its own activities—but this will not be easy for either. So the threat of contempt proceedings hangs over newsmen, editors, and proprietors despite the Supreme Court's impressive record of generally slapping down such citations when they are appealed.

6. Pressure Points for Managing the News

Anyone who has taken first aid lessons knows that there are certain specific spots at which it is possible to apply pressure and stop emergency bleeding. So it is in the journalistic process—but without such beneficial objectives. Applying pressure at any of four points will interfere effectively with the flow of information and news to the public. Those who desire to manage the news are fully aware of these points and do not hesitate to use this knowledge for their own purposes. These four points are:

(1) The news source itself.

(2) The reporters with all their individual mores, prejudices, and ideals.

(3) The news "gatekeepers": some editors and proprietors, especially those individuals who set broad editorial policies and then see that they are carried out. As used here, the phrase "editorial policies" does not mean what gets support or disapproval on opinion pages or broadcast commentaries but the guidelines for the whole publication or broadcast. This need not be something sinister—as some cynical critics of media often seek to describe it. It is just that somebody has final authority for setting policy.

(4) The ultimate "news consumers," especially those with indelible stereotypes or "pictures in their minds," to borrow from the phrases of Walter Lippmann. Preconceptions may make it difficult, if not impossible, to accept new viewpoints that do not square with the old and familiar. Some individuals just won't believe what is there in the news dispatch or broadcast.

In the procession from news source to ultimate reader or listener, each step represents a nearly irreversible decision. For instance, if a news source can successfully block release of information, then the reporters, "gatekeepers," or readers can do little to remedy the deficiency. On the other hand, stereotypes existing in minds of the reading and listening audience may unravel most, if not all, of the effective efforts of those who have handled the news previously.

Since most newsmen are primarily writers—either for print or for broadcast—the derogations of the news sources have been fairly well publicized during the years since it has become respectable to cover and tell. Various approaches to news gathering fall into four categories: embargoes that physically inhibit, if not prevent, the gathering and dissemination of news; deliberate misrepresentations that are either outright lies or a neat blend of omissions and half-truths; the keeping of news (or at least the key points of it) out of reporters' sight and hoping that they won't discover the remainder; and a frank, "open door" policy that honestly tells what is going on.

Possibly the simplest way to manage the news is not to admit reporters, at least those who may ask probing and possibly embarrassing questions. The Soviet Union tried this during the cold war years when Josef Stalin set the rules. Even this was not completely successful because the less than half dozen representatives of the Western press in Moscow during that era often told more than the Soviets wanted known. The Russians probably carried control of newsmen to the ultimate when Stalin died. They simply had a workman rip out the backboard connections at the Moscow international switchboard and thus broke all the outgoing lines that reporters might have used to get the news out of the country. In that case, newsmen had their facts but they lacked any chance for releasing them. A reporter without a channel for distributing his news is as ineffectual as no reporter at all—for the time being. Eventually, however, he does leave the country or the war front where the embargoes apply.

The Spanish American War was the last involving U.S. troops in which a wealthy publisher could simply charter a yacht and sail away to cover the fighting on land and sea. That was what William Randolph Hearst did. In this century, the Pentagon and, earlier, the War and Navy Departments have demanded accreditation before admitting newsmen to most war areas. Of course, it has been possible in some cases for correspondents to go to the fighting scene on their own—but without quarters, post exchange privileges, communications, and transportation, all provided by the U.S. government, their lives have not been pleasant and their exclusive news has been rare. Probably too much should not be made of these restrictions by the military but Vietnam reporters have confessed that their reporting was not always effective when accreditation was withdrawn.

Harassment of newsmen can very effectively create an environment which makes objective information gathering close to impossible. Police action in Chicago during the 1968 Democratic convention was an example. The following are all remarks of Chicago law enforcement officers, taken from newsmen's statements printed in *Rights in Conflict,* the Walker Report to the National Commission on the Causes and Prevention of Violence:

"Fuck your press cards." (By a policeman to a reporter being clubbed in the back.)

"Get the man with the camera." (Directed to a news photographer.)

"Give me your god dam notebook you dirty bastard." (Remark to Claude Lewis of the Philadelphia *Evening Bulletin,* who was clubbed four or five times and treated at a hospital for "a contusion and abrasions of the scalp.")

One television reporter at the Chicago convention recalled that two police detectives, separately, had warned him "the word is being passed to get newsmen" and "be careful—the word is out to get newsmen." And "get newsmen" the police did; a total of forty-nine newsmen are described in the Walker Report as having been hit, maced, or arrested, "apparently without reason," by the police. In more than forty instances, the report said the newsmen involved were clearly identifiable as such. The performance of Chicago law enforcement officers during convention week was described by the Walker Report as "a police riot."

Embargoes may arise from reasons that have only tangential relation to news coverage. For instance, civil rights groups and later the Black Panthers have barred or ejected white newsmen from some of their strategy sessions but have been willing to admit blacks employed in media. Various motivations cause this reaction to "whitey" members of the so-called Establishment press and broadcast media. Since blacks are underemployed by all media in comparison with their proportion in the total U.S. population, refusal to admit white reporters forces many personnel officers to look harder for qualified blacks. (Mrs. Franklin D. Roosevelt utilized a comparable rule about women reporters when she first went to the White House in 1933 and her enforcement of that admission requirement brought about greater job opportunities in Washington for females in those depression years.) Many blacks have antagonism against the predominantly white Establishment media and barring white reporters simply reflects this emotion. Also just enough white "informers" for federal agencies have posed as reporters for some activists to be suspicious about allowing any but black "brothers" to sit in on such councils.

Earlier, Northern white reporters assigned to cover the civil rights news in the South were attacked and beaten by segregationists who felt that such tactics would force media to leave uncovered what was happening in Dixie. However, the beatings did not generally curtail such news.

Broadcasters also have encountered their difficulties. When the National Broadcasting Company was filming a 1968 documentary on racial and poverty problems in metropolitan areas, film crews shot scenes of the black area of Boston with telephoto lens—instead of close-up as done in other cities—because, as Frank McGee explained in the narrative, organized community groups had promised to hold demonstrations during the filming unless they could pick participants and then edit the processed film. NBC refused to surrender its editing prerogatives and thus the telephoto lens was used.

If truth has its uses, so has untruth. When a news source tries to manage information, he may give some of the "truth" but fall far short of the whole truth. When the fuller story is revealed, those who trifled with the facts may have to face the consequences.

The "cover story" on the U-2 incident during the last year of the Eisenhower Administration is a classic illustration of a news diversion that backfired with international consequences. On May 1, 1960, just two weeks before a scheduled Big Four summit conference in Paris, a U.S. plane was brought down over the Soviet Union and thus did not reach its scheduled destination in Norway on a flight from Pakistan. The United States announced that one of its weather reconnaissance ships from Turkey was missing. On May 5, Soviet Premier Nikita Khrushchev said that a U.S. "spy plane" had been brought down by antiaircraft fire and accused this country of "rekindling the cold war." Through the White House press secretary, this government denied the Russian interpretation and the U.S. State Department added that no American planes had deliberately crossed the Soviet border. Then Khrushchev produced the plane's pilot, Francis Gary Powers, who had parachuted to earth, and also claimed that Powers had confessed to an espionage mission. Khrushchev demanded that President Dwight D. Eisenhower admit that the United States had committed "aggression" against the Soviet Union and that "the guilty" who had ordered the flight be punished. The President refused and the Paris conference collapsed before it began. Powers was convicted after a widely publicized trial in Russia and was sentenced to ten years' confinement. Much later, Ike's press secretary, James Hagerty, was quoted as commenting, "If there was any mistake in the U-2 affair, it was that we moved too fast on our cover story."

During the Cuban missile crisis, President John F. Kennedy told his press secretary to announce that he was suffering from a cold and was discontinuing his Midwestern tour; his real reason, it turned out later, was to obtain the latest information in Washington on the Cuban build-up in weapons. Back in the national capital, the President still kept a lid on news releases because he feared premature publication of what the United States was doing might jeopardize the impact of its response, possibly alerting Premier Khrushchev before U.S. ships and troops were in place for possible military action.

News tinkering, of sorts, accounted for much of President Lyndon B. Johnson's lack of credibility with press and public.

On April 1, 1965, for instance, the President and his advisors made "the decision . . . to change the mission of our ground forces in South Vietnam from one of advice and static defense to one of active combat operations against the Vietcong guerillas," according to a memo from John A. McCone, director of the Central Intelligence Agency, which was included in the Pentagon Papers. That same week, the President told reporters at his news conference that this country sought no wider war, adding, "I know of no far-reaching strategy that is being suggested or promulgated" to commit U.S. troops to ground fighting in Vietnam.

Documentation for this example did not come for some years but other cases were exposed within a week or less. To illustrate, President Johnson was asked at his televised news conference on March 9, 1967, whether there was any truth in reports he was searching for a successor to U.S. Ambassador Henry Cabot Lodge at Saigon. The President replied, "No, there is no truth that I am looking for a successor," adding that no definite date had been set for Lodge to leave. Less than a week later, Ellsworth Bunker was named as Saigon ambassador. The White House press secretary, George Christian, was queried about the President's televised answer and replied that LBJ's response was "absolutely accurate" because he had chosen Lodge's replacement by March 9 and thus was not looking for a successor. A *Chicago Daily News* editorial protested, "Accurate, perhaps, but not truthful. . . . Newsmen were put off the track, the country misled, by a technical escape hatch."

So often did such word games with the press take place in the late 1960's that William McGaffin and Erwin Knoll, both respected Washington correspondents, summed up a not uncommon feeling about the Johnson Administration when they said in their book, *Anything but the Truth* (G. P. Putnam's Sons, New York, 1968):

> What set the Johnson administration apart from its predecessors, in fact, is merely that the dissemination of half-truths and untruths has become a matter of day-to-day routine.

Evasion and lack of candor was applied to areas far from combat and politics. For instance, during March 1968, approximately 6,000 sheep mysteriously died in Skull Valley, Utah. Eventually the cause was shown to be exposure to nerve gas from the nearby Army Dugway proving ground, at which the military tested chemical and biological warfare agents. But repeatedly during congressional questioning, Army CBW officials denied that nerve gas was involved in the sheep's deaths—even after government agents had agreed to indemnify the animals' owners. Finally, in May 1969, a Chemical Corps representative admitted to a House of Representatives subcommittee that his fellow officers had lied from the beginning.

At President Franklin D. Roosevelt's 1937 press conference to disclose his proposals for reorganizing the federal courts, the main thrust of his discussion was on the need to bring new blood into the judiciary without pointing up the impact it would have among the Supreme Court's "nine old men," a majority of whom had held unconstitutional large portions of the New Deal's legal basis for reform. At least one long-time White House press association reporter failed to recognize the potential implications for the nation's highest court—until he was interrupted while dictating his news story and questioned sharply by his news superiors.

Then a new lead stressing the Supreme Court angle was substituted hurriedly for the earlier version from the White House correspondent. Thus did an alert copydesk cut through the camouflage.

When First Lieutenant William L. Calley, Jr., was retained on active duty so the Army could proceed with charges arising from the My Lai slayings, the Fort Benning public information office simply added that this case would be referred to court-martial trial for "violation of Article 118, murder, for offenses allegedly committed against civilians while serving in Vietnam in March 1968." Specific details of the massacre were omitted and the news about Calley got printed at the bottom of page 38 of the Sept. 8, 1969, issue of *The New York Times*. As released, it seemed fairly routine and when reporters asked about the number killed, the Fort Benning PIO referred them to the Pentagon in Washington or replied, "No comment." When the full import of the massacre finally was unearthed, it received major front-page play in dailies across the nation on November 13, telling about at least 109 Vietnamese civilians "deliberately murdered." It was another case of "murder will out," this time on the country's front pages, but the basic facts had to be dug out from behind the Fort Benning news release.

A managed leak of news may serve special purposes and, infrequently, it may be a street on which traffic moves two ways. To illustrate, Secretary of Interior Walter Hickel's letter calling upon President Richard M. Nixon to "consider meeting on an individual and conversational basis with members of your Cabinet" was leaked to the press the same day it was dispatched to the White House. The general impression presented was that of a lack of communication between the President and his cabinet officers. This was helped along by further confidences to reporters that Hickel had had only two private meetings with Nixon during fifteen months. What was not said? According to John Osborne in *The New Republic* (May 30, 1970), "The reason Mr. Hickel had seen the President alone only twice in 15 months was that he had asked for only two meetings in that time." As Osborne wrote, it was "one of the more interesting episodes of the Nixon Presidency." It also was an intriguing example of managing the news leak.

In all of the above cited examples, the reporters won at least minor victories and told their stories despite a wide variety of methods to manage the news. The public was informed in the classic traditions of journalism. However, one has a gnawing doubt as to whether all the efforts at controlling information are thwarted as simply. How many times does the news source get away with his plan? How many cases are there that nobody knows about, in which there is no chance to ask the probing and embarrassing questions that penetrate the surface calm?

The very way a news source releases information may fix what impact it will have on the public. This is a subtle means of managing news. For illustration, suppose there is something to be told about a new U.S. policy toward Mexico. Should it come from the White House, the Department of State, or the American Embassy in Mexico City? In the first, should the president himself announce it at the beginning of a nationally televised news conference? Should his press secretary talk about it at his daily news briefings? Should it be handed out as a mimeographed release? The answers to these questions will have a great deal to do with whether the resulting dispatch appears on front pages of the nation's dailies and in every newscast on television. Of course, the display the news receives is also related to how much impact it will have on U.S. readers and listeners. But news may be subtly managed simply by who says it and how.

Even the timing of a presidential news conference may determine whether the easy or the tough questions are asked. President Johnson utilized this during the late 1960's. Since the reporters regularly assigned to the White House are, as a rule, specialists in president-watching, they are not likely to be acquainted with all the fine points of British fiscal policy, relations between East and West Germany, or the ecological effects of oil spillage near our ocean shores. Thus the chances for pointed, probing questions from news experts in those subjects are reduced at restricted, almost private, meetings. This unquestionably was part of the rationale for substituting such procedures for the well-announced, all-media conferences. (In fairness, it should be pointed out that President Johnson did have a number of these full-dress, advance-notice news conferences during his six years in office but they were less frequent than with most of his recent predecessors.)

News sources often feel that they have sufficient reasons—one frequently heard from government officials is "national security"—to keep certain happenings out of the media. Not infrequently, correspondents have been willing to delay announcements for what seemed to them and their bosses good and sufficient reasons. For instance, reporting on overseas trips by President Roosevelt for conferences with Winston

Churchill and Josef Stalin; President-elect Eisenhower to Korean fighting areas; and President Johnson to behind-the-lines bases in South Vietnam, were held up so as not to endanger the life of the chief executive.

Appeals to newsmen's patriotism have been used by some officials who felt some events should not be probed extensively during interviewing. For instance, Secretary of State Dean Rusk turned to a group of Washington reporters questioning him about official Vietnam policy and asked, "Whose side are you on? . . . I'm on our side."

In other instances, noncooperation with media has just been a news source's effort not to rock the status quo with a possibly complicating incident. Mrs. Elizabeth Carpenter, former news secretary to Mrs. Lyndon B. Johnson, told a story of why Harry Truman would not allow himself to be interviewed in Greece when he was there as emissary for the Johnson Administration during the funeral of the late King George. Reporters in Athens were anxious to question the former President who had been responsible for launching United States aid to Greece and Turkey in the early post-World War II era, but Mr. Truman refused. Finally, in desperation, they appealed to Mrs. Carpenter. She took their request to the former President and suggested that he meet the press. "No," she quoted Truman as replying, "some damn fool reporter will ask some damned fool question and I'll give some damned fool answer." Correspondents did not interview him.

On the other hand, Ivy Lee, a pioneer in corporate public relations who won praise from some reporters and the nickname of "Poison Ivy" from others, early in his career demonstrated how cooperation with newsmen could pay off. During 1906, an accident occurred on the Pennsylvania Railroad's main line near Gap, Pa. Lee, who had just recently become executive assistant to the railway president, reversed the traditional procedures of trying to enforce complete news suppression. He provided a special car to take reporters to the wreck location and ensured that they got help from employees on the scene. The Pennsylvania had seldom, if ever, received such a favorable press response. The impact of this payoff was not lost on other corporate publicity men, even two-thirds of a century later, but top management and government officials sometimes have failed to go along with anything approaching an "open door" policy in releasing information to media.

At worst, those who release the information may be trapped by their own ambiguities and deceptions. Writing about his Vietnam experiences as a public information official at the U.S. Embassy, John

Mecklin in *Mission in Torment* (Doubleday, 1965) claimed that if a man from Mars had visited inner government circles in either Saigon or Washington in the mid-1960's the visitor could easily have gotten the impression that newsmen, as well as the Viet Cong, were the enemy. Mecklin said that "to the best of my knowledge" no responsible U.S. official in Vietnam told newsmen a "really big falsehood" but rather supplied "endless little ones," sometimes almost instinctively if that seemed the only way to get rid of the reporters. "They seemed to regard a journalist as a natural adversary who was deliberately trying to sabotage the national interest, or as a child who would not understand and should not be asking about grown-up affairs in any case." Eventually, this misinformation, "morally marginal and thus difficult to dispute," seeped into government thinking and officials themselves began to believe their own colored versions of the news and thus were trapped into an unjustified and tragic optimism about how the war was going.

Reporters, too, may be one of the barriers to effective and efficient transmission of news and information. They are step two in the news process. Censorship and suppression by newsmen, for whatever the reason, does hinder dissemination of the world's happenings.

Seymour M. Hersh, who won the 1970 Pulitzer Prize for his reporting of the My Lai massacre, put it this way in the *Columbia Journalism Review* (Winter, 1969-70):

> I honestly believe that a major problem in newspapers today is not censorship on the part of editors and publishers, but something more odious: self-censorship by the reporters.
>
> There is no doubt that many reporters had heard of the Pinkville [My Lai] incident (at least many have told me so).

Why do reporters become involved in such "self-censorship"?

Partly because it is easy not to want to alienate a news source that one is assigned to work with for months, possibly years, in the future. If a newsman has to dig up all the background facts on his own, each story can become a time-consuming enterprise that prevents him from reporting others that are equally or more important. If the story is a major news development, it may be worth investing all the extra time required to dig it out. Usually, however, it behooves a harried newsman to stay in the good graces of the sources that can provide him with the essential details of a dispatch.

Partly because a quiet, sympathetic, pool-type operation may exist unofficially among the assigned reporters. A persuasive argument may go: "Why make life too tough for all of us? Let's all work together instead of trying to cut each other's throats." It usually prevails—unless one is willing to be a lone wolf news operator, and that requires a lot of hours and energy.

Partly because press facilities at such places as the United Nations headquarters in New York City and at the White House in Washington, for example, can be very comfortable indeed. Special office space, even separate rooms for each of the news agencies and most larger metropolitan dailies; individual telephone connections with their offices; and the privileges of using such nonpublic areas as the Delegates bar at the UN —all these make a reporter's life more enjoyable than on some other news beats to which he might be shifted. There is a subtle pull toward conformity.

Robert H. Fleming, who left his job as Washington news director for the American Broadcasting Company to become deputy press secretary for President Johnson, had this to say about his former news colleagues:

> They want comfort; they want reliable lids [embargoes that no further news will be released that night]; they want transcripts; they want advance travel plans; they want jet-speed airplanes to jet-age hotels where they hope to have a leisurely horse-and-buggy schedule.

The seduction by an accommodating news source may be insidious, pervasive—and all too enjoyable. It can take place without any feelings of guilt, at least at the time. When I was a Washington reporter during the middle New Deal period, I enjoyed an acquaintanceship with Rep. Maury Maverick, Dem., Texas, which yielded some news exclusives that received front-page display in newspapers across the nation. As I look back I wonder what I would have done if some scent of scandal or "bad news" about the Texas liberal had come to my attention while covering other news beats. It never happened to me but a comparable situation has confronted quite a few newsmen, some of whom, I am sure, opted for a comfortable flow of future news stories. Those responsible for assigning reporters try to overcome this hazard by shifting newsmen on beats. When this applies to a foreign correspondent, such factors as intimate knowledge on who to see for a candid assessment of some new development, where to gather the behind-the-scenes background, or even how to get the information out of the country with maximum speed have to be balanced against the reluctance to antagonize important somebodies who are his friends. Just determining who will be shifted to what country can be a complicated and demanding decision for those who set the ground rules for correspondents and the news they are to cover.

Even the quirks of accent may sometimes cause confusion—or, in a few cases, errors—in spreading the news. The Associated Press sent out word that James Meredith, the black civil rights leader, had been killed during his 1966 march through Mississippi. It was, according to Wes Gallagher, AP general manager, a real case of misunderstanding. The news executive explained later:

> This is what happened. Our reporter in Memphis was listening to a telephone call from a member's reporter in the field. The caller, in a wonderful Mississippi drawl, said Meredith had been shot in the *haid.* Our reporter thought he said shot *daid.* The bulletin that Meredith was *daid* stood for some 30 minutes before we discovered the error and corrected it.

Most newsmen as part of the news-gathering machinery make their own individual decisions about how and what to report and each, to some degree, determines irrevocably what the final product will be. For instance, facts uncollected by a newspaper or magazine reporter can be salvaged later only by expending a lot of time and effort (which sometimes is done). Pictures and television film can not be duplicated later unless the scene is reenacted and thus becomes, at best, synthetic and less real; at worst, blatant faking.

In telling about the motion picture version of his best seller, *The Making of the President 1968,* Theodore H. White, Pulitzer Prize-winning political reporter, provided a case history of this danger in news coverage in the *Columbia Journalism Review* (Winter, 1969-70):

> I did the movie version of *The Making of the President 1968.* We had two crews on the road all the time. They were young and wonderful cameramen. I was busy writing my book and reporting and I couldn't direct the film crews, so about nine months later when I finally got to Hollywood to put the film together, I found that these young people absolutely adored Eugene McCarthy and Robert Kennedy, and there was not a bad shot of either Gene McCarthy or Bobby Kennedy in the thousands and thousands of feet that we took. The images were glowing. On the other hand, these people who worked with me did not bring back one human shot of Hubert Humphrey. Everything that was taken looked sinister. He has an angular face, a

pointed chin, and if you want to shoot Hubert badly, it's the easiest thing in the world. I have a personal fondness for Hubert Humphrey. I have known him for fifteen years. But I had to work with film that showed Hubert Humphrey only as a sinister character. Such problems are even more pointed when you come to the daily TV shows. You're in the hands of the hundreds of people who are feeding material to you. No single person controls television.

Infrequently, reporters may take a long, hard look at their performances and decide that they were too rough on a news source. Apparently this happened for Mr. Nixon when the newsmen reevaluated their dispatches on his vice-presidential years and his unsuccessful campaigning for the California governorship in 1962. At any rate, the press was inclined to deal more friendly with him when he sought the 1968 Republican presidential nomination. Jules Witcover of the *Los Angeles Times* Washington bureau summed up a widely held reaction when he wrote in *The Resurrection of Richard Nixon* (G. P. Putnam's Sons, 1970):

> Nixon reached the White House without ever saying what he would do about the one major foreign policy issue facing the nation—Vietnam; part of the reason he managed to do so was that he successfully bluffed the press out of applying toward him the same fierce and unremitting pressure for straight answers that undid [George] Romney. If there was press irresponsibility in 1967 and 1968, it existed just as much in giving Nixon a free ride on Vietnam as it did in hounding Romney to political death on the same issue.
>
> In a comeback full of ironies, one of the greatest surely was this: that the press that Nixon in 1962 had charged with giving him "the shaft" was now playing a prominent role in the undoing of the man who was the first major barrier to Nixon's success.

The blatant effort to bribe a newsman into, in effect, selling news space for some selfish interest's cause is rare these days but it is one possible form of pressure on reporters. One of the few instances that has been publicly exposed is described in the following remark at a University of Pennsylvania symposium by Alton Blakeslee, Associated Press science writer, who has received practically all the awards possible for outstanding performance in his field of coverage:

> Recently I was approached by a man who said he had an opportunity for me to place an article in a magazine on a free-lance basis. He described very frankly his own rather curious organization. He

and his associates were representing a company which had developed a new product to treat a very common ailment. They guaranteed to find the medical researchers who would test it, and had done so. Further, they had a method of getting it published more quickly in a medical journal than might otherwise be done, so that it became "legitimate" news.

At this point he went to a magazine and suggested a story on the general topic, and told the magazine editor that the company would place a large amount of advertising with them if the story were used. He also volunteered to find a science writer who would write the story, and this is what he was talking to me about. He said I would make my deal with the magazine editor, and perhaps be paid $1,500 or $2,000 for the article, and all I had to do was to mention this new product by trade name twice, and never mention any other product. The company, he said, knew that writers were never paid what they were worth, so the company would give me $5,000 on the side. Then if the article were picked up and reprinted by a certain outlet, I would get that reprint fee, and the company would be so delighted with the advertising achieved that way they would pay me $10,000 more.

This added up to $17,000—as I mentally kept track of the arithmetic—but apparently something else showed because when he had finished this explanation, he asked, "Why are you looking at me like I just crawled out from under a rock?" And when I tried to explain to him, as gently and as easily as I could, why I didn't want to have any part in such a planted story I simply said that I'd like to be able to sleep at night. He had a curious answer. He said, "I wish I could."

One of the more under-discussed aspects of who and what determines the news that gets into print and on the air involves the so-called "gatekeepers": those individuals who make the decisions, either broad determinations of policy or specific choices of whether a certain item is to go on page one, inside, or into the wastepaper basket. Obviously, appearance on the showpiece front page of a daily newspaper insures far greater readership than publication on page 28 next to a half-page advertisement. Such decisions have to be made on hundreds or, on larger papers, possibly thousands of stories every day. No one master mind really could do it everywhere all the time—as has been demonstrated by a few publishers and editors who tried. Consequently, such choices generally depend on the prejudices and background of copyreaders and news editors rather than some dominating owner or news executive.

To illustrate, one internationally known science writer confessed that he could always ensure massive play for a story if it dealt with hangovers, hemorrhoids, or sex impotency—because at least one copyreader around any sizeable desk suffered from each of these conditions. By way of contrast, copyreaders with massive backgrounding in ecology, oceanography or the peacetime uses of atomic energy are difficult to find, except on a couple of the larger metropolitan dailies, and news in these fields may not be getting the space it deserves. Such may be the bases on which news positioning is made. As more and more college-trained employees are coming to copy editing and makeup, progress is being made but there is still room on most papers and broadcast stations for even less subjective decision-making.

A built-in bias toward the Establishment viewpoint may exist on many copydesks and, as spotlighted in the following case concerning the possibility of sniper fire just before the National Guardsmen shot Kent State students, this attitude may conflict sharply with findings and opinions of reporters at the scene.

During the evening of the shootings, Bill Schmidt of the *Detroit Free Press* was trying to wrap up a story for the following day's paper and interviewed Brig. Gen. Robert H. Canterbury, Ohio assistant adjutant general and commander of the National Guardsmen who fired on the students. The general told newsmen that he was not sure whether a sniper had fired but that his men were justified in shooting because their lives were endangered by stones thrown by Kent State students. This was a backdown from earlier reports of certain sniper fire. At 10 P.M., with a deadline at hand, Schmidt telephoned the *Free Press* with Canterbury's comments for a new lead. A rewrite man in Detroit said that a statement from Maj. Gen. Sylvester T. DelCorso, the Ohio adjutant general in Columbus, claimed flatly that there had been a sniper and that this should top the next day's story. Schmidt argued for Canterbury's comment backing off the sniper-fire theory, pointing out that Canterbury was at Kent while DelCorso was miles away in the state capital. The *Free Press* rewriteman contended that DelCorso outranked his junior officer on the scene, and thus the Tuesday morning story featured the sniper fire—because that was the ranking voice of the Establishment. The following day DelCorso, too, backed off from the sniper theory and Wednesday's *Free Press* led with his change of mind. Schmidt later said that he felt vindicated but that strong doubts should have been cast on the theory a day earlier through giving prominence to Canterbury's comments at Kent on the night after the shootings.

A booklet prepared by the Knight Newspapers for distribution by the American Newspaper Publishers Association included this pointed viewpoint:

> In a matter of hours, the nation had been told that snipers were a contributory element of the Kent State incident. In the months since, neither independent journalistic investigations nor the work of Ohio law enforcement agencies and the Federal Bureau of Investigation have produced any evidence whatever to substantiate the sniper claim. Yet many readers believe to this day that revolutionary gunmen were really responsible for the events that culminated in Kent State's deaths.

Headline writers generally set a frame of reference into which readers then fit the text of a news story. However, writing headlines is as much an art as a science; it involves subjective judgment to a high degree in selecting what points to emphasize a well as mathematical exactness (so that the heads will fit the unrelenting demands of metal slugs and type sizes). As a result, the headlines used for a single news event sometimes show a wide range of ideas as to what took place or was said.

An illustration of this was provided when a Creighton University researcher in preventive medicine and public health told a science writers' seminar of the American Cancer Society during the spring of 1969 that some families seemed prone to cancer while others appeared to have a natural resistance. Here are some of the headlines that appeared in daily newspapers around the nation on reports of his findings:

me Families Resistant to Cancer Omaha (Neb.) *Evening World Herald*

Some Families Charleston (W.Va.) *Gazette*
Cancer Prone

ereditary Cancer Link Found *Boston Globe*

Cancer Risk
Inherited?   Nashville (Tenn.) *Tennessean*

Doc: Heredity Has Role in Cancer New York *Daily News*

In this selection of headlines, some writers focused on the increased hazards in some families; others picked out the possible resistance; at least one left the reader, as the headline, with a question mark. While this confusion may have done little public damage, it is symptomatic of what may take place.

A few publishers have tried to impose their bias and prejudices upon their copydesks—not always with success—as if they were feudal barons managing their domains in the Middle Ages. Documentation is not often provided but enough exists to substantiate the specific operations of two newspaper publishers: the late Col. Robert R. McCormick of the *Chicago Tribune* and Walter H. Annenberg, publisher of the *Philadelphia Inquirer* and *TV Guide* during the 1960's before he was named ambassador to the Court of St. James's by President Nixon. Since Annenberg's record is the more recent and has been studied by various critics of the media, it is given here in some detail.

Annenberg used his paper to punish individuals who, for some reason (often unknown to any of the paper's regular working reporters), had incurred his displeasure. He thus created a list of "bad guys," who were not to be mentioned, no matter what they did in the news. This blacklist was known indelicately in the *Inquirer*'s city room as "Annenberg's shit list."

Although Annenberg provided the original endowment for a school of communications at the University of Pennsylvania, its president, Gaylord P. Harnwell, was on the list. This required some fancy writing because a prestigious university's head is much in the news. Thus the Wharton School Alumni gold medal, a highly regarded award at the university, was presented, during the time that Harnwell was on the list, by an anonymous "high university official," without mention of the president by name or title in the *Inquirer*.

Another time a columnist had to request permission to attribute a quotation in a story to a Philadelphia-Baltimore Stock Exchange vice-president because the head was on Annenberg's list. A ban on singer Dinah Shore extended to *TV Guide* as well as the *Inquirer* and her broadcast program, for a long time near the top of the ratings, was listed simply as "Variety Show," without the name of its star. When Philadelphia's professional basketball team was on the list, the 76'ers received no pregame coverage and only one paragraph if they lost, two if they won.

As long ago as the mid-1940's, Gunnar Myrdal, sociologist who wrote the classic study *An American Dilemma* (Harper, 1944), said that his most important sources of information about race relations were Southern reporters who knew the facts but did not use them for publication. A 1969 study for the Commission on the Causes and Prevention of Violence blamed this Southern refusal to print much news about local blacks to "the parochial attitudes, ignorance, and, in some cases, venality of Southern publishers." The same report then added about later developments in black coverage:

> The campaign of sit-ins, parades, and picketing at least provided some news coverage of black problems. White Americans, for the first time, were learning that blacks existed as humans, not chattels, and were unhappy about something. Whites also learned that the Negro proposed to do something about his discontent.

Most media executives do not have to compile a so-called "shit list"; the always-present desire to please the boss exists among a vast majority of those on any payroll. It all may be rather subtle but it doesn't have to be outlined in office memoranda. And the concept that one can always quit if too much professional misconduct is asked in return for salary, may be better in theory than in practice, especially if one has a wife, two children in college, and a large mortgage. There are instances where writers, editors, and producers have quit over a matter of ethics and principle, as they saw it, and then in storybook fashion have gone on to better-paying and more prestigious jobs. It doesn't always turn out that way and so some people in media, as in other vocations, develop a certain elasticity of conscience.

The mores, either real or fancied by the editors, of the potential audience often influence how the news is presented and even what news is given. J. Anthony Lukas, Pulitzer Prize winner for his 1967 story of a Greenwich, Conn., debutante who was slain in the East Village, was assigned by *The New York Times* to cover the Chicago Conspiracy

Trial and recited how perceived sensitivities influenced that paper's coverage. On Feb. 4, 1970, the Chicago Deputy Chief of Police, James Riordan, was testifying about how he saw David Dellinger, one of the defendants on trial, lead a group of militants in Grant Park on Aug. 28, 1968. Dellinger, at the defense table, exclaimed, "Oh, bullshit!" Judge Julius J. Hoffman later that afternoon reprimanded the defendant for using "that kind of language" in court and revoked his bail.

Lukas wrote as follows about what happened to his coverage of the incident:

> Knowing the *Times'* sensitivity about such language, I called the National Desk and asked how they wanted to handle Mr. Dellinger's phrase. The editor on duty said he didn't think we could use it and suggested I just say "an obscenity." I objected, arguing that it wasn't, strictly speaking, an obscenity; that if we called it that most people would assume it was something much worse; and that since it was central to the day's events we ought to tell our readers just what Mr. Dellinger had said. The editor thought for a moment and said, "Why don't we call it a barnyard epithet?" Everything considered, that seemed like the best solution, and that was the way it appeared in the *Times* the next morning.

Whether he is functioning as a news source, a news gatherer, or a "gatekeeper," each individual can not help being subjective about his activities. In brief, people are human. The same also applies to the audience. Its members bring their biases and prejudices to their reading, listening, and viewing of the news. They select what appeals to them, read in detail what intrigues them, and retain in memory that which they consider important or interesting to them. In the social scientists' language, these traits are known as selective perception and selective retention.

One classic study a generation ago indicated that Republicans tended to read and listen to their party's candidates, paying little attention to Democratic appeals while the Democrats ignored the Republican speeches. Anyone who has worked in newspaper offices and broadcast stations can tell about all sorts of inquiries about events that did not happen as the caller reported them.

Our minds play tricks on us. This is not to say that "news consumers" do not pick up, possibly unconsciously, some of the implications that get into print and on the air and react with strong feelings. But selective perception and selective retention do provide distorting influences on large segments of the mass audience and any realistic observer of the media should be aware of them. Classroom testing has shown that believability and retention are greater if the idea is attributed to a generally approved news source, less credibility when from a disapproved source.

All of which should add up to the conclusion that everybody in the news process—from news sources to "news consumers"—needs to do a more professional and as completely honest a job as humanly possible. This is especially necessary in any democratic society where the people really do need to know.

7. Breaking Out of the Straitjackets of Journalistic Practices

Up until the early 1920's, daily newspapers were virtually unchallenged in public communications. They monopolized the informational function of U.S. society, except for weekly news opinion magazines and a few books. In the half century since then, however, have come a huge range of competitors: news magazines, radio, television, and a batch of specialized publications for almost any subject. Thus a single medium has expanded into a wide range of means for obtaining news and information —and, for a lot of the mass audience, opinions, too.

The current jockeying for public attention and for advertising dollars has led to exposing many of the defects that went unnoticed in calmer, less competitive times. So those who now attend professional meetings of reporters, editors, publishers, and station managers hear a great deal about the "new journalism," where the writer becomes advocate as well as reporter. Some of this has real pertinence and high idealism; some of it is just hopeful rationalization that there must be an easier way to get the money (or to capture readership or ratings) that might slide over to a media rival. Increasing interest is being shown in these analyses as the rosy glow of the affluent 1960's fades into the less certain 1970's.

A major part of the troubles in today's journalism arise from the fact that it is a fairly inexact science with a large dash of the arts thrown in. In mathematics, two plus two always equals four, but in reporting a news event, anything that comes between three and a half and five is considered an entirely satisfactory result. Thus if you gave a dozen professionally qualified newsmen a sample, there would be remarkable agreement about how well it fitted journalistic standards because traditions and conventions are so loose that instincts and emotions provide acceptable answers—at least for colleagues in the newsroom.

Yet these measures of competence often have become figurative straitjackets that prevent creative innovations that would better transmit the import of happenings to the readers and listeners, which basically is what communication is all about. Thus strong pressures exist for following often antiquated techniques rather than experimenting—with a chance for errors as well as improvements. For instance, a summary lead paragraph which demands that the "guts" of an event be told in fifty words or less arose during the Civil War when Confederate raiding parties cut the newly laid telegraph lines and Northern editors wanted to be sure their papers could print who won the battles, just in case the wires were severed. This now-stereotyped practice which deadens the drama and suspense of any reporting still persists in an era of space satellites and instantaneous broadcasting around the world. News magazines long ago discarded the summary lead but papers still cling to it. The processes of journalism aim at developing an informed public which can thus make the intelligent decisions needed for a democratic society, but if readers and listeners are so uninterested or bored that they stop after the second paragraph or shift to a motion picture rerun on another channel, all the processes clank in a void.

Amazingly, for many of the daily newspapers (where I reluctantly confess the deficiencies cry out most flagrantly for repair), standard operating procedures have changed little in the century since telegraph lines were placed and the linotype was perfected to replace human typesetters. That statement may seem overly simplified but, for at least partial documentation, consider the old-fashioned concepts of what makes news in an age of urban sprawl and technological profusion, the heavy reliance on the Establishment viewpoint, and the stilted and fundamentally dull organization of all supplementary information in an inverted pyramid format so that the last segments can be discarded during any hurried page makeup. And while newspapers have failed to modify their practices in competition with television, broadcast personnel have too willingly adopted print procedures for their medium. Broadcasters, like newspapermen, may concentrate on the easy-to-get news that floats to the surface in their communities and then fill the rest of their "news hole" with press association wire stories and features. Still others just rip and read copy from the news service tickers and forget the local scene. A superior television documentary, like a good print series in daily papers, may be tremendously effective in-depth journalism. Unfortunately they are not plentiful in either medium.

The tenets of the traditional philosophy of journalism are under attack—and they deserve it. Many reporters with print and broadcast have worshipped at the altar of a god of impossible objectivity. Since philosophy and definitions are more basic than specific techniques, let's look at them first; then we can turn to the frustrating and self-defeating practices that have grown up in newsrooms.

For several generations, at least, working newsmen have had difficulties explaining just what sort of operations they were practicing. Among other names, newspapering—and now broadcasting, too—has been called a "profession," a "craft," a "trade," and a "business." To some, it became just "THE business," in tribute to its often irresistible appeal and fascination.

Prof. Daniel P. Moynihan, former counsellor to President Richard M. Nixon, expressed a common viewpoint when he paid tribute at a funeral service for a journalistic friend and tried to describe what he had done. Moynihan spoke of journalism as "that most underdeveloped, least realized of professions." Then he added:

> Not a profession at all, really. Rather, a craft seeking to become such out of the need to impose form on an activity so vastly expanded in volume and significance as desperately to need the stabilizing influence of procedure and precedent and regularity. Events have overrun this quest, and the result is an occupation no longer the one and not yet the other.

Part of the cause for this search for an identity in journalism is due to the uncertainties—even by those practicing it—about just what it is supposed to do. Much is heard about informing the public—and that is true and necessary. Much also is said about helping the mass audience to make up its collective mind in a democratic society and the need to provide the background and facts on which sound public opinion rests. Some observers talk about educating the public—and this, too, has some foundation in fact despite the refusal of quite a few reporters to agree that they do any teaching. Yet if readers and listeners are not educated along the way, they will not comprehend the events and trends in such advanced areas as scientific research, medicine, educational procedures, urban planning, and contemporary economic theory. In these news fields, an effective reporter has to carry piggyback the recent findings (which were not in anybody's textbooks or classroom lectures when the "news con- sumers" went to school) or it will be impossible for the public to under- stand what happened. Even less is heard about another socially required function: to alert the general public and to send them to other less-general channels for additional facts and information if they are interested.

For example, a physician and his patient may both read about some new drug or surgical procedure in a daily paper or a news magazine. The doctor thus is informed about something which is yet to appear (or has just been printed) in his specialized, professional journals. If a patient asks about the news item, the M.D. has another shove to do his occupational home work. The result may be better medicine. One of the uncollected bits of survey research would be the number of patients who enjoy health today because the mass media have alerted their doctors to the possibilities of new treatments or recently discovered drugs. Some physicians complain about "the trash that gets into the papers" but the survey results would be illuminating reading, I feel.

Thomas Griffith, who edited both national affairs and foreign news sections for *Time,* wrote in *The Waist-High Culture* (Harper and Broth- ers, 1959) that journalists had problems because, unlike historians, they were writing in time for the news to be acted upon and because they were recording events "while the facts are not all in." The first brought "its temptation to passion and its besetting sin of partisanship." The second demanded efforts to dig out enough information in time to take action. "If journalism is sometimes inaccurate and often inadequate," Griffith wrote, "ignorance would not be preferable."

As changes escalate in the modern world, some practitioners and even more students of journalism have embraced what is known as the "journalism of advocacy." Many others have their doubts about this im- plied shift in goals for newsmen. The choices are: Should the press, in the broad definition including print and broadcast, provide a mirror of the affairs in today's (or this week's or this month's) world, thus serving merely as the chronicler? Or should the press use its news columns for improving the world and bettering mankind? Is the situation so bad that everyone, including newsmen, has to stand up and be counted? (What the media say in editorial comments is not involved here; what is being discussed is the proper utilization of news columns.)

Despite the best intentions, reporters do not attain absolute objectivity. It is like a perfect vacuum—approachable but unattainable. All this was not so obvious a generation ago. Between the two World Wars, objectivity was a widely heralded goal of journalism. But when Sen. Joseph McCarthy, Rep., Wisconsin, was hunting supposed Communists or their sympathizers in the U.S. government service during the 1950's, responsible newsmen had to take a new and hard look at what had passed for objectivity. Among the discussants, one of the most perceptive was the late Elmer Davis, broadcast commentator and head of the Office of War Information during World War II. Davis summarized his thinking this way:

> This striving for objectivity was in its beginnings a good thing; but it went a little too far. From holding that newspapers ought to present both sides it went on to the position that it was all right to present only one side, if nobody happened to be talking on the other; and it was not the business of the newspaper to tell the reader if that one argument happened to be phony. . . .
>
> This kind of dead-pan reporting—so-and-so said it, and if he's lying in his teeth it isn't my business to say so—may salve the conscience of the reporter (or of the editor, who has the ultimate responsibility) as to his loyalty to some obscure ideal of objectivity. But what about his loyalty to the reader? The reader lays down his nickel, or whatever, for the paper, in the belief that he is going to find out what is going on in the world; and it does not seem to me that the newspaper is giving him his nickel's worth if it only gives him what somebody says is going on in the world, with no hint as to whether what that somebody says is right or wrong.

The "journalism of advocacy" differs from what Davis was discussing. There are certain topics where background information is needed—even demanded, in the eyes of responsible newsmen—so that the audience can get the full picture and put the facts in perspective. It would be a lot easier to throw perspective out the window and try to do the reader's or listener's thinking for him but that would merely give free rein to the reporter's personal bias and prejudices. In their news writing, reporters are not supposed to grind political, partisan, or personal axes; they are supposed to provide the informational grindstones on which their audiences may sharpen their own thinking. The newsman's assignments today are tough ones as he steers between both the "journalism of advocacy" and "dead-pan reporting."

On the question of a newsman's involvement with the news he is reporting by using the "journalism of advocacy," some have questioned whether editors and reporters could reasonably ask for "the privilege of being on both sides of the footlights, actors on the stage and critics in the audience at the same time." That was how J. Russell Wiggins, former editor of the *Washington Post,* described it. Early in 1971, that Washington paper's "resident commentator on the news business," Richard Harwood, left no doubt of his verdict when he wrote in his publication:

> Newspapers and the people involved in their production cannot have it both ways. They are no longer confronted with an illiterate or indifferent audience. The audience of the 1970's is educated, aware and concerned. It is not tolerant of publishers or editors or writers who compromise themselves financially and politically and then parade their "integrity" and "fairness" in demanding the respect and influence that comes with *belief.* The audience, in those circumstances, will not believe.
>
> . . . The remedy is in ourselves as journalists, in the self-discipline we are willing to accept, in the ethical standards we are willing to observe, in the example publishers and editors are prepared to set.

Thus, if a newsman wants a pulpit or a soapbox, let him become an editorial writer, columnist, or broadcast commentator—or let him go into another vocation. Those journalists who insist on "being on both sides of the footlights" undoubtedly will have to pay some penalty in lesser public trust.

If there is confusion about a philosophy for journalism, utter chaos exists when it comes to drafting a satisfactory definition of what is meant by "news." One of the oldest (and least satisfactory) was phrased by a New York City editor a century ago: "When a dog bites a man that is not news, but when a man bites a dog, that is news." Even the specifics are just not true. If President Nixon's latest pet were to gnaw away at the leg of the Vice-President, extensive media coverage would be one of the surest bets of the month. Obviously, media are concerned with the unusual. This journalistic fascination about the off-beat reflects an anticipated curiosity by the readers and listeners. Airplanes that arrive, clergymen who behave themselves, rivers that do not flood, and stock markets that float slightly upward—none of these are considered "hot" news; "cool" probably would be the adjective preferred by Prof. Marshall McLuhan. Anyway, none is unusual enough to merit much media mention. This concentration on the off-beat can, too often, project a drastically false impression of a news event and of the real world.

One of the well documented illustrations of this emphasis on the sensational and its potential for bad public reactions concerned a meeting of blacks in Athens Park during the Watts rioting in Los Angeles in 1965.

In an effort to calm down black community emotions, John Buggs, executive director of the Los Angeles County Human Relations Commission, and others scheduled a meeting for early afternoon at Athens Park. They wanted to organize teams and send them out "to talk peace." When Buggs arrived he found television cameras focused on the microphones and at least "100 kids"—not expected to attend. Under this changed situation, the session shifted into a public forum in the hope that the group thus could vent emotions. As Robert Conot reported in *Rivers of Blood, Years of Darkness* (Bantam Books, 1967), "The gripes of the Negro community, both relevant and not, now started bouncing freely through the room."

During discussions, a teen-ager grabbed the microphone and shouted, "It ain't going to be lovely tonight whether you like it or not! . . . They going to do the white man in tonight! And I'm going to tell you—!" Catcalls from the audience drowned him out. Other blacks dragged him away and at least a half dozen youths began to pummel him until adults intervened. Other blacks spoke up that all they wanted was a fair hearing and that the recent speaker did not reflect community opinion. A group, led by a black female police sergeant, asked television crews not to show the boy because his was an isolated opinion. It certainly was potentially inflammatory and the most dramatic quotation from the whole meeting. Camera crew members were noncommittal. "Everybody has it. We can't say we won't use it, and then have some other station put it on the air."

Here is what happened on the newscasts that night, as told by Conot:

At 6 o'clock, most of the city's seven television stations launched their evening news programs.

A meeting had been held, viewers were informed, at the instigation of the County Human Relations Commission, in the Negro community that afternoon, and television news cameramen had been present.

"We the Negro people have got completely fed up," a boy was orating. "They not going to fight down here no more. You know where they going? They're after the Whiteys! They going to congregate. They don't care! They going out to Inglewood, Playa del Rey, and everywhere else the white man supposed to stay. They going to do the white man in tonight!"

That was the complete television report of the Athens Park meeting, not only to the citizens of Los Angeles, but to those of the nation, CBS carrying the film on the network.

Both blacks and whites reacted. One of the youths who had been approached to calm down the community saw the broadcast and commented, "If that's the way they want to read it, that's the way we'll write the book." That night the theme was "Burn, baby, burn."

To illustrate some of the flawed definitions of news that come close to rivaling the "Man bites dog" variation, here are some of the others that get into discussions of working reporters:

News is accelerated literature. The newspaper is the shuttle weaving the tapestry of history on the loom of time.

News is anything that makes a reader say, "Gee whiz!"

News . . . is such an account of events as a first-rate newspaperman, acting as such, finds satisfaction in writing and publishing.

Two cynical ones but certainly with a heavy coating of realism are:

News is what the city editor says it is.

Women, wampum, and wrongdoing. (Attributed to the late Stanley Walker, one-time city editor of the *New York Herald Tribune*.)

Any satisfactory definition would have to include several elements: (1) "new-ness," freshness, or no prior release plus (2) interest or use to the potential audience, either as serious information or as amusement. "New-ness" or no prior release does not mean only a highly dramatic happening such as a fire or a street demonstration. For instance, a report on young people's changing mores regarding premarital sex relations has "new-ness," too, if the facts were not published or broadcast previously. Often the slow-moving trends may have more impact, even immediately, than the seemingly spectacular trivia that got on the police blotter during the past twenty-four hours or what an overly excited speaker said at this week's Rotary Club luncheon.

Rather than try further to determine what news is, it probably would be more helpful to look at the new audience that has to be attracted and retained. The population and the education explosions combined for a fantastic impact on the mass media audience. The U.S. total population is increasing by approximately two million a year. At the same time that more people are living beyond 65 years of age, the nation as a whole is "younging" with approximately half of the total population now under 25 years. (Of interest here is Cecil King's remark that he built Britain's largest daily circulation for the London *Daily Mirror* by "not giving a damn about anybody over 30.") More than half of all those students who complete high school now go on to college; this contrasts with one in three twenty-five years ago. Approximately two-thirds of the country's population live in the 215 metropolitan areas, comprising less than one-tenth of the physical land area. The shift from the urban centers to the suburbs and the westward "tilt" in the population are scheduled to continue through the 1970's. California already is our most populous state, surpassing New York. The gross national product is bouncing above the trillion dollar a year level. The lessons of all this for media are constant change and adaptation to a new audience, which will be increasingly youthful, well educated, and more sophisticated.

In partial recognition of this new audience, both print and broadcast have made concessions and improvements—but not rapidly enough. The world, in most of its aspects, is changing with accelerating speed. While communications have left the horse and buggy, they have not yet reached the supersonic stage.

Among the more dramatic changes has been expansion in coverage of such formerly underplayed topics as science, education, religion, economics, and the arts. The first landing of men on the moon highlighted the tremendous impact of that technological performance for media audiences. An estimated one-fifth of the global population *simultaneously* watched the American explorers walking on the moon. The National Aeronautics and Space Administration (NASA) accredited 3,497 news personnel for that Apollo 11 flight—although honesty compels one to mention that all of these were not really "working" media representatives. *The New York Times,* a showpiece of American newspaperdom, displayed the largest type it ever printed in a banner headline, having to photograph and enlarge a smaller size for a metal engraving because the composing room lacked what was wanted. For the three space flights in 1969, the National Broadcasting Company preempted approximately 118 hours for news; spaced over the full year, which it definitely was not, this represented about nineteen minutes every single day that year. Less spectacular have been the shifts in coverage from school board and PTA session to the "new math" and other curriculum improvements, from sermons to the Roman Catholic Vatican Council II and so-called "rebellion" in the churches, from stock market tables to assessments of ideas underlying the "new economics," and from some "canned" copy of motion pictures and plays to an array of items on little theater groups, museums, dance, symphonies, and art auctions.

How well are communicators doing their job? There is considerable discontent, an undercurrent for the need to do better.

William B. Dickinson, executive editor of the Philadelphia *Evening Bulletin* and past president of the Associated Press Managing Editors Association, told the 1966 APME annual convention:

We fill most of the columns of our newspapers with spot news—much of it trivial to the point of absurdity. We deluge our readers with undigested facts. We report the events—and we do it especially well if they are dramatic—and we overlook the causes and the consequences of those events. We cover the violence in the streets, but not the conditions that are responsible for that violence. We cover the wars, but not the threats to peace.

Partly we act this way because we are conditioned by long habit, because our staffs are set up to do it this way. We have become accustomed to covering certain beats: police and fire, the city hall, the courts, the Chamber of Commerce, and so on. We are not yet accustomed to covering the new beats, the very people who are transforming our world—the scientists, the physicians, the economists, the engineers, the architects, the educators, and management elite, the planners, the thinkers. . . .

I think we must define the meaning of news. We must somehow take a broader view, see events and people in a larger sense, paint with our words and pictures on a wider canvas. The challenge to us is that of increasing man's understanding of man. I do not underestimate the enormity of this task. We shall not move easily and straightly toward our goal.

Speaking at Memphis State University for a 1968-69 M. L. Seidman Town Hall Memorial lecture, Howard K. Smith of the American Broadcasting Company pointed out that the journalist was becoming more than "just a collector of interesting items that people want to hear about." In an increasingly complex world, he said, news coverage was far too important to be performed by the late-movie stereotype of a reporter, "a press badge sticking out of the band of his hat and cigarette on his lips as though it had grown there." Smith continued:

> Now we simply have to have reporters who are scholars, and who are not cynical but deeply concerned and compassionate. They need training and profound continuing scholarship, and they need a background of wide experience.
>
> We are getting such people; and in time, we will get them in numbers. If we are, then what is my complaint? Well, my complaint is that we are still letting our journalists, old and new, be tied to traditions of journalism that have lost their value and lost their meaning. It is a remarkable thing that in a nation so continuously changing as ours, news writing, in newspapers in particular, is hackneyed, frozen into stereotypes that have not changed for over half a century. We are still taught and we still practice in all our newspapers that the way to present news is to pack the 'who, what, when, and where' all in the first paragraph, then let the rest trail off into a dull listing of less essential details. The faith of American journalism in that formula would be touching if it were not so deadly.

To the ABC commentator "the first requisite" of journalism was that one knew how to tell a story in an interesting way. "It so happens that we live in a fascinating time," he said, "and if journalism doesn't teach journalists to write up to the dramatic level of their times, then it doesn't have any purpose."

Local station broadcasters were criticized for their reliance on stereotypes and for unimaginative performances when the first Alfred I. duPont—Columbia University Survey of Broadcast Journalism [1968-1969] was released. There was high praise for network handling of such news events as the assassinations of Dr. Martin Luther King, Jr., and Senator Robert F. Kennedy, the Apollo flights, the Nixon inauguration, and the Eisenhower funeral. Performance, the survey report said, reached "an all-time high in technical proficiency and editorial resourcefulness." However, documentary programs that originated with the local stations were described as hitting "a new low." To illustrate the reasons for that poor rating, specific comments from survey correspondents included these:

Salt Lake City: "All stations are still event-oriented, and documentaries and depth reports are comparatively rare."

Phoenix, Arizona: "Essentially, radio and TV stations in Arizona do little more than cover the old-fashioned police beat with cameras and tapes—the fires, accidents, violent deaths of all kinds."

Cincinnati: "The three commercial TV stations with news operations devoted an inordinate amount of time to run-of-the-mill crimes of violence, traffic accidents and the like . . . political coverage is limited to the surface of the news. Seldom do the TV stations try to get behind the statements of public officials."

Honolulu: "There is always talk of producing locally made documentaries by various stations and invariably they fall by the wayside."

Providence: "There is very little initiative on the local level here for production of any documentaries."

The point cited in the Cincinnati evaluation, "Seldom do the TV stations try to get behind the statements of public officials," opens up a whole corridor of complaints that have been explored by recent critics of the media's performance. It applies to print and broadcast journalism alike and it provides a base for criticism from the left, the right, and the curious center. In this age of the rebellious, resentful, and suspicious, even accurate quotations of what officials say provides little sympathy for the working newsman as too many of them have been inclined to accept the Establishment's viewpoint without much questioning and checking. This, possibly more than any other single reason, has fueled the tremendous growth of the underground press and its decidedly anti-Establishment stance.

Disturbances and disorders during the late 1960's and early 1970's comprised some direct, head-on confrontations with the Establishment. How were the media to cover them? If in the conventional way, then they could rightly be accused of "selling out" to the *status quo*. Newsmen were bothered about how they could handle such events and maintain a sense of fairness.

One attempt to face up to this problem was discussed at the 1970 convention of the Associated Press Managing Editors Association in Honolulu. It was a symposium by staff members of the Knight Newspapers based on their experiences in Detroit during the 1967 summer disorders and the 1970 shootings of students at Kent State University.

Neal Shine, city editor of the *Detroit Free Press,* told how the "comfortable kind of formula reporting" just did not apply to such coverage. He added:

> One of the major things we learned in 1967 was that we can no longer rely on official reports from official sources when the sources themselves are parties to the conflict. According to every police and National Guard source during the Detroit riot, sniper activity was rampant, deadly and organized.
>
> The official reports detailed it, and we bought it. In one lead story, based on police reports, we had Negro snipers launching an offensive from the west side of the city to the borders of Grosse Pointe.
>
> Phrases like "nests of snipers" and "sniper teams" kept popping up in the paper. When the police said a death was a sniper death, we reported it as such. Official police reports listed at least 15 of the 43 riot deaths as caused by snipers.
>
> A six-week investigation by a three-man team of Free Press reporters uncovered no evidence of massive sniping. When the smoke of the riot had cleared, there was one confirmed sniping incident—a drunk with a pistol who was killed by the police.
>
> Reporting conflict has taught us that a riot is not just a succession of facts and the tendency to report it uncritically and without asking the tougher questions is an abdication of everything a newspaper should stand for.
>
> A riot is a civil war being fought in your own back yard and a critical role is essential lest the riot itself be used as an excuse for acts that would, in another situation, be intolerable.

Shine said that he and his *Free Press* colleagues had learned that covering the news from behind police lines got "only half the story." Even at the risk of sending newsmen into dangerous assignments, he said, editors in their offices had to have the personal reactions, impressions, and experience of reporters on the scene to shape the news judgments that had to be made about what to print.

Discussing the Kent State shootings, Robert Files of the *Akron Beacon Journal* told the AP editors that that event suggested the press should be more careful about the accuracy of the information it disseminated. He continued:

In normal times the statements of government officialdom may automatically be news—reportable per se simply for the fact of their happening.

But when the established bureaucracy is under attack and the system itself is being challenged, the truth requires that both versions be examined and judged on their merits.

In covering campus conflict, a secondary conflict tends to arise in the office. This conflict is between reporters and editors. Back from the trenches come the reporters, convinced they can explain the underlying causes of the outburst. But their explanation often doesn't square with accepted formulas of confrontation. Thus the editor, who has been sitting on his fanny in the office all day, hesitates to accept the view of young reporters that National Guardsmen over-reacted and fired into the students. If the editor's own instincts prevail, he is likely to find himself confronted with two problems:

First, there is the inevitable erosion of staff confidence when the reporters' accounts of what they saw are rebuffed or edited to match the accepted pattern that law enforcement agencies are right and demonstrators are wrong.

Second, the newspaper's own report of what happened becomes suspect, particularly by readers who also were witnesses.

Here is a recommended solution: put an editor in the field. In other words, go find out for yourself.

Going out into the field, however, would not change one of the other cherished traditions of contemporary journalism that has received criticism: the devotion to the summary lead paragraph that answers the five W's and H—Who, What, When, Where, Why, and How.

Some critics have argued that editors and publishers construct their publications as if they were trying to shortcircuit their readers' attentions, sometimes after the very first paragraph of the lead. Research some years ago by Dr. Wilbur Schramm of Stanford University documented that stories of five paragraphs, for instance, lost more readers if they were written in inverted pyramid form than if they were treated as features; that generally a steady attrition of attention took place as more and more readers turned away at the end of every single paragraph; and that high initial readership of a story did not guarantee that a large percentage of readers would stay with the news. Broadcast media, on the other hand, do not provide any chance to divert attention in the middle of one item to something else. With radio and television the news consumer has to listen all the way through—or shut off the program entirely. Print provides a smorgasbord of choices; broadcast offers a chance to bid or pass—and that is it. Newspapermen may praise the chance for variety but there is a built-in opportunity to "tune off" on every single item.

Ernest Hemingway, a Kansas City newspaperman before he became a world known storyteller, once reminisced about his early writing experience, recalling, "After I finished high school I went to Kansas City and worked on a paper. It was regular newspaper work: Who shot whom? Who broke into what? Where? When? How? But never Why, not really Why." The comment pointedly illustrates one of the major faults of journalism of that period. Reporters, editors, and publishers have paid lip service to the "five W's and H" but often omitted the elusive "Why?" That answer is the most difficult to dig out, honestly and accurately, and so it sometimes just is left out. Yet, as Elmer Davis said in the cited quotation, the background materials that answer the question, "Why?" may be the needed ingredient to put all the other answers into a realistic and truthful perspective for the readers.

In his 1968 presidential address to the Associated Press Managing Editors convention, David N. Schultz of the *Redwood City* (Calif.) *Tribune* said that readers in our fast-moving world were constantly asking, "What is it all about?" Discussing the response to that request, he said:

> The newspaper that tries to cover the "why" of each news story runs the risk of being labeled a biased interpreter. But we cannot slacken our responsibility in explaining the meaning of all the advances of these technologies and sociologies for fear of being called names that are uncomplimentary.
>
> Each day there is an increasing clamor from those who plead: "What does it all mean?" We must find out what it means and tell the people.
>
> As society becomes more complex newspaper reporting will also become more complex. Complexities breed wider differences of opinion and the newspaper must report these differences. . . .
>
> What I'm trying to say is that the newspaper, long recognized as a living day-to-day textbook on current history, must also be the voice through which its writers explain that history and its readers debate it.
>
> If the folks back home feel that that is what our product is

accomplishing, then maybe we are changing along with the changing times, and we'll be better able to cope with tomorrow's problems.

Pleas for more "Why?" background in newspapers have not gone unanswered. In recent years, longish stories—often presented as features —and whole series have been devoted to answering the "Why?" of important news events and trends. The press associations, which service practically all of the daily papers and broadcast stations in the United States and a great many in other countries, have done this increasingly. The first team report was carried on the United Press International news wires in 1961 and more have been written each year. The Associated Press has established news task forces to move in on a major event and produce massive copy.

How far UPI has moved away from the traditional summary lead and inverted pyramid organization is shown in a dispatch written in response to the challenge in the report of the National Advisory Commission on Civil Disorders—sometimes known as the Kerner report. The Commission's text said that media "have not communicated to the majority of their audience—which is white—a sense of the degradation, misery and hopelessness of living in the ghetto." UPI sent John L. Taylor, a black graduate of Lincoln University, to spend three days with a Harlem slum family. These are the opening paragraphs of the dispatch, distributed April 7, 1968, under the byline of Taylor and H. D. Quigg, a senior editor based in New York City:

> NEW YORK—Cold spring rain wets the car tops and the streets. On an avenue in Harlem, hand-lettered window signs are prominent in the shop fronts. "Jesus Saves" . . . "U.S., Get Out of Vietnam" . . . "Hell no, Black won't go."
>
> One of New York's new buses, equipped with panels for advertising on the outside, mutters along the avenue. The panels on one side have not been sold yet, and they bear two of the phrases of whimsical urging that the ad agency uses to fill unused space.
>
> "Dream a Butterfly," the bus advises. And: "Explore a Street."
>
> At this place, and in this time, that is a strangely cruel combination of commands. Anyone who explores a side street here is not going to dream a butterfly. He's going to dream a cockroach or a rat.
>
> It is a gray and cold late afternoon. You're guided down a side street by a neighborhood worker who warns you not to be surprised at anything you might see. The block seems quiet enough. A candy

store, real estate office, barber shop, beauty shop, apartment houses, a public school.

You enter the apartment building that is home for the family that has consented to let a stranger share an ordinary day with them. In the downstairs hallway a group of about 10, including several teen-agers, are shooting craps—the smooth hardstone floor is alive with $5 and $10 bills and several pairs of dice.

They don't even notice you, except to move aside when you say "excuse me."

The air in the elevator to the seventh floor is heavy with the smell of urine. It's a little self-operating elevator that rises very slowly. The corridor of this top floor has a depressed spot. In it is a pool of water of undetermined origin. Beyond that lies the apartment door of our family, whose name is being withheld from this account. . . .

After the Detroit racial disorders during the last week of July 1967, the *Free Press* took an introspective look at what had taken place to cause such violence and forty-three deaths. For Sunday, August 20, Philip E. Meyer of the paper's Washington bureau, wrote a near-definitive study of the rioters, who they were, what their attitudes and grievances were. Freshly back from a Nieman year at Harvard where he studied computer and quantitative research techniques, Meyer was able to apply social science methodology to his inquiries. Four weeks after the outbreak, an eighteen-column report was published. In the Sunday edition of September 3 appeared a wrap-up with a case history of each of the forty-three deaths during the disorders. An investigating team of three *Free Press* reporters had checked and double-checked details on each one. The conclusion was: Most of the forty-three deaths were unnecessary and could—or should—have been prevented. The *Detroit Free Press* operation became the basis for a sixty-page booklet distributed by the American Newspaper Publishers Association.

Despite efforts such as those by UPI and the *Detroit Free Press,* newsmen generally felt a great deal still remained to be done in covering the black communities. For instance, a survey of 388 news outlets by the Anti-Defamation League of B'nai B'rith and the *Columbia Journalism Review* (Fall 1968) found that, almost a year after the 1967 racial disorders, a lack of analysis and interpretation about news of black affairs still existed, although there were "definite signs of progress." News media executives, in general, felt that media had failed—up to that time—to keep demonstrations and riots in perspective. Some news organizations said they had broken from "traditional reporting methods" when they became aware of shortcoming after "decades of neglect."

Two in-depth stories in *The New York Times* during the 1960's attracted such national attention and acclaim that they set a pattern for other newsmen.

As part of his preparations for becoming the new metropolitan editor, A. M. Rosenthal early in 1964 called upon the then police commissioner who was concerned over the death of twenty-eight-year-old Catherine Genovese while walking to her Kew Gardens home early one morning. Thirty-eight witnesses had seen or heard the slayer at work during the more than a half hour it had taken him to stalk and repeatedly stab the young woman. Although urban apathy is well known and widespread, the inaction of these thirty-eight citizens disturbed the commissioner because he believed a single call to the police might have saved a life. Rosenthal was appalled and assigned Marty Gansberg to investigate the case as a special assignment. Results of his inquiry about the silent witnesses appeared on *The Times'* front page two weeks after the slaying; the story shocked the city and the nation. Rosenthal wrote a *New York Times Magazine* article about the wider implications of apathy and eventually a book, *Thirty-Eight Witnesses* (McGraw-Hill, 1964), appeared and was translated into several foreign languages.

Nearly four years later, J. Anthony Lukas, another *Times* reporter, was assigned to investigate the slaying of a Greenwich, Conn., debutante who was found slain in the East Village beside a hippie friend. In studying the background of Linda Fitzpatrick, Lukas interviewed members of her family at their thirty-room home in Connecticut and ran down clues furnished by East Village habitués who told him of her experimentation with drugs. "The Two Worlds of Linda Fitzpatrick," which contrasted her two lives, appeared in *The Times*. It won the Pulitzer and George Polk Memorial prizes and a condensed version appeared in *Reader's Digest*.

Many other papers have broken from the conventions of the summary lead and the inverted pyramid organization format—but these techniques still dominate the bread-and-butter reporting of the nation's press, especially the smaller papers where salaries and talent frequently are less than on the metropolitan ones. As long as the daily newspapers were the initial channel for learning what was going on in the world, there was some basis for these practices' extensive use. Now television can cover the anticipated news—and much of the unexpected, too—well before the presses begin to print. That means the dailies, like the news magazines, have to turn to backgrounding, explaining, illuminating what took place. For that, they should not employ a century-old traditional approach. Unfortunately, a lot of them do.

Another idea that has encountered little acceptance by the daily press is departmentalization of the news, except for sports, women's interest, and financial-business sections. News magazines have done this since *Time*'s Vol. 1, No. 1, issue in 1923. During the past several years, network television has experimented with a "magazine"-type program and the National Educational Television's offering "Black Journal," directed chiefly at covering black communities and race activities, attracted enough favorable attention and approval to win an Emmy award in 1970. Among the great circulation successes of the recent past have been specialized magazines, along with the so-called mass circulation variety. Consider, for example, *TV Guide, Better Homes & Gardens,* and *Scientific American.* Yet newspaper efforts to adapt departmentalization and specialized appeals have been almost nonexistent beyond the conventional special sections, such as sports. Possibly readers' resistance to change may account for part of this inaction but some valid arguments can be made for further departmentalization of inside pages. Since the front page still is regarded as a show window for important news of that day's events, it may have to continue as a jumble of unrelated items chosen rather subjectively by the daily's chief news executives with the view of attracting typical readers. But must the inside pages be put together solely on the basis of where the slugs of type will conveniently fit? The contention that newspapers must be doing something right in their arrangement of news items because they are selling more than 60,000,000 daily does not really hold. Subscribers probably do not even know there is another (possibly better) way to package the news.

Broadcasting has somewhat different problems but it, too, has inhibiting practices.

News announcers are trapped by the clock, even more than most print-oriented colleagues are by limited news space. A thirty-minute or hour long program can only include a dozen to twenty news items—and on most newscasts that means sports, weather forecasts, and often market quotations besides the top news. As Richard Salant, head of CBS News, said, "We can't give stories enough length or depth. Things are always left out." The "bang-bang" type of news more easily adapts to compression but what about, say, the complexities of mounting tensions between two Central American neighbors which have not yet broken out into actual fighting or the implications of education reforms that concern new ideas rather than new equipment or buildings?

If an event has little or no visual and audio possibilities and, as the medium's critics say, no "show biz" potentials, then television and, to a lesser degree, radio tend to pass it by in their coverage. A lot takes place in the world that does not lend itself to a quickie, visual (or audio) presentation. How do you tell how people's thinking is changing? Of course, a graphic table may hint at it. Possibly one might get a particularly articulate person to talk about his ideas for a few seconds—or even a couple of minutes. A panel talk show might do it. It is not an easy assignment and probably the efforts will be both expensive and ineffectual. So what does a local broadcaster do? Sometimes, just forget it and cover a fire, demonstration, or wreck.

On the networks, television has superbly displayed the rituals of the past decade—Apollo flights to the moon, political conventions, presidential inaugurations, investiture of Charles as Prince of Wales, Earth Day activities, and those anti-Establishment demonstrations on campuses and at the nation's capital. The Vietnam war took on almost ritualistic aspects of military men in action, dead, captives, airplanes, and bombs.

Broadcasters' ingenuity has been at work, just as it has among print newsmen. Some hour-long TV documentaries in recent years have demonstrated that, when networks find the funds and when local stations air the resulting program, in-depth reporting can come close to the ideal through a happy blending of sight and sound, insight and intelligence. But each affiliate station has to grant its own clearance when the networks offer a program. These clearances are not automatically given. For example, six New York state network-affiliates during 1968-1969 declined to clear at least one out of every three network news programs offered by their own colleagues, according to the duPont—Columbia survey. Thus innovations often may be blocked at the local level because—let's face it—some of the audience would rather watch a comedy rerun.

On radio, the all-news phenomenon, which started in the 1960's, stabilized at eight stations across the country as the decade ended. All were in major population centers and economic influences appeared to militate against expansion of this type of broadcasting into smaller markets.

As the media reexamined their conventional ways of presenting the news, many of the old, familiar straitjackets were altered though not discarded completely. Undoubtedly even more changes would be beneficial for a truly democratic society. Readers and listeners, while sensing these shifts, do not entirely understand what is happening to the processes by which they get their information about what is happening in the world. At worst, opportunities for newsmen to air their biases and prejudices are strengthened. Even in the best of circumstances, an uneasiness has grown because change is always uncomfortable. So a ferment has arisen which offers plenty of chances for exploitation by those who want to make a profit of some sort, economic, social, ideological, or political. Thus it is that the media in the 1970's have become a real and potential scapegoat for the trouble that Americans currently are facing. Illumination of what is happening may light the way for a solid public opinion.

8. Cluttering Up
the News Picture

Two of contemporary journalism's most complicating trends arose from advancing technologies and recent media affluence when they brought (1) an explosive use of pictures in print as well as on television and (2) massive hordes of newsmen or, as some observers called it, "herd" coverage. The first gave the audience more of a sense of "I was there" and the second, on its plus side, provided a greater variety than ever before possible.

Improvements in camera equipment, film, and wire transmission combined to make available photographs so that individual newspaper editors, if they wished, could counter television with the assertion that the press was at least a quasi-visual medium. This wasn't true of all papers, however. The *Wall Street Journal* with its million-plus circulation uses no photographs at all, only sketches and charts. And, as one journalism school expert in graphic arts noted, "As I study newspapers today, all I see are fundamentally the same basic designs that were used as long as 40 years ago. Most newspaper designs have not been changed very much even though everything around the newspaper is changing."

With mounting circulations and listenerships (and their resulting advertising revenue increases), more money for editorial content brought so many reporters and photographers on assignments to cover the really big news stories of the 1950's and 1960's that they not infrequently got in each other's way to such an extent that they changed the focus of the event itself by their very presence.

Photographs are frozen moments of action. Sometimes the results are dramatically significant and capsulate the theme of an event; other times the pictures are blatant distortions and spread misinformation to the public. Each tells its own story, true or false, and to do the job properly a good news picture must:

★ Tell a story, and clearly.

★ Have impact, combining, it is said, "the interest of a miniskirt, the shock value of a punch in the nose, and the visual excitement of a parade."

By and large, the flood of pictures by local cameramen and by wire photo syndicates provide today's publications with a wide range of possibilities for selection. Although a "cheesecake" photograph of a beauty queen still has its local appeal and minimal impact elsewhere, a whole group of socially significant photographs have profoundly helped to shape U.S. public opinion during the past decade.

For instance, four batches of photographs out of South Vietnam played truly key roles in shaping attitudes, in each instance against American involvement. They were:

(1) A Buddhist monk killing himself by self-immolation.

(2) U.S. troops setting fire to thatched huts of Vietnamese natives.

(3) A Saigon police officer shooting a Viet Cong suspect, arms tied behind his back.

(4) Photographs taken at the time of the My Lai slayings.

In all cases, viewing was unpleasant and Americans only reluctantly admitted the implications. The Buddhists were able to force this country to face up to the unpopularity of the Diem regime and thus helped to pave the way for acceptance of its eventual overthrow. The destruction and barbarism of the others brought home to the U.S. public the brutality of war as few other things had and undoubtedly helped to increase opposition to the conflict itself. When the Cleveland *Plain Dealer* published the first My Lai pictures on Nov. 20, 1969, many phone calls of protest were received during the following twenty-four hours; readers felt the displays of bodies should not have been printed. Thus the cameramen in South

Vietnam may have proved more powerful than newspaper columnists and television and radio commentators in molding American opinion about the war and this nation's involvement there.

Much the same case for photographic power over people's minds could be made for domestic events. The still and television pictures of police dogs in Birmingham and the sheriff's deputies of Selma activated the public, especially in the North and West, and the 1964 Civil Rights Act became law partly because of the pressures aroused by the picture coverage. The shooting of Lee Harvey Oswald on live television two days after the assassination of President John F. Kennedy added to the fantastic public shock, although much of it was personal and not transferred directly to such forms of reform as stricter regulations on firearm sales. Scenes of ghetto rioting and student demonstrations on campuses during the late 1960's were powerful prods on the public mind.

But any person who sees only pictures may have a very simplistic view of what is happening in the world—and the viewer may never know that it isn't a completely true and accurate picture. Some word reporters get a slight satisfaction from this but they need not gloat because a happy combination of words and pictures or film and script can be among the most powerful instruments yet devised.

Let's examine some cases of pictures that told considerably less than the whole truth.

During the demonstrations of black students at Cornell University in April 1969, one widely used photograph distributed by the Associated Press showed a group emerging from the union building on campus where the students had secluded themselves. The picture showed blacks carrying rifles and shotguns and with a belt of bullets draped around one of them. It was publicized on front pages around the world, including the front page of *The New York Times* and the cover of the following week's *Newsweek*. The impression that most people got was of black students with guns on campus, ready to shoot it out if they didn't win their confrontation with administrators and policemen. Was this true? Not so, said several individuals who doublechecked on the situation weeks later. For instance, Terry Ann Knopf, research associate at the Lemberg Center for the Study of Violence, Brandeis University, wrote in the Spring 1970 issue of *Columbia Journalism Review*:

> Certain facts were largely ignored: prior to the disorder a cross had been burned in front of a black women's dormitory; the students had heard radio reports that carloads of armed whites were moving

Wide World Photos

toward the campus; when the students emerged from the building their guns weren't loaded. What was basically a defensive response by a group of frightened students came across in the media as a terrorist act by student guerrillas.

The Lemberg Center reported on another example, this one arising from disorders at York, Pa., in the middle of July 1968. The Harrisburg Bureau of United Press International asked its part-time stringer at York for picture coverage and it then distributed a photograph of a motorcyclist with an ammunition belt around his waist and a rifle strapped across his back and a small object dangling from the rifle. The *Washington Post* of July 18, among many dailies, printed the picture with the cutline shown on the next page.

The implication was that the "armed rider" was up to no good, at best, or a possible sniper, at worst. Actually it showed a sixteen-year-old

ARMED RIDER—Unidentified motorcyclist drives through heart of York, Pa., Negro district, which was quiet for the first time in six days of sporadic disorders.
Washington Post, July 18, 1968, and United Press International.

boy who was fond of hunting groundhogs. He strapped a rifle across his back with a hunting license dangling so that all would see he was hunting animals, not people. Unfortunately, that was not the impression readers got.

What has become another classic example of misinformation conveyed from a widely reproduced photograph and captions is the "co-ed screams" picture from the Kent State University campus after the slaying of four students by National Guardsmen. During the morning and afternoon of that tragic May 4, 1970, John Paul Filo, a six-foot-three photography student with an Abraham Lincoln beard, exposed six rolls of film—a total of more than two hundred shots. As Filo put it later, he simply had to have "something important" because he had tried to stand at the heart of the actions, even being gassed, knocked down, and clubbed over the head as he clicked the shutter. Troubled by rumors that vigilante groups were stopping cars to search for guns and cameras, he hid his exposed films in various parts of his Volkswagen and started driving for his home town of Tarentum, Pa. Across the state line, he called the editor of the daily there, the *Valley Daily News,* and was told to bring his film in and they would develop it. In the group was that of what James Michener called "the girl with the Delacroix face" in his narrative, *Kent State: What Happened and Why* (Random House, 1971). It showed an anguished young woman, her arms outstretched over the body of Jeffrey Miller. Cutline writers assumed that she was a co-ed apparently stunned by the slaying of her fellow student. The next day across the country were such cutlines as:

Student Discovers Classmate Lying Dead
After Guard Fired on Crowd of Protesters
St. Petersburg (*Fla.*) *Times* and Wide World Photos.

A COED SCREAMED OVER THE BODY OF DEAD CLASSMATE
ON THE CAMPUS OF KENT STATE UNIVERSITY
National Guardsmen opened fire on a crowd of
demonstrators yesterday at the Ohio school
Seattle Post-Intelligencer.

"He's Dead!" Coed Screams as Classmate Lies Slain
. . . on campus of Kent State University Monday
Daily Press, Utica, N.Y.

The assumption that Mary Vecchio was a "co-ed" vanished later when it developed that she was a fourteen-year-old runaway from a junior high school at Opa-locka, Fla., who just happened to be in Kent during the weekend of disturbances. After Filo had won a Pulitzer Prize for news photography in the spring of 1971, one letter writer to the trade journal, *Editor & Publisher* (May 29, 1971), asked:

> Was this photograph, I wonder, thoroughly checked to be sure that it was not in the least posed? I should think that the [Pulitzer] judges would have required affidavits from John Paul Filo, the youthful photographer, and the runaway girl who purportedly did the screaming—affidavits that would guarantee (almost) that the photograph was completely unmanaged.

If the cutline writers in early May of 1970 had been as careful as the letter writer proposed for the Pulitzer judges, the initial impact of this photograph might have been considerably blunted. In the rush to get it into print (and by competitive standards, justifiably so), a distortion was projected and, for many Americans, it remains that most recalled symbol of the Kent State shootings, if not all campus disruptions. Cutline writers may start viewers along a line of thought that leads them to "see" more in a photograph than is really there; this need not be a photographer's fault.

How the emphasis on the dramatic and the violent may distort the true circumstances was well illustrated in *Mass Media and Violence,* a staff report to the National Commission on the Causes and Prevention of Violence. Both still and television cameramen shot an incident at San Francisco State College shortly after Dr. S. I. Hayakawa took over as acting president there. The nation's audiences saw pictures of him atop a sound truck ripping out wires and surrounded by a group of apparently hostile students. The report commented as follows:

> The television newscast gave the impression that the entire university was in turmoil. If the viewer read the *Los Angeles Times* account the next day, he learned that the event on television represented only one episode that lasted eight or ten minutes. The rest of the day, Dr. Hayakawa was in his office receiving groups of students seeking to restore order on campus. The same day, 16,000 students attended

class and did not participate in the disturbances. A few words by the television commentator would have provided the perspective necessary to communicate a representative portrayal of what had happened at San Francisco State College that day. Those words were missing.

This business of picking the unusual, be they students, hippies, or militants, has become a common practice of both still and television photographers. It adds color and enhances usability through appealing to stereotypes. Even to explain that 500 or 50,000 took part in a parade or a demonstration does not completely erase an initial impression that kooks dominated what, in fact, may have been a basically peaceful and highly conventional affair in this era of dissent. Consider the few hundred militants who descended on the Department of Justice building in Washington during the Moratorium demonstrations on Nov. 15, 1969. It was on them, not the peaceful tens of thousands, that the Attorney General targeted his vocal comments. On the other hand, earlier that year during the Nixon inauguration, cameras were focused primarily on the central event although limited attention (as it should have been) was paid to dissenters and their actions at their own "In-Hog-Uration."

The National Advisory Commission on Civil Disorders in its 1968 report indicated that most newsmen were "aware and concerned that their very physical presence can exacerbate a small disturbance" but that others had acted with "a startling lack of common sense." The report recited one incident where a photographer during the Newark disorders staged events "for the sake of the story" and thus may have contributed to the already high racial tensions. The text said:

> Reports have come to the Commission's attention of individual newsmen staging events, coaxing youths to throw rocks and interrupt traffic, and otherwise acting irresponsibly at the incipient stages of a disturbance. Such acts are the responsibility of the news organization as well as the individual reporter.
>
> Two examples occurred in Newark. Television cameramen, according to officials, crowded into and in front of police headquarters, interfering with law enforcement operations and "making a general nuisance of themselves." In a separate incident, a New York newspaper photographer covering the Newark riot repeatedly urged and finally convinced a Negro boy to throw a rock for the camera. Pushing and crowding may be unavoidable, but deliberate staging of events is not.

We believe every effort should be made to eliminate this sort of conduct. This requires the implementation of thoughtful, stringent staff guidelines for reporters and editors. Such guidelines, carefully formulated, widely disseminated, and strictly enforced, underlie the self-policing activities of some news organizations already, but they must be universally adopted if they are to be effective in curbing journalistic irresponsibility.

Persuading a youngster to throw a rock on camera, of itself, may seem no major breach of journalistic ethics but when it is done against a backdrop of high emotions, then it takes on added dimensions. By the 1970's, most responsible media managers had carefully considered how their cameramen should behave in tension-charged situations and issued highly specific guidelines. How well they were carried out depended on decisions made—sometimes literally—under fire.

Most infrequently, television crews have arrived at a news event with signs, carefully prepared to simulate amateur hand-lettering, which they handed out for participants to use. On one such occasion, the crowd came even better prepared than the cameramen; on signal for them to "perform" for filming, they switched to previously hidden signs denouncing the network by name for faking. Obviously, that film never made a national broadcast but rival reporters told the story with relish for months and years. Such actions are most unusual but they have happened.

Photographers can pick their spot for shooting pictures so that they achieve a predetermined goal. If, for instance, a cameraman, on his own or under instructions, wants to favor a certain prominent individual, he can do so in many ways. For instance, a friendly photographer never would show a political candidate from the back of a partly empty hall; he would move right in where the crowd was. A vengeful cameraman could capture an entertainer with his mouth open or with an unflattering smirk on his face.

At times, picture coverage may be created—by more than the conventional professional techniques. On Nov. 1 and 2, 1967, the Columbia Broadcasting System's Chicago station WBBM-TV broadcast a report of a marijuana party held in nearby Evanston, site of Northwestern University. The resulting storm brought hearings by the Federal Communications Commission and a Special Subcommittee on Investigations of the House Committee on Interstate and Foreign Commerce. Deeply involved was John Victor Missett, a 1967 Northwestern graduate and, in the words of the FCC hearing examiner, "a young, ambitious reporter" for the station's news staff. The examiner's report held that the pot party broadcast "was prearranged for the benefit of CBS, and that this particular party would never have been held but for Missett's request."

The FCC itself found that Missett had, without the station management's knowledge or consent, gotten Northwestern students to hold the marijuana party but the commissioners ruled that they could not review the "journalistic judgment" displayed in such programing. However, the Commission told CBS to issue guidelines so its personnel would not again stage a news story for broadcasting. It further said that stations "are entitled to show through investigative journalism that substantial segments of society are flouting a particular law."

The pot party case raised some of the key questions about pictorial journalism. Staging of an event—in less polite words and in other circumstances, one might say, "faking" the news—is beyond the scope of normal reporting procedures. Obviously, responsible journalists for either broadcasting or print can not so deceive their audiences. However, the right to show legal violations as "a facet of investigative journalism" was upheld by the Commission's majority. Viewers may have difficulty, especially if they are displeased, distressed, or disgruntled by what they see on television, in distinguishing these journalistic procedures, clear as they apparently were to the FCC. The impact of a pot party broadcast on a puritanical viewer may be just as violent whether the program is an event to which a TV camera crew was invited after it was scheduled or one which was arranged originally by "a young, ambitious reporter."

A picture editor can select the photograph to achieve the impression he wants to create. For example, two Chicago papers showed pictures of Edward F. Kratzke, jury foreman, after the 1969-70 conspiracy trial arising from demonstrations at the time of the Democratic convention. The cutlines read:

(1) *Chicago Daily News:* "Happy to get home again. Edward F. Kratzke, jury foreman in the Conspiracy 7 trial, carrying baggage, arrives home in Forest Park, after 4½ months' absence."

(2) *Chicago Tribune:* "Edward Kratske, jury foreman, shields himself from photographer as he arrives home."

The *Tribune*'s picture displayed the foreman's bag hiding his face; the *Daily News* showed a smiling individual holding his hat, bag in hand.

One of the most discussed—and rightly so—aspects of the impact of photographers involves what happens when cameramen confront what may become their performing audience. The biggest effect, by far, is a television crew with its massive equipment and lights, sometimes with mobile truck. So television has received most of the recent criticism, a share of it for actions during the Chicago convention. One critic said, "It is questionable if TV is capable of reporting the news objectively." In apparent anticipation of television coverage of the demonstrations during the 1968 Chicago convention week, many policemen removed their badges to avoid possible identification and smashed cameras as one way to eliminate possible evidence of their misconduct. The full story is told in *Rights in Conflict* (Government Printing Office, 1969).

If the cameramen are there and if they do record what happens, they have been, in some cases, a restraining influence on possible violence by authorities. Former Attorney General Nicholas Katzenbach cited this two-edged impact of television coverage when he was quoted as saying in *Race and the News Media* (Frederick A. Praeger, 1967):

> The bitter segregationists' view of this [civil rights movement] is that the demonstrators are following the cameras, not vice versa. To them, it is the Northern press and the television networks which seem to be the motive force in the civil-rights movement. This idea apparently motivated many of the toughs during the 1961 freedom rides in Selma and elsewhere. Almost their first moves were against the cameras.
>
> Yet news coverage has been a powerful deterrent to racial violence in the South. For every assault on newsmen, many more incidents have been defused by their presence. Reporters and cameras, particularly the network-television cameras, which symbolized the national focus on Southern violence, have had a tempering as well as instructional effect.

Regardless of how media allocate their film, their air time, and their print space, they may come under attack. To paraphrase Abraham Lincoln, you can't please all the people all of the time with all you do. It always has been somewhat that way but it just seems to be increasingly so for media, especially in photo journalism. Unless one wants to become involved with the sophistication of communications, pictorial or otherwise, it may be easier for readers and viewers to hit out at all the media that do not report the "good news" that they want to read and see. That, unfortunately, is what some members of the mass audience are doing. It is not enough for editors just to "let the film tell the story" and the public is making that point clear. The commentary or the answers to the question, "Why?" just have to be included. For instance, suppose a film shows policemen swinging their batons at rioters. How to handle the photographs? The report *Mass Media and Violence* gives these suggestions:

> The film cannot tell the story. It represents a very small slice of the disorder. It does not tell why the police were cracking skulls; whether they were attacked by the mob; whether the mob had been ordered to disperse and refused to do so; whether they were trying to rescue an officer or another threatened person; or whether they had just lost their senses and, for no apparent reason, decided to beat up some people. Just showing the film clip openly invites each viewer to supply his own reason why, and it will be the viewer's preconceptions about rioters or police that will determine what story he receives—not the film. Just showing the film may be the easy way out of a difficult decision for the reporter, but just showing the film is not enough.

A television crew with its obviously conspicuous equipment and the single news photographer with his camera in hand or dangling around his neck can influence the news event, as pointed out earlier in this chapter. But the mere presence of a reporter with his pencil and note paper can subtly modify what is happening. The fact that they are, either literally or figuratively, "on camera" changes the way people behave. With enough money in business office tills to afford it, news executives have been sending their own reporters to cover the big news stories instead of depending on press associations or other sources that service many outlets. Despite some few exceptions since the early 1950's and even including the less affluent early 1970's, most newspapers and television have dispatched correspondents with fairly lavish freedom. This has created the problems of "herd" journalism.

This is not a unique journalistic development, as witness the 1935 trial of Bruno Hauptmann on charges of slaying Charles A. Lindbergh, Jr., when more than 300 reporters filed more than 11,000,000 words during a twenty-eight day trial, and the earlier Hall-Mills murder case, when even *The New York Times* printed verbatim question and answer testimony. But the extent to which this mob coverage has expanded is a variation from the past.

Documentation is easy to provide from recent press performances. For instance, presidential voyages always have been a favorite assignment —and still are. The thirteen-day trip of Chairman Nikita Khrushchev of the U.S.S.R. to this country in 1959 attained a level of chaotic confusion not previously witnessed here and President Dwight D. Eisenhower's trip to India matched the Russian's in many ways. But the event that raised the loudest protests from nonjournalists was the media's performance after the assassination of President John F. Kennedy in Dallas in 1963. The Warren Commission's report includes "Activity of Newsmen" (five text pages and three illustrations), "News Coverage and Police Policy" (nine pages and one picture), and "Responsibility of News Media" (three pages).

Let's look at a couple of these in greater detail:

The Khrushchev Visit of 1959: Even as the Soviet Chairman landed in Washington, the scramble began because he alighted from the far side of his plane away from the reporters and photographers. Newsmen had to fight to catch up with Khrushchev—and did. Correspondents were to shift the pattern of his visit as they followed him everywhere he went. More than 300 newsmen from seventeen countries traveled with him cross country and dozens or hundreds more from local and regional media joined the group at each major stop. For instance, the Columbia Broadcasting System estimated that a total of 375 of its cameramen and technicians took part in some phase of the visit to the United States.

Not untypical were the reporters' reactions when Khrushchev entered the press car on the way from Los Angeles to San Francisco. Advance arrangements said the newsmen were to remain seated and silent. But when the visitor entered the car, as *Editor & Publisher* said, "Newsmen hurdled the backs of seats like mountain goats, while others burrowed through the aisle."

On a visit to Roswell Garst's Iowa farm, the tour reached its climax as a roadshow. During a trip to a nearby Des Moines meat-packing plant, newsmen had to work around slabs of beef with note pads, cameras, and even television microphones. At the Garst farm, photographers climbed trees, perched in a barn loft, and even on haystacks to record the Khrushchev smile and a Garst scowl. Finally, the farmer-host lost his patience; he hurled silage at one group of newsmen he thought were too close and landed a kick on Harrison Salisbury of *The New York Times.* Ironically, Salisbury, a former Moscow reporter for *The Times,* had a reputation as one of the fairest observers of the Soviet scene.

James Hagerty, Eisenhower's press secretary, admitted that the reporters got in each other's way but argued, "I have no right to decide who can go." One network executive estimated that the total production costs for all three surpassed $2,000,000 for the entire thirteen-day visit. Both print and electronic newsmen agreed that something had to be done to bring some kind of order during future events of this type but few suggested how it could be done.

The Kennedy Assassination and Oswald Shooting: Although a presidential trip always has its quota of accompanying newsmen, an estimated 300-plus representatives of news media were in Dallas within twenty-four hours after the assassination. "Upwards of 100 newsmen and cameramen," according to the Warren Commission report, crowded Friday night into the third floor corridor, into which Lee Harvey Oswald was brought on his way to interrogations. Agent James Patrick Hosty, Jr., of the Federal Bureau of Investigation testified later that the police station was "not too much unlike Grand Central Station at rush hour, maybe like the Yankee Stadium during the World Series games." Dallas Police Chief Jesse E. Curry called it "a bedlam of confusion."

To get the flavor of the scenes (because they provide a basis for much of the attacks on media "herd" performance), the following include descriptions from the Warren Commission report with interspersed comments from Darwin Payne's careful study, *The Press Corps and the Kennedy Assassination* (Journalism Monographs No. 15, February 1970, published by the Association for Education in Journalism). Payne, who participated in covering the assassination and following events as a Dallas newsman, wrote his study "based strictly on verifiable evidence," much of it from the twenty-six volumes of testimony and exhibits collected by the Warren Commission.

The Commission reported:

In the lobby of the third floor, television cameramen set up two large cameras and floodlights in strategic positions that gave them a sweep of the corridor in either direction. Technicians stretched their television cables into and out of offices, running some of them out of the windows of a deputy chief's office and down the side of the building. Men with newsreel cameras, still cameras, and microphones, more mobile than the television cameramen, moved back and forth seeking information and opportunities for interviews. Newsmen wandered into the offices of other bureaus located on the third floor, sat on desks, and used police telephones; indeed, one reporter admits hiding a telephone behind a desk so that he would have exclusive access to it if something developed. . . .

The corridor became so jammed that policemen and newsmen

had to push and shove if they wanted to get through, stepping over cables, wires, and tripods. The crowd in the hallway was so dense that District Attorney [Henry] Wade found it "a strain to get the door open" to get into the homicide office. According to [Secret Service Special Agent Winston G.] Lawson, "You had to literally fight your way through the people to get up and down the corridor." . . . The television cameras continued to record the scene on the third floor as some of the newsmen kept vigil through the night.

[Payne wrote: Except for two instances—the Friday night Oswald press conference and the attempted Sunday transfer of the prisoner—the press centered its activities on the building's third floor. This was the information center: the homicide office where detective [sic] interrogated Oswald, the key administrative offices and the small press room equipped with three telephones and two typewriters. The press room normally served two local police reporters; it was wholly inadequate to accommodate the 100 or more newsmen who stationed themselves in the third floor corridor. This hallway, 7 feet wide and about 140 feet long, was the scene of chaos and congestion. . . .

[Through this hallway police escorted Oswald 16 times over the three-day period between the jail elevator and the homicide office, a distance of about 20 feet. Each time, the prisoner and his armed escorts were besieged by shouting newsmen, many of whom thrust microphones before him in hopes of eliciting some response. Some of the questions contained slurs. The prisoner invariably heard shouts which assumed his guilt: "Why did you kill the President? Why did you kill the President?" Police Chief Curry testified before the Warren Commission that the detectives and Oswald were "almost overrun" by the news media each time they moved the suspect down the hall. Yet, police placed no limitations on the press' activities other than to forbid the newsmen to enter the homicide office. Moreover, the police failed to vest a specific officer with responsibility for liaison with the press, and this added to the chaotic atmosphere. . . .

[Amid the confusion, the dominant factor that emerged was television with its harsh lights, cables, tripods, cameras, microphones, technicians and enterprising newsmen. The television newsmen who were so successful at leading the interviews with official spokesmen left a vivid impression. Police Chief Curry elaborated at length for the Warren Commission on the aggressiveness of television newsmen in obtaining interviews with him. Astonishingly, he could not recall a single interview with a newspaper reporter during the weekend. . . . Most descriptions of the press' activity placed similar emphasis on the particularly disruptive nature of television coverage.]

The Commission report continued:

Oswald's most prolonged exposure occurred at the midnight press conference on Friday night. In response to demands of newsmen, District Attorney Wade, after consulting with Chief Curry and Captain [J. Will] Fritz, had announced shortly before midnight that Oswald would appear at a press conference in the basement assembly room. An estimated 70 to 100 people, including Jack Ruby, and other unauthorized persons, crowded into the small downstairs room. No identification was required. The room was so packed that Deputy Chief M. W. Stevenson and Captain Fritz who came down to the basement after the crowd had assembled could not get in and were forced to remain in the doorway.

Oswald was brought into the room shortly after midnight. Curry had instructed policemen not to permit newsmen to touch Oswald or get close to him, but no steps were taken to shield Oswald from the crowd. Captain Fritz had asked that Oswald be placed on the platform used for lineups so that he could be more easily removed "if anything happened." Chief Curry, however, insisted that Oswald stand on the floor in front of the stage, where he was also in front of the one-way nylon-cloth screen customarily used to prevent a suspect from seeing those present in the room. This was done because cameramen had told Curry that their cameras would not photograph well through the screen.

[Payne wrote: At approximately midnight Friday, police displayed Oswald to the clamoring newsmen in a basement assembly room. Oswald was brought to this much-publicized confrontation, according to Chief Curry, primarily so reporters could examine him closely and help forestall rumors that the police were mistreating the prisoner. . . .

[Most descriptions of the brief midnight conference assumed that the press was responsible for the extreme congestion; however, approximately half of those attending were not associated with the news media. The Warren Commission concluded that from 70 to

100 persons attended the conference, although individual estimates were as high as 300. . . .

[Some police officers attended the session from curiosity rather than duty. One private citizen who entered the unguarded room and took part in the press conference was Jack Ruby, who also had been seen on the third floor earlier.

[. . . But this confusing and much-criticized conference was not solely the result of press importunities, for Chief Curry sought help for his investigation from the confrontation. He hoped that some of the newsmen might have seen Oswald at the assassination site, the airport or some other location and therefore could help confirm his supposed connection with the crime. The Warren Commission failed to acknowledge this motive in its criticism of the newsmen, and attributed the midnight confrontation only to police acquiescence in press demands.]

The Commission said:

The decision to move Oswald to the county jail on Sunday morning was reached by Chief Curry the preceding evening. Sometime after 7:30 Saturday evening, according to Assistant Chief [Charles] Batchelor, two reporters told him that they wanted to go out to dinner but that "they didn't want to miss anything if we were going to move the prisoner." Curry came upon them at that point and told the two newsmen that if they returned by 10 o'clock in the morning, they wouldn't "miss anything." A little later, after checking with Captain Fritz, Curry made a similar announcement to the assembled reporters. . . .

By the time Oswald reached the basement, 40 to 50 newsmen and 70 to 75 police officers were assembled there. Three television cameras stood along the railing and most of the newsmen were congregated in that area and at the top of the adjacent decline leading into the garage. A group of newsmen and police officers, best estimated at about 20, stood strung across the bottom of the Main Street ramp. . . .

Someone shouted, "Here he comes!"; additional spotlights were turned on in the basement, and the din increased. A detective stepped from the jail office and proceeded toward the transfer car. Seconds later Fritz and then Oswald . . . came through the door. . . . Though movie films and video tapes indicate that the front line of newsmen along the Main Street ramp remained fairly stationary, it was the impression of many who were close to the scene that with Oswald's appearance the crowd surged forward. According to Detective [L. D.] Montgomery, who was walking directly behind Oswald, "as soon as we came out this door . . . this bunch here just moved in on us." . . .

After Oswald had moved about 10 feet from the door of the jail office, Jack Ruby passed between a newsman and a detective at the edge of the straining crowd on the Main Street ramp. With his right hand extended and holding a .38 caliber revolver, Ruby stepped quickly forward and fired a single fatal bullet into Oswald's abdomen.

[Payne wrote: Police instituted more rigid security measures on Sunday morning in preparation for Oswald's transfer, but they were by no means adequate. A Philadelphia reporter recalled being asked "four or five times" for credentials, but other opinions as to the rigidity of security precautions varied among the newsmen, evidently depending on whether or not their own credentials were examined. At least eleven newsmen entered the basement on the morning of November 24 without having to present identification. These figures reveal that, at a minimum, one out of four newsmen in the basement did not have to present credentials for admittance. The Warren Commission acknowledged only that "several newsmen" entered the basement without having to identify themselves. The Commission pointed out that the double doors from the interior police station hallway leading to the basement were not guarded, apparently because of an oversight. However, some of the newsmen who entered unchallenged came in through other entrances.

[Press congestion does not appear to have been severe enough to have caused the security breakdown. Entry to the third floor was possible only by two elevators side-by-side in the center of the hallway and directly across from the only stairway leading to the floor. Had the press been responsible for Ruby's entry to the third floor, Dallas police had opportunity to correct the security lapse later upon seeing and talking to Ruby, but they did not. . . .

[Not enough persons, whether newsmen or officers or both, were present in the basement on Sunday morning to obscure Ruby as he entered and walked down the ramp to join the group waiting for

Oswald's appearance. Ruby joined the crowd easily without having to push or shove since the congestion was not that substantial.

[The officer who was handcuffed to Oswald also discounted the possibility that the congestion and glare from television lights prevented officers from stopping Ruby before he could fire. In his opinion, Ruby acted so suddenly that even a man equipped with prior knowledge of Ruby's intentions could not have reacted quickly enough to stop him.

[Warren Commission members gave Dallas police officers ample opportunity to express their opinions as to whether the press should be blamed for the security breakdown, but key police officials declined to do so. . . .

[In conclusion, the press in Dallas presented an aggressive but less formidable force than commonly has been supposed. The massive presence of newsmen was a constant factor to be considered, and the journalists became more than mere observers in creating certain events, notably the midnight press conference for Oswald and the open transfer of the prisoner. Certainly, the newsmen's clamor on the third floor of the police station constituted a troublesome atmosphere in which to solve the assassination of a President. Yet, it cannot be said that the press was guilty of more serious interference. Rather than being unwelcome participants at the Dallas police station, the newsmen were there not merely because they insisted, but because city and police officials wanted them there for their own reasons. The press did not obstruct the investigation as significantly as did the visiting lawmen who crowded into the homicide office, nor were the newsmen so numerous or disruptive as to prevent the police from enforcing effective security measures within the police station. While the press clamor was responsible for the public transfer in the basement, newsmen were not the majority there, nor did they prevent adequate security measures from being taken. That the press directly facilitated Ruby's attack on Oswald is by no means clear. In reaching its critical conclusions, the Warren Commission discounted the observations of key police officials and substituted its own opinions without developing substantiating evidence.]

Such are two, somewhat conflicting, discussions of the coverage and the slaying of Lee Harvey Oswald. Since a considerable base for recent criticism of media grew out of these activities, they have been extensively quoted. Newsmen, law enforcement officers, and attorneys all could have performed with more idealistic manners. Press representatives, particularly television crews, certainly put on flawed performances at Dallas but one can rightly ask whether the law enforcement officers' and lawyers' actions were so superb that their associations should set the ground rules for reporters in action? Should they contribute to pressures on the press? There is plenty of blame to spread around so that neither attorneys nor reporters would seem to have the perfection to force their views on the others. Since all groups comprise human beings, both sides in the controversy should —probably, must—make greater efforts to be responsible. The general public will benefit when this is done.

Herd coverage brings politicians and newsmen into potential conflicts during coverage of the quadrennial conventions to pick a presidential nominee. The grist of negotiations between various party leaders comprises much of the news that reporters seek and sometimes the spokesmen are less than ready to have all this publicized.

The size of the problem is told in the figures on requests for passes to the 1968 Democratic convention, for example. The Standing Committee of the Congressional Press Galleries, which was coordinating arrangements for newsmen, told the Democratic National Committee that two thousand working passes would be needed. Teletype operators and others of that sort of back-up workers were not included in the request because they do not clutter up the convention floor; messengers to carry copy from reporters were. When passes were handed out, only 375 were available. Protests were violent and finally the Standing Committee got 1,600 working passes and 80 floor passes. A lot of smaller publications just gave up the bother and depended on the press associations and syndicates for their copy.

The question here again is, does the newsman become part of the event itself, as he did in the Khrushchev visit and the Kennedy-Oswald shootings? And, if so, what should be done about it? Obviously, if curtailment of witnesses is because newsmen find out too much, the answer has to be: "Keep up the fight for coverage." If curtailment really promotes the democratic process, then the answer should be: "Okay, let's go along." But the evidence is not crystal clear and so honest men can have different opinions.

Vermont Royster, then *Wall Street Journal* editor, believed that many of the 1968 convention restrictions were "purely annoyances designed to discourage reporters from too much getting around, and perhaps finding out too much." Then he added, "The truth of the matter, I suspect, is that we are not only unloved but unwanted, and the disarrangements are made accordingly."

The late Ralph McGill, when publisher of the *Atlanta Constitution,* witnessed the jam-up of newsmen and photographers at both 1968 political conventions and advocated "changing the convention from entertainment to a condition of dignity and an opportunity for delegates to function uninterrupted." He proposed:

All media should be barred from the floor during convention sessions—reporters, television cameramen and commentators and radio reporters. It cannot be said that sessions of the Congress of the United States are lacking in meaning. But even at their more electric moments, aisles are not jammed with media reporters, cameras and mikes.

Frosty Troy, associate editor of the *Tulsa Tribune* and a newsman accredited to the 1968 Democratic convention, was even more blunt. He argued:

I don't buy the theory that the press is a sacred bug with the right to perch in the ear of the elephant or the donkey. We keep on preaching restraint to the public while going beyond those same restraints in the interest of getting the news. Being for good, tough, accurate reporting isn't enough if it means my unlimited freedom to cover a convention is going to create great difficulties for the election system under which my freedom is preserved.

Is pooling—whereby a selected small group cover the event—the answer to "herd" coverage, whether it is pretrial events, the trials themselves, presidential travels, or political conventions?

The arrangement sounds better than it usually works out although it may be necessary in some cases. When President Franklin D. Roosevelt traveled to Big Three conferences during World War II, representatives of the then three major press associations went with him most of the time —but not always. A hardy select band accompanied President-elect Eisenhower when he went to South Korea in secret to fulfill his 1952 campaign promises. So far so good. But what about the selection arrangements? When Vice-President Spiro T. Agnew went to Southeast Asia in December 1969, he arranged to take along enough correspondents to fill the empty seats of his jet. But when the *Baltimore Sun,* one paper which had opposed Agnew for governor and for vice-president, applied for one of its newsmen, it was told that there wasn't any room available. Many of the places had gone to friendlier publications although the Vice-President's staff could point out that a representative from *The New York Times,* which Agnew had blasted a few months earlier, was included. Certainly editorial nonendorsement should not become the sole basis for a seat in a vice-president's plane. However, the problem of who will go and who will stay behind will be around for some time with its resulting complications.

By their technological improvements and because of recent affluence, the media have created problems which generate pressures for themselves. For some dramatic events, still and television cameramen can capture bits of reality that are far more graphic than anything a word artist can hope to achieve. Admittedly an oversimplification, the saying, "A picture is worth ten thousand words," does have increasing significance as photographers get to scenes of the action faster and faster. Yet the fact that pictorial journalism seems so realistic and true breeds a fallacy because its very simplicity may misrepresent what really happened. Worship of speed may stimulate inaccurate interpretations when caption writers and broadcast commentators fail to provide accurate and truthful background.

It is false to claim that pictures can not lie. They must rest in a frame of reference and for most of them that requires captions and commentary. Here misinformation and faulty attitudes may be built up for the mass audience. The photographer, like the writer, can not possibly report everything. For better or worse, both have to focus on a segment of the available data and this is bound to lead to some malpractices even with the best intentions in the world. Readers and viewers must be aware of this, even if they are unwilling to forgive how the process of selection operated in any particular case. Now the media also are flooding their Big Event coverage with massive crowds of newsmen to take pictures and to write stories, thereby creating the complexities of herd journalism. If those concerned with the communication processes do not keep attention focused to eliminate all kinds of distortions and misinformation, there is little chance for the public to be accurately informed. Without at least a near approach to that goal, the whole operation has failed.

9. Mass Media as Big Business

To contemporary readers, it seems well-nigh incomprehensible that anyone was surprised when Lincoln Steffens, one of the greatest of the turn-of-the-century muckrakers, wrote in *Scribner's Magazine* in 1897, "Journalism today is a business." But people were and that fact suggests how far we have traveled in seventy-five years. Things that shocked Steffens and his readers now are accepted as matter of course. The communications industry today is indeed Big Business (with capital letters to give fanfare effect) and no knowledgeable observer for at least the past fifty years has had the temerity to maintain otherwise. Some of the rationale for journalistic procedures thus rests firmly on economics.

Like much of the rest of American business, the mass media have become bigger but not more numerous and, in some ways, more conformist as they have appealed to larger and larger audiences. On the other hand, some recent technological developments that could be adapted to communications promise the probability of segments of diversity—but usually with a lesser chance of big profits than with the giant corporations.

This chapter will examine these Big Business trends and two resulting developments: the thrust of competition and the quiet but persistent push to conformity. The next chapter will look at how these changes have created multimedia ownerships for many communities and the burgeoning threat from the large conglomerates when they venture into journalism.

That the media have become Big Business is easily demonstrated; the day when a printer with a batch of second-hand type could become a publisher has all but vanished. As for the size of the industry, look at these statistics:

★ Daily newspapers are almost an $8,000,000,000 industry, with approximately $2,000,000,000 coming from the public and the remaining, larger share from advertisers.

★ Television is supported by the $3,660,000,000 paid by advertisers and sponsors in purchasing air time or paying production costs.

★ Magazines receive $2,500,000,000 annually with $1,321,000,000 coming from advertising revenues.

★ Radio gets $1,278,000,000 yearly.

These statistics show that mass media income has climbed upward beyond $15,000,000,000 a year and this did not include such channels of public affairs information as the "instant" paperback books on contemporary issues. Figures thus are equivalent to about a penny and a half out of every dollar in the U.S. gross national product. Of the total advertising expenditures of $19,000,000,000-plus, including direct mail and other nonmedia formats, the print and broadcast media received more than half. Just after World War II, advertising expenditures were approximately $3,000,000,000.

For further proof of the bigness of current journalism consider the following: The Times Mirror Company of Los Angeles paid an estimated $65,000,000 in 1970 for *Newsday,* the prosperous Long Island paper—largest suburban daily in the country—started by Alicia Patterson and her husband, Harry F. Guggenheim, in 1940 with an initial investment of $70,000; some months earlier the Los Angeles company paid approximately $90,000,000 for the *Dallas Times Herald* and its Columbia Broadcasting System-affiliate broadcast stations. Dow Jones & Co., which owned the *Wall Street Journal* as well as financial news services, entered the general daily newspaper field in 1970 by acquiring nine papers from Ottaway Newspapers Radio, Inc., with a combined circulation of 242,695 daily, in a transaction involving more than $35,000,000. In 1967, Roy Thomson, the British media lord, paid $75,000,000 for the Brush-Moore group of Ohio dailies with total circulations of 363,000 and that same year S. I. Newhouse spent $54,200,000 for the Cleveland

Plain Dealer, with a circulation of 388,000 in an intensely competitive market. In 1971, the Gannett Co., Inc., issued more than $70,000,000 in common stock to merge the Federated Publications, Inc., into its organization. Federated, with headquarters in Battle Creek, Mich., publishes seven newspapers in Michigan, Indiana, Idaho, and Washington.

During the early 1970's, broadcasting stations were grouped together and sold for prices running into hundreds of millions of dollars. Some of these were highly complicated transactions since the Federal Communications Commission limits the number of stations any one owner may garner and also restricts managements to one-to-a-customer when they enter a new community. After months of hearings and discussions, the FCC approved license transfers in 1971 from Walter H. Annenberg, ambassador to the Court of St. James's in the Nixon Administration, of three Triangle television stations, some Philadelphia real estate, and a syndicate service to Capital Cities for a reported $110,000,000. These switches involved WFIL in Philadelphia, the nation's fourth ranking market; WNHC in New Haven, twenty-first ranking market; and KFRE in Fresno, Calif., sixty-ninth ranking market. To gain control of these new stations, however, Capital Cities proposed to yield some of its previously owned five television and eleven AM and FM radio stations in lower ranking markets. It agreed to sell WSAZ in Huntington, W.Va., to Lee Enterprises for $18,000,000 and WTEN in Albany, N.Y., plus its satellite station WCDC at Adams, Mass., to Poole Broadcasting, Inc., for $19,000,000. Before the FCC acted, Capital Cities further had agreed to spend up to a million dollars over three years to develop programs reflecting community minority groups and thus damped down some of the citizen groups' opposition to the new ownership. In April 1971 the FCC commissioners, by a 4 to 3 vote, authorized transfer of five Corinthian television station licenses to Dun & Bradstreet, Inc., data and business-information service. When the proposed sale was announced in December 1969, the stock that John Hay Whitney and his Corinthian associates would have received in Dun & Bradstreet was valued at $134,000,000 and when the FCC acted in April 1971 the stock had a market value of $137,000,000. Time-Life Broadcasting, subsidiary of the magazine publishers, sold off five television properties in the Midwest and California for $80,000,000 but remained active in CATV in many areas. Scripps-Howard Broadcasting bought KVOO-TV in Tulsa, Okla., for $6,600,000. Columbia Pictures purchased WNJU-TV in Newark and Linden, N.J., for $8,100,000. Field Enterprises, owner of half of WFLD-TV in Chicago bought the other half for $2,500,000 and was slated to sell the entire station to Metromedia for $10,000,000 but the option lapsed before negotiations were completed.

Another revealing index of the growth of communications-oriented corporations is publication of stock market price ranges in each issue of the newspaper business' *Editor & Publisher.* As of late 1971, this weekly chart included thirty listings from the New York Stock Exchange, eleven from the American Stock Exchange, and twenty-one from over-the-counter tradings. The New York Stock Exchange list included such print and broadcast organizations as Cowles Communications; Gannett Co., Inc.; Knight Newspapers; Time, Inc.; and Times Mirror Company, with its Los Angeles, Long Island, and other properties. Other media-related corporations on the Big Board included Eastman Kodak; Fairchild Camera; Foote, Cone & Belding, the advertising agency; Great Northern Nekoosa; Harris Intertype; and J. W. Thompson, another advertising agency. *The New York Times,* long closely held by the Ochs-Sulzberger family, now is listed on the American Stock Exchange. Booth Newspapers; *Boston Herald-Traveler;* Dow Jones & Co.; Doyle, Dane, Bernbach; and Multimedia, Inc.—all were available for purchase over the counter. And in keeping with its sometimes antitelevision stance as a print spokesman, *Editor & Publisher* omitted stocks of all three of the major networks from its New York Stock Exchange listings: American Broadcasting Company, Columbia Broadcasting System, and Radio Corporation of America.

Figures on profitability among the mass media were even more impressive than the overall totals. The following facts from *Mass Media and Violence* (Government Printing Office, 1969) show average before-taxes earnings ratios:

All U.S. industry (1964-65)	13.5%
Broadcast networks *	16.
Publishing industry (including papers, magazines, books, and allied printing trades)	18.
All independent broadcast stations	30.

* Principal earnings of networks come from wholly-owned and operated stations, not network operations.

Two items should be kept in mind in viewing these percentages. First, to make a profit certainly is no crime in a capitalistic society, but there can be results of less than social benefit if the urge to make money is pushed too far and too fast. Second, since a time lag always exists in compiling economic statistics, these figures do not reflect the real distress of staff curtailments and other cutbacks in media during the recession of 1970-71. Individual key corporations reported lower earnings—but there still were profits.

Touching on implications of the Big Business aspects of the communications industry, Derick Daniels, executive editor of the *Detroit Free Press,* wrote in *The Quill* (July, 1970):

Today, newspapers and networks are big business. They cost money to operate, and make money when they do, and they are dangerously near forgetting why they're operating and who they're operating for. While the communications industry has grown, it seems to me its willingness to pay attention to little voices has diminished.

But the times are changing. We're going to wake up or we're going to be woken up and the process won't be pleasant. We need to take a look at what belongs to whom.

Every time a reader spends a dime for a newspaper and every time a viewer switches channels, he participates in the relationship that is the economic and moral basis of our being. We are a service industry and those little voices out there delegate to us all our power to accomplish—to sell advertising, to make money, to exercise influence, to survive. . . .

The only vested interest to which we should respond—the one that deserves our ultimate attention—is that of our collective readers. And we haven't been doing a very good job.

The search for high profitability in electronic journalism during the affluence of the late 1960's undoubtedly led the 1968-69 Alfred I. duPont–Columbia University jurors to cite the broadcasters for pollution of "our minds, talents, and souls, our spiritual environment" and then to add:

Of all those Americans who are trying to get more out of life than they have put into it and who are laying waste their country in the attempt, none in recent years have appeared more successful as a group than the broadcasters. In what other business can a moderately astute operator hope to realize 100 percent a year on tangible assets, or lay out $150 for a franchise that in a few years' time he can peddle for $50 million—should he be so foolish as to want to sell? The most fantastic rewards associated with broadcasting in many instances grow from enterprises that do as little for their fellow country men as they legally can.

Media today pervade our culture, as truthfully said in *Mass Media and Violence,* "to a degree unmatched by any other social institution." For instance, an adult may choose from among some 1,750 daily newspapers, more than 8,000 weeklies, more than 22,000 periodicals, some 850 television stations, 4,200 AM and 2,250 FM radio stations. Such a selection would assume that a New Englander might want to listen to an AM or FM station in California, an Oregon resident might select to read a suburban weekly from upstate New York, or a Hoosier might pick a Texas regional journal for ranchers. In effect, the individual's area of choice is limited by geography as well as by his interests. Even within this narrower range, there is less competition than meets the eye. This is due to each publication's or station's dependence on the ancillary services of Big Business journalism: press associations for nonlocal news, networks for most of the broadcast programing, and syndicates for their comic strips, columnists, cartoons, photographs, and miscellaneous advice on almost any subject from manners to postage stamps.

The two press associations—Associated Press and United Press International—overwhelmingly service the nonlocal news needs of the thousands of newspapers and broadcast stations. According to recent figures, the Associated Press sells its report to 1,238 newspapers and 3,045 television and radio stations while United Press International provides news to 1,175 papers and 3,209 broadcast stations. Despite some recent Federal Communications Commission efforts (see Chapter Five), the three major networks rule a dominant portion of the prime-time hours and provide much material for other broadcasting. Although there are close to three hundred syndicates, a half dozen of the largest ones share more than 40 percent of the gross revenue total of $100,000,000-plus.

As in other segments of U.S. business, economic pressures, primarily, have brought the bulk of activities to a limited number of communications concerns. For example, the fifty most widely circulated daily papers accounted for 39 percent of the total daily circulation. The three television networks were seen by 92 percent of the audience during the peak viewing hours from 7:30 to 11 P.M. before the new prime-time cutbacks took place in the fall of 1971. The twenty largest consumer magazines garnered 41 percent of the total magazine circulations.

Daily newspapers without press associations are all but inconceivable. Even the most affluent metropolitan dailies could not manage to cover the wide world without some help from the news agencies. The globe is just too large a place for any publication or station (or even most groups of publications or broadcasters) to cover by themselves. Financially such an operation would be staggering. For instance, UPI operating costs during 1969 totaled $52,077,000. That means that the press association spent approximately a million dollars a week to tell its thousands of clients what was going on in the world: politicking in Washington, fighting in Vietnam and Middle East, foreign policy decisions from European capitals, the landing on the moon, sports in all the major leagues, price ranges in Wall Street, and all that variety of features from humorous to educational background that round out a news agency's report. So, to handle the high costs of news gathering and distribution, the media have combined to share expenses. This is nothing new because it was economics that drove New York City publishers into their first efforts at cooperative news gathering in 1848 when the initial Associated Press was founded. Then each of the city's publishers found that it was just too expensive to send out his own boats to meet incoming ships from Europe and so they pooled their resources—and tried to save money without losing news. It has been much the same ever since.

Figures on specific payments by individual newspapers for press association and syndicate copy are hard to obtain but, after the *World Journal Tribune* suspended in New York City, the Subcommittee on Antitrust and Monopoly of the U.S. Senate Committee on the Judiciary obtained key documents under subpoena dated Dec. 5, 1967. Thus it is possible to authenticate just how much the defunct paper contracted to pay for various services. To United Press International, the corporation agreed to pay $4,200 weekly so the projected *World-Journal* could have UPI wire services (two national or main trunks, both New Jersey and New York regional wires, Greater New York wire, sports wire, and Unirace wire six days weekly and a radio wire on Sundays only). For generally similar services for the proposed morning *Herald-Tribune,* the contract called for $2,612 additional. That totals $6,812 weekly for the seven morning and six evening editions. The Newspaper Enterprise Association, Inc., one of the larger syndicates, was to provide its full six-day Feature Matrix and Proof Service for $700 weekly and eight four-color NEA Sunday comics for $680 weekly. The Hearst Headline Service was to supply all its syndicated materials for $55,000 a year. All this added up to slightly less than half a million dollars a year for various contracts to supply wire service dispatches and syndicated features. Subcommittee testimony gave a rarely visible view of what a large metropolitan daily had to pay to obtain dispatches and features to fill its news hole beyond items from local staff reporters. Metropolitan journalism is indeed expensive.

As an index of the Big Business aspect in syndication, several of the more popular columnists in recent years have earned salaries of at least $100,000 yearly. Probably most successful of all the distributed features is "Peanuts," which has been descibed as "a truly remarkable feature"— and it is. It has spread to television, radio, and even Off-Broadway theater. During some years, an estimated gross income of as much as a million dollars annually was split by Charles M. Schulz, the artist, and United Feature Syndicate. Most top public affairs commentators get a high guarantee plus a percentage of the syndication payments, frequently a 50-50 split. Since they along with the popular comic strips are the bait for sales, the promotion costs and sales efforts may eat rather heavily into the syndicates' share. When possible, newspaper owners try to purchase exclusive rights to syndicated material for their entire circulation areas and this often increases the fees they have to pay but insures that competition will be minimal where most of their papers are sold. This makes it difficult for new suburban dailies to wedge into the field of familiar syndicated features, thus introducing a monopoly factor into newspaper operations of many a geographical area. After the *World Journal Tribune* stopped publication in New York City in May 1967, a hot contest developed over who was to grab up the more popular features that were under contract to the defunct publication. Were the syndicates to sell their wares exclusively to the single highest bidder or would they package them into various allocations to segments of the large New York metropolitan area? The answer was that both developments took place, depending mainly on how the bidding went and which way was most profitable for the syndicates.

Although there are only two major press associations, a professional and skillful wire-copy editor who is backed by a publisher willing to spend money for additional news input and for sufficient competent copyreaders does have more elements of selection than might appear to the nonjournalistic observer. AP or UPI supply far more than a typical daily can print in any one day and there are a wide range of distributors of special news such as Religious News Service and financial wires. *The New York Times* receives approximately 2,000,000 words daily and, on an average week day, publishes about 250,000. Thus about six or seven items may be discarded for every one that gets into print. This statistic is slightly deceptive because with its subscriptions to most of the news agencies, *The Times* may receive a half dozen or more versions of any major news development, with repetitions—besides stories on the event from its own correspondents. In addition to discarding whole dispatches, another extensively used technique is to combine the several versions into a single report and mark it, "From our various news services."

The men who decide whether to assign a news agency reporter to cover an event and then determine how much to send to subscribers or clients play almost godlike roles in the information-dissemination process. Fortunately, almost without exception, these key editors have been and are today of highest integrity and subscribe to the recognized standards of good conduct. The importance and high performance of these men was cited by Richard L. Tobin in *Saturday Review* (May 13, 1967):

> The most powerful man in the United States is not the President, the Secretary of State, a member of Congress, a Senator, a Governor, the chairman of AT&T, or the head of Harvard University. The most powerful person in the United States is the key man on the general desk of AP or UPI, by whatever name at whatever hour in the twenty-four. For most rip-and-read radio broadcasters (which is to say virtually all the small stations in this country) depend utterly on the competence and integrity of the wire services and their news tickers, and only the very best of our 1,754 daily papers have available to them anything but wire service copy from out of town. The responsibility is an awful one, though less frightening when one realizes that [these individuals are persons] of utter integrity and objectivity . . . Truth is their religion and an informed democracy their goal, whether they would admit it or not. The nation could not function long without them.

However, some observers feel that only two such wire service editors are too few despite their generally recognized "utter integrity and objectivity." For instance, why was a smaller, independent news agency the one that broke the full impact of the My Lai massacre, not either AP or UPI? But, by and large, as long as the present competition and intense rivalry continues between the two major U.S. press associations, the American public has a superb chance of maintaining the freedom of its information channels, and wire-news editors and broadcasters will have a true choice of what to print in their papers or to use on the air. If this competition ever weakens, the impact on the entire U.S. communications structure would be monumental and could be catastrophic for all, including the reading and listening public and the democratic system.

One minor restraint may occur on rare occasions when a paper will buy a comic strip or a columnist and then not publish it. This, as competing publishers have found out, does not allow them to purchase the unprinted material. Harry Horvitz, publisher of four Ohio dailies all within eighty miles of Cleveland, told the Subcommittee on Antitrust and Monopoly of the U.S. Senate Committee on the Judiciary in 1967 that he had tried to buy "Little Orphan Annie" earlier that year when the Cleveland *Plain Dealer* discontinued its use. The syndicate said it would have to check what the *Plain Dealer* proposed to do. Horvitz continued, "So several months after the Cleveland Plain Dealer stopped using this comic, they were preventing the Chicago Tribune from selling it to us, preventing the author from having his works seen in this area, and preventing the public from obtaining the enjoyment of reading the comic."

A really serious problem for the television networks concerns procedures that require a local station clearance before any offering may be aired, regardless of whether it is for an evening news program, special documentary, or an entertainment show. Thus, even if a program has news and information that the public needs to know, no requirement forces a broadcaster to carry it on his station. Somewhat the same problem confronts a wire-news editor and/or his publisher. Network programing, however, does not regularly include the slack provided by the news agencies. Where papers have a smorgasbord of ready choices, broadcasters are locked into choosing the network show, a locally-produced one, or a previously recorded tape. Often a network offering may attain somewhat higher overall standards than the local production but suspected sensibilities, such as white audience attitudes toward blacks in the South, may induce a manager to opt out. Obviously, local stations should broadcast their own works—this is a tenet supported heavily by the current FCC commissioners—but these should not be scheduled to eliminate network scheduling with "public service" values just because they may turn away viewers and listeners. Station managers' attitudes are imperatives because networks provide under half of the news that gets on the air. Local broadcasters may argue that they have to earn a profit but figures cited earlier in this chapter show that, on the whole, they were in no economic distress during the 1960's. On the other hand, no one should expect the mass audience always to rise in wrath if a public service program is left off the air. For instance, when the late Hugo L. Black, then senior associate justice of the U.S. Supreme Court, was interviewed after years of refusals, only 9 percent of the New York audience tuned in while 44 percent were viewing a Brigitte Bardot special on another network. That's a viewer ratio of one to five.

Other press critics complained that smaller U.S. papers and broadcast stations were as alike as peas in a pod and there is some truth in the comment. Few news outlets have a resident James Reston, Joseph Alsop, William F. Buckley, Jr., or George Gallup on the staff and, if they did, such individuals would be paid far less than under the shared fees of national syndication. Economics thus pull the experts and exploitable features away from local papers and stations. Some of the larger publications, such as *The New York Times, Washington Post, Los Angeles Times, Chicago Tribune,* New York *Daily News, Newsday, Des Moines Register* and *Tribune,* have kept their newsmen on the home staff but offered them syndication. Much the same happens to a successful local broadcaster and certainly the additional fees and exposure of national network performances lure television newsmen. (This may, in some cases, lead to overreaching and the sensational so as to capture the eyes and ears of the editors and producers of a national broadcast or syndicated service.)

Press association wire filers who decide what news to send ahead and which to delay, wire-copy editors who choose which items to play on the front page and which to place inside, and station executives who determine whether a network project is to be aired or not—these are the key decision-makers in the communications process. Many media observers feel that, with obvious and generous exceptions, those with news agencies and networks who understand the national, broader picture may be more responsible than those who manage the smaller operations. Developing technologies, however, may come to the rescue of the audiences for more diversity among media, especially broadcasting, since relays from satellites and cable television during the 1970's will change the whole scheme of news dissemination. Already a renaissance of strictly local print media, including most of those grouped as the "underground" press with its multimillion circulation, has expanded tremendously during the past decade.

Even without the new technologies, the service agencies of the communications business—the press associations, networks, and syndicates—have not been unresponsive to changing popular attitudes.

For example, the mounting interest in ecology and conservation has risen while the final phases of the Apollo space shots were attracting less attention. "Earth Day" on April 22, 1970, got local coverage in major communities, plus national round-ups ranging to National Education Television's six and a half hours of programing. News of the events was broadcast in every one of sixty-seven cities and towns monitored by correspondents for a duPont–Columbia University survey. In contrast, the members of the press corps assigned to the Manned Spacecraft Center at Houston for the Apollo 15 flight was slimmed down about two-thirds from the all-time high for the 1969 Apollo 11 initial moon landing and about half from the three intervening moon journeys.

With rising interest in and additional space for news about blacks in the late 1960's after the Kerner Commission report on civil disorders, syndicates obtained additional columns and comments from such black leaders as Roy Wilkins of the National Association for the Advancement of Colored People; Carl Rowan, former Minneapolis newsman and government official under both Presidents John F. Kennedy and Lyndon B. Johnson; and L. F. Palmer, Jr., a regular *Chicago Daily News* writer. According to one knowledgeable news executive, Rowan's column was "one of the most widely distributed and valuable properties." Despite this syndication and other changes in coverage of black communities, militants view the mass media as distinctly white-oriented. Spreading of this attitude among minority groups accounts for much of the inattention and outright rejection found in ghettoes and other localities where these groups congregate.

In the routine, day-to-day operations of the news machinery, however, considerable repetition and redundancy occurs. News competition, formerly among rivals of the same medium (because radio was in its infancy and television was not yet in operation), now is chiefly among representatives of the different media. This produces an echo effect in coverage.

To illustrate, *The New York Times* of Sunday, July 12, 1970, printed the results of a nationwide survey on the front page under a two-column headline which read:

Black Exodus to Suburbs
Found Increasing Sharply

An Emerging Pattern, Running Counter
to Expectations, Discerned in Study—
Negro Growth in Cities Declines

The Monday night news program on the National Broadcasting Company's local station, the first full scale one after the Sunday paper, picked up the survey and then interviewed a black family in New Jersey to humanize for television what had been printed as an impersonal study of national urban-suburban trends. As if to demonstrate that the practice was a two-way street, *The Times* of Monday, July 13, played a two-column front-page headline based on the appearance of Joseph J. Sisco, Assistant Secretary of State, on NBC's Sunday "Meet the Press" program. When they have exclusive developments or special interviews, the three news magazines and *Life* all are quoted by daily newspapers and television commentators.

Thus multi-media competition exists today but it is much more sophisticated than in the older days when "Front Page" journalism set a pattern of flamboyant rivalry in Chicago and dozens of other cities by simply kidnapping witnesses and playing a not-entirely-adult "cops and robbers." It was fun for the participants but not particularly beneficial for readers, unless they wanted vicarious thrills, which still remain among the rewards of "news consumers."

Competition between two rival morning papers in the same community is relatively easy to spot, especially for those with experience in print media. But when different media borrow from each other, the echo effect may be so skillfully concealed by a professional rewrite man or news director that it is difficult to trace the connections as coverage shifts from a morning daily to an evening newscast and then on to a news magazine. Yet competition of a type is still there—and so is the conformity bred by borrowing from a common reservoir instead of adding new bits of news to the supply available to the public.

The news distributing system may, in itself, shortchange the readers, listeners, and viewers despite the best intentions of the people who work in it. As more and more privately owned papers, magazines, and broadcast stations come under public shareholding, a subtle shift in priorities frequently occurs. A family such as the Sulzbergers of *The New York*

Times, the Knights in Ohio, Philadelphia, Detroit, and Miami, the Binghams in Louisville, and the Meyers in Washington may be able to afford the price of the highest standards of responsibility—even when it means losing money from annoyed advertisers or irate subscribers. A public corporation by the impersonal rules of Wall Street is evaluated chiefly in either short or long range earnings per share. The impact of this substantial shift from private to public ownerships may be one of the greatest pressures on the press during the rest of the twentieth century. So while this trend may ease the financial problems of publishers and editors, it may bring less fortunate results for the public. Can the mass media be, as one observer asked, "godless, profit-making corporations" and still function as impartial conveyors of news the public needs to know?

10. The Threat of One-Newspaper Towns—and All That

To defend the increasing monopoly or duopoly among newspapers in U.S. cities is comparable to attacking American motherhood, one of the few institutions against which the militants have not mobilized their heavy artillery. Yet, to be perfectly frank about it, newspaper monopolies may prove to be blessings in disguise although it is natural to look askance at any decrease in the number of channels for getting news to the general public.

Much of this ambivalence was displayed during the late 1960's in testimony concerning the Failing Newspaper Bill, which eventually became a law. Some, cynics no doubt, contended that it was properly named because the adjective quite accurately modified the word "bill" and not the publications themselves. One witness, Eugene Cervi, gadfly Denver editor and weekly publisher, called S-1312 "the millionaire crybaby publishers' bill." But, on the whole, witnesses before the Subcommittee on Antitrust and Monopoly of the U.S. Senate Committee on the Judiciary supported the proposals and that probably explains why it got majorities in both houses and went on the law books as the Newspaper Preservation Act. (Some critics credited what they considered effective lobbying by publishers and owners whose employees could control access to publicity in elected officials' home districts.)

Much of what was lamented so loudly would have been entirely to the point half a century ago but we live today in an age of electronics, news magazines, and instant books. There are many ways to receive the news besides daily papers and it is senseless not to recognize this. Again, little evidence exists that competition—just any kind of rivalry, regardless of how impotent—insures better journalistic performances. In some cases, it definitely does; in others, there is ample room for arguments, either way. Not without relevance is the fact that when the "great" newspapers of the country are cited, those in Des Moines, Kansas City, Louisville, Milwaukee, and Minneapolis—all communities where there is a common ownership of dailies—are almost always on the lists. In the language of a popular saying, publishers and editors must be doing something right, even when there aren't rival owners.

What can not be discounted are these dominant facts: (1) The number of U.S. dailies declined markedly after World War I and then reached a plateau for the past twenty-five years and (2) one-newspaper towns have increased as a result. Whether the general public has grievously suffered is, in my opinion, still open to some debate and depends to a greater degree on the location than on philosophical concepts. Yet one should not forget that the words in a thirty-minute broadcast news program would fill only slightly more than half of a full page in the standard-sized daily if they were set in type and pasted against that format.

Obviously, under anything like normal circumstances, a reader or listener has a chance to learn more about the world in which he lives if there is wide diversity among the mass media. This accounts for concern about the decline in the total number of U.S. dailies during the twentieth century. Such concern presupposes that the typical individual has both the desire and time to spend informing himself and then, as a good citizen, making up his mind on important public issues. And if one looks only at daily newspapers, the situation does indeed appear ominous. A 1971 survey showed that only 37 of the 1,511 newspaper communities had two or more fully competing dailies and that the remaining could be termed noncompetitive as far as dailies were concerned. That is not the full media portrait, however. An earlier study which included the competition of television and radio found a total of 5,079 competing voices and 202 communities with common ownerships. If weekly and suburban publications were included, the "single-voice" towns dropped to

61. And one should always remember that news "input" may come from beyond the boundaries of any individual's city or town. Overconcentration upon the evils of one-newspaper towns distorts the total picture, deceiving the general public into seeing bogies that are not there and blinding it to others that do exist.

Trends in daily newspaper ownership and related statistics are subject to possible misunderstanding. The total number of U.S. daily newspapers declined almost steadily for the first fifteen years after World War I, and then stabilized, while the country's population growth and daily circulations climbed, practically uninterrupted, except during the 1930's depression. This meant fewer papers purchased by more individuals. One might anticipate that a rising population would increase sales but the decline in ownership mirrored another trend: increasing concentration of U.S. business into larger and larger organizations.

Comparing the statistics for the half century 1920-1970, one gets the following:

U.S. total population	Up 92 percent.
Total daily circulation	Up 123 percent.
Number of daily papers	Down 14 percent.

Translated into actual figures this means that the total number of daily newspapers declined from 2,042 to 1,748, according to *Editor & Publisher International Yearbook,* a standard reference for journalism research. And the downward trend already had set in after the high of 2,461 in 1916.[1]

This peaking in the number of dailies indicates how people with money avoided the risks of a new publication. Thus economics was taking its toll in daily ownership years before the first radio newscast was transmitted in 1920 and the appearance of Vol. I, No. 1 of the earliest of the currently successful news magazines, *Time,* in the spring of 1923, as well as several decades before commercial television came on the communications scene after World War II.

As the nation's population concentrated in urban areas, there has been an increase in the number of communities that could boast their own daily paper, going from approximately 1,200 in 1910 to 1,400 in

[1] The *Editor & Publisher* current series of statistics was not compiled prior to 1919 and this earlier figure is taken from N. W. Ayers & Son data, which generally is comparable but does have approximately two hundred trade and special publications excluded by *Editor & Publisher.*

1930 to 1,500 currently. During the 1950's and 1960's new dailies were born in the satellite suburbs and not in the urban cores; thus the total reached a plateau as mergers and sales were offset by these new suburban papers. It seems unlikely that the total number of U.S. dailies will decline drastically again.

These new trends gave a decided push toward one-newspaper towns. A study by Prof. Raymond B. Nixon of the University of Minnesota published in *Editor & Publisher* (July 17, 1971) showed:

Total number of dailies	1,748	
Total number of cities with dailies	1,511	
Total number of one-daily cities	1,304	(86.3%)
Total number of cities with single morning and single evening paper under the same ownership	141	
Total number of cities with "joint operation" but separate ownership of morning and evening papers	21	
Total number of cities with two or more competing dailies	37	(2.5%)

Thus, with a total of 1,748 daily newspapers in 1,511 communities, 1,304 cities and towns have only one daily paper plus 141 more with the same owner putting out a combination publication. Some critics would include the 21 with separate news departments but common business and printing facilities as noncompetitive. (Still others argue that even this listing should read 24.) Furthermore, twenty-seven of the fifty states have no communities with commercially competing dailies.

Even a figure of five communities with three or more dailies is somewhat deceptive. New York City and Washington, D.C., each have three papers with three separate ownerships. On the other hand, Chicago has four papers but only two owners, each of whom publishes a morning and evening version. Philadelphia has three dailies but two owners. Including the nationally distributed *Christian Science Monitor,* Boston has four papers with four owners. In the simplest terms that means that in the entire United States there is not a single community where a potential reader has more than three choices in locally published dailies in the morning or again in the afternoon. That is indeed a vast contrast with fourteen general-circulation, English-language dailies with ten owners in New York City in 1920, nine after the depression-induced closings of the early 1930's, and seven in the early 1960's. In 1913, Philadelphia had eight dailies.

News and comments do not come from print alone—and that is how people in many communities can check on their single local paper. Increasingly, competing media provide the public with greater choices despite the contraction in the number of locally competing dailies. According to other information submitted at the same U.S. Senate subcommittee hearings, approximately 2,100 communities in metropolitan areas have AM or FM radio stations and of these, 1,480 have only a single outlet and approximately 600 possess competing AM or FM stations. For television's top 250 TV markets, approximately 162 are competitive—or well over half the total, compared with approximately four percent for daily newspapers. As some Federal Communications Commission members have emphasized, there is a lot more competition because of the diversification of broadcast ownership than if the newspaper trends toward single-ownership towns had been allowed unchallenged into broadcast operations. Yet there is tarnish in even this presentation. In 82 of the 1,500-plus newspaper market areas, a television station belongs wholly or in part to the local paper and in 216 of these communities, a radio station is owned by a publication. Furthermore, in 25 cases, there is no independent local TV competition and in 35, no competing radio station owner. Even where a local daily faces competition from an independent station, the broadcaster may not cover his community as thoroughly as the print newsman. Recognized critics of media do not agree on the efficacy of print-broadcast competition as witness these comments:

★ From Prof. Nixon of the University of Minnesota:

The extent to which radio and television compete with newspapers in bringing news and opinion to the public varies according to locality. Most broadcasting stations at least subscribe to a news service such as the Associated Press or United Press International and regularly broadcast news summaries. Even this much news service serves as a "sword of Damocles" over the head of any newspaper publisher who might be tempted to withhold or distort news that he had received from the same service. In addition, the broadcasting of political events and speeches in many ways gives the public a better check on the accuracy of newspaper reporting than was possible in the pre-electronic era of hotly competitive but violently partisan local papers.

When news magazines, suburban papers and other new types of specialized print media are brought into the picture, along with radio and television, there can be no doubt that more American communities now have daily access to a far larger volume of information, opinion and entertainment than ever before. The principal media not only compete vigorously with each other: they also supplement and complement each other in a manner that was impossible when newspapers alone were the chief means of mass communication.

★ From Ben H. Bagdikian, *Washington Post* assistant managing editor and commentator on the U.S. press:

The reduction in newspapers is serious. We need local papers because our society concentrates more responsibility at a local level than any other modern state. We do not have national papers as do other countries that have a few huge papers in the capital blanketing the country. We have local papers because our localities control their own schools, police, taxes, highways, welfare distribution, and other functions handled in other countries by centralized government. No matter how much we may admire the New York Times, the Wall Street Journal, and the Christian Science Monitor, and no matter how quickly they can be delivered in other cities, they cannot tell the local citizen what he needs to know to govern himself intelligently in his own town. . . .

Broadcasting has been a failure so far in filling the function of adequate local news and commentary. The local newspaper is still the best instrument we have for daily contact among citizens of the modern community. . . .

I think the typical local news effort of the typical broadcasting station in the United States is an incompetent reading of the first line of a few front page stories of the local paper. Most radio stations have no separate news staff. This is not talking about the few who concentrate on news or who make unusual efforts. Most of them consist of an announcer who spends some time compiling a 5- or 3-minute summary of the news. This either comes off his wire service ticker, which he reads verbatim, or he reads maybe first lines of stories in his local newspaper. If he is enterprising he paraphrases the first sentences and if he is not, he simply reads them verbatim.

I do not think I am the only newspaper reporter who went to work in the morning feeling badly as he saw that in his story in the paper he used the wrong middle initial of a public official and then heard the announcer give the same story but use the same wrong middle initial because he is reading your story verbatim.

In local news commentary, most American broadcasting stations are so deficient that I am quite surprised the FCC has not moved into this area.

Broadcasters are not competition on local news.

★ From Newton N. Minow, who had definite ideas about the "vast wasteland" of television programing as FCC chairman but who was less rigid about multi-media ownership when he told a congressional hearing:

I believe the public would be the loser if we sought to make every relationship between broadcasting and the press conform to any one notion of what is appropriate. Though I could not document this, it is my personal impression that some of our licensees which are affiliated with newspapers and periodicals are among those broadcasters most serious about service to the public interest. Some of them who have come to broadcasting from a tradition of journalism rather than entertainment have set high standards of independence from advertisers, of emphasis upon informative broadcasting with extensive news staffs, and upon dedication to meeting community needs and advancing community projects.

Generally (but not always, unfortunately), the growth of one-newspaper towns brought at least one beneficial side-effect. The partisan political press of a century ago is now largely dead and buried. As publishers and editors turned to making more money, they aimed at gaining the largest possible audience to insure a necessarily broad base for advertising revenues and circulation sales. Thus, again, economics played a key role, this time in killing off much partisan news coverage simply because there are more Democrats and Republicans together than separately. Many owners choose the larger market rather than vent their bias and drive away customers to other media. This is not to say that *all* current political reporting is impartial. It isn't. However, the financial profits of balanced news reporting—and this applies to broadcasting, too, and also to coverage other than just of politics—are greater than the profits from partisanship. Editorializing in columns and comments, where it properly belongs, has backfired among some unsophisticated readers and listeners who have not learned to separate news reporting from opinion writing.

A socially responsible publisher with a competent staff in a one-newspaper town has the opportunity—if he wants to seize it—to provide highly informative coverage and community-beneficial comments and opinions. A study by Prof. Nixon of representative competitive and non-competitive dailies indicated that a lone paper with its increased income could provide more "news hole" for articles, more skillful reporters, and more highly desirable features.

As an attempt to avoid further increases in one-newspaper towns, the Failing Newspaper Bill became the Newspaper Preservation Act of 1970. The measure had been introduced originally after the U.S. Department of Justice began antitrust action against two Tucson, Ariz., dailies which had established a joint operation in 1940, and the efforts intensified when the courts upheld some of the government's objections to price-fixing and division of profits between the two papers by a predetermined formula.

When a newspaper is losing money, its owner has four possibilities: he may merge by selling to a rival in the same town, sell to someone from out of town, just close shop and go out of business—or he may set up a "joint newspaper operating arrangement," as it was called in the legislation. Since 1940, the *Tucson Daily Citizen* and *Star* had been published under such an "arrangement" with distinctly separate news and editorial enterprises but as one commercial entity for mechanical production, advertising, and distribution. William A. Small, Jr., owner of the *Daily Citizen,* claimed the joint operation enabled the two "completely separate" papers to exist in a city of 315,000 population, which he said was not large enough to support them if they were "competing commercially as well as editorially."

How did the arrangement work?

Both dailies put their production equipment into joint ownership of a third corporation, Tucson Newspapers, Inc. (TNI), with each paper having equal stock holdings. On behalf of the *Citizen* and *Star,* the TNI operated production, advertising, circulation, and business departments, set all type, printed both papers, received all advertising and circulation revenues, and paid production and operating costs. Each paper paid salaries and expenses of its own news and editorial operations. Thus the joint management needed only one printing plant, one typesetting department, one press, one fleet of delivery trucks—instead of the two that would have been necessary had the dailies remained independent. Profits of TNI were distributed according to a predetermined formula. The activity that got antitrust attention was that circulation and advertising rates for both papers were set by TNI directors.

Over the decades, the arrangement succeeded and by the late 1960's when Congress was considering the Newspaper Preservation Act, the two Tucson papers were on "a sound financial footing," as Small testified. Among newspaper groups involved in "joint operating arrangements" of their own were Cox, Hearst, Knight, Newhouse, and Scripps-Howard. Such enterprises were thus generally supporters of the legislation. Included were seven such combinations among Scripps-Howard's seventeen dailies. Other publishers and newsmen were less than enchanted with the proposal. The *Wall Street Journal,* certainly no radical, called the plan "special interest legislation for newspapers" and *Saturday Review* editorialized that a newspaper that could not make it competitively should go out of business and that America's free press had "no right to expect the Constitution also to guarantee its profits through monopoly." Only the future will determine which arguments are correct.

Beyond the issue of one-newspaper towns looms—much more ominously—the advancing threat of media groups (or "chains," as the critics call them) and of conglomerates, either primarily in multimedia communications or those marriages of media properties with completely unrelated businesses.

The well known names in U.S. journalism long have been enamored with the idea of owning a whole series of newspapers in different communities. Centrally directed, as they generally were in the earlier period and by some managements today, this setup provided a powerful national voice for any ambitious publisher. With such machinery under his command, William Randolph Hearst could dream—unsuccessfully, as it turned out—of becoming president as he dispatched directives to editors from his California castle. At the peak of the Hearst organization's ownership in 1935, the copy for every fourth Sunday paper printed in the United States passed, figuratively if not literally, under the blue pencil of the Lord of San Simeon. Others whose reputations rest, at least in part, on their group or chain operations include E. W. Scripps, Frank E. Gannett, James S. Copley, James M. Cox, John S. Knight, S. I. Newhouse, and the McCormick-Patterson combination.

The number of groups owning two or more newspapers in different cities has grown consistently this century, except for the 1930's depression period. Here are statistics on the subject, as prepared by Prof. Nixon:

Year	Number of Groups	Number of Group Papers
1910	13	62
1930	55	311
1940	60	319
1945	76	368
1954	95	485
1961	109	552
1968	159	828
1971	155	883

Thus more than half of the dailies in the country now are owned by groups and, more important, 63 percent of weekday circulation and 65 percent of that on Sundays are under group control. This introduces absentee ownership except when the papers happen to be printed at the location of the group's national headquarters. This doesn't happen very often because the number of papers averaged 5.7 in each group. Most group operations have certain economic advantages and this is the reason generally given for setting them up and then increasing their size. Arguments in favor of a group setup are much the same as for any multioutlet business—rapidly rising labor costs, centralized headquarters, and lower (through sharing) management expenses. However, unless local officials can overcome resentment toward outsiders who control that intimate relationship of selecting the news a community is going to obtain, any group organization may be storing up difficulties for the future. To meet this attitude toward absentee owners, some groups loosen the reins and permit a sort of local autonomy for each locality. The Gannett, Newhouse, and Thomson groups especially are known for this autonomy and it seems to be countering some of the psychological disadvantages of absentee ownership.

Newspaper chain owners may set up feature news services or even supply editorials to all their members. This may cut down on the costs of paying writers on each individual paper but it often breeds trouble when an identical viewpoint is presented in an industrial New England community, a Southern metropolis with strong ties to its surrounding agricultural areas, and a Midwestern locality where a state university is the largest activity. When such copy is supplied, local managers usually are given the right to discard the copy if they think that advisable. Political endorsements at the national level are a most sensitive area and here some groups take their stand and let the chips fly while others allow each paper's editorial director to set his own course. Thus, for some groups where autonomy is widespread, various members at presidential election time may support different candidates. Few, if any, group executives have followed William Randolph Hearst's example of entering the political area and then mobilizing his papers to support the effort. However, some have tried their skill at trying to mold public opinion in the communities where they published chain dailies—if the decisions did not run so counter to prevailing mores that they would cost their publication substantial circulation or advertising losses.

The Chicago Tribune Company group, which includes the New York *Daily News,* highest circulation paper in the country, among its total of eight dailies, leads with the largest circulation of any U.S. group. Its weekday circulation of 3,615,725 combines with Sunday circulation of 4,678,360 for a combined seven-day total of 26,058,015. In second place is Newhouse Newspapers with weekday circulation of 3,087,775 for its twenty-two papers and a seven-day total of 21,400,027.

The Chicago Tribune Company-owned dailies had 5.8 percent of the 1971 weekday circulation of 62,100,000-plus and 9.5 percent on Sundays. During Hearst's heyday in 1935, comparable percentages were 13.6 percent daily and 24.2 percent Sunday. The Hearst group had twenty-six dailies and seventeen Sunday papers for its record in 1935 and was down to eight dailies and seven Sunday papers in 1971.

Listing of newspaper groups in order of the number of dailies published showed the following as of late 1971:

Name of Group	*Number of Dailies*
1. Gannett Newspapers (including Federated Publications and Honolulu Star-Bulletin, Inc.)	52
2. Thomson Newspapers (including Thomson-Brush-Moore)	43
3. Scripps League Newspapers	31
4. Donrey Media	25
5. Newhouse Newspapers	22
6. Freedom Newspapers	22
7. Worrell Newspapers	21
8. Scripps-Howard Newspapers	17

Of the top eight groups in numbers of dailies owned, only Newhouse, Gannett, and Scripps-Howard (with 2,321,028 weekday circulation and 1,589,097 on Sundays) had combined weekday circulations in excess of a million copies.

Influential as newspaper groups or chains are, those companies with multimedia properties wield even more power in forming U.S. public opinion. For instance, the Chicago Tribune Company with the largest newspaper circulations in both New York City and Chicago also holds licenses for two television stations in these same cities—WPIX in New York and WGN (an acronym from the *Tribune*'s slogan of "World's Greatest Newspaper") in Chicago. S. I. Newhouse, with a variety of dailies, holds the maximum permissible number of television station licenses—seven—and most of them are in the communities where his organization publishes the local daily. Newhouse is the only one with a full quota of both VHF and UHF licenses but eight companies own the maximum of five of the more valuable VHF television stations.

The Gannett Co., Inc., with fifty-two papers extending from Hartford, Conn., to Honolulu and Guam, also owned a television station in Rochester, N.Y., where it publishes both morning and afternoon papers, plus a radio station at Danville, Ill., where it also owns the daily. During 1971, Gannett followed a recent trend and bought two other groups to merge into its own. It acquired the seven dailies published by Federated Publications, Inc., in four Midwestern and Western states and then agreed to exchange Gannett common stock to get control of the Honolulu Star-Bulletin, Inc. The Hawaiian concern had purchased the morning and evening papers in Huntington, W.Va., earlier in the same year during its own expansion. These new acquisitions gave Gannett a weekday distribution of approximately 2,175,000 and Sunday circulation of approximately 1,450,000.

Tax regulations currently encourage a media group to invest its accumulated earnings in related enterprises rather than pay out extra dividends or build up larger surpluses, and the seller of one "public" organization may profit more from a stock exchange than an outright cash deal.

Before he began liquidating his communications empire after he was named ambassador to the Court of St. James's in 1969 by President Richard M. Nixon, Walter H. Annenberg held the reins on the Triangle Publications, Inc., which had an estimated income of approximately $235,000,000 in 1969 and ranked among the top twenty-five privately held concerns in gross sales in the country that year. Included were such properties as:

(1) Print—*Inquirer* and *Daily News* in Philadelphia; *Morning Telegraph*, New York racing daily; five regional editions of the *Daily Racing Form;* the weekly *TV Guide;* and the monthly *Seventeen* magazine.

(2) Broadcasting—Television and radio stations in Philadelphia; Binghamton, N.Y.; New Haven, Conn.; Altoona, Pa.; and Fresno, Calif.; a television station in Lebanon, Pa.; and cable television holdings in most of the same cities.

According to trade reports, Annenberg received an estimated $55,000,000 when he sold his two Philadelphia dailies to John S. Knight and his associates.

Time, Inc., with a magazine stable including *Time, Life, Fortune,* and *Sports Illustrated,* has been seeking to purchase a daily in one of the larger metropolitan areas. Negotiations for the *Newark Evening News* broke off in 1968 after preliminary publicity of an impending sale to Time, Inc.

Many of the various multiple holdings included highly profitable VHF stations in metropolitan communities but not a single UHF station in a remote, isolated location. The five television stations owned by the Columbia Broadcasting System, one of the Big Three networks, might appear as a minor possession out of approximately 850 stations but these five alone reach seven percent of the total U.S. viewing audience during prime-time hours on weekday evenings; the entire network's share of the national audience regularly is somewhat more than a third of all households owning sets.

The Radio Corporation of America, parent company for the National Broadcasting Company and its network, operates such diverse holdings as a book publishing concern, one of the nation's big automobile rental services, five television stations in the larger cities, and a huge manufacturing line of television, radio, and other electronic goods. When CBS bought the New York Yankees professional baseball team, some media watchers speculated what sports commentators would say when the team fell from its near-monopoly on league championships, but the news came through without visible taint when that fate overtook the players.

Some of the projected dangers of conglomerate ownership loomed very real when the International Telephone and Telegraph Corporation sought to purchase the American Broadcasting Company with its network facilities and motion picture properties. At FCC hearings, one of the questions asked was whether ITT with vast business interests in the United States and abroad would try to tamper with ABC's news coverage in cases where the parent company's interests might be at stake. ITT executives promised that, if they received FCC permission to control ABC, attempts to influence or bias the news would never take place.

When the FCC was considering whether to reopen the merger proceedings in February 1967, ITT naturally watched what Washington correspondents were writing, but what was far from routine was that they complained to the two press associations, *The New York Times, Wall Street Journal,* and *Washington Post* about news coverage. According to one report among Washington newsmen, an ABC representative complained to the Associated Press and United Press International. The concern's public relations men argued that ITT executives were dissatisfied because some of the coverage was "incomplete and unfair." After his editor got an irate telephone call, one reporter was quoted as saying, "It is incredible that guys like this want the right to run ABC's news operation." The *Columbia Journalism Review,* watchdog of media performance, said bluntly that "ABC News often sounded as if its stories about the mergers were dictated by management."

When the FCC announcement on a delay in effective date of the merger was released, an ABC official is reported to have called AP in New York to complain about a story on the wire from Washington. As Prof. William L. Rivers of Stanford University and former Washington correspondent told a U.S. Senate subcommittee, "The Washington reporter was in the middle of his sixth paragraph when ABC's request that the first paragraph be changed was relayed to him. He refused to change it." Rivers concluded that the ITT efforts not only showed the corporation was "extremely sensitive about news reports" concerning it but that "it will make unusual efforts to shape the reports to its liking."

Summarizing for the senators, Rivers said:

> That a company should seek to influence news coverage of its activities is not unique, but veteran Washington newspapermen consider the extent and intensity of ITT's efforts extraordinary. A hallmark of big companies like ITT is a sophisticated PR policy. Their press agents employ the suave soft sell, knowing that if they push too hard they will alienate the journalists they are trying to influence. But there has been no policy or subtlety about ITT's campaign; it has been a frontal assault.

Because of governmental objections on antitrust grounds rather than concern about activities of the ITT public relations men, the proposed merger did not go through, but it does provide an intriguing case history on what may be ahead for coverage of news conglomerates.

Another example surfaced in 1968 when *The Permissible Lie,* a book described as mildly critical of advertising, was scheduled for publication by Funk & Wagnalls, then a subsidiary of *Reader's Digest,* mammoth of the magazine world with six percent of the country's entire consumer magazine circulation. After decades without advertising, the *Digest* in 1954 first opened its pages for sale instead of raising its price and now counts on advertising for a large share of its income. When *Digest* executives found out about the book and its criticism, they told the subsidiary not to publish the book although the press run already was completed for the first printing of 5,500 copies. However, the story has a happy ending, at least for the author, because another publishing house, without a parent company saying "No," took over the printed books and distributed them. Thanks to the publicity, the book got more attention than if *Reader's Digest* had never played the suppressive parent company role. Possibly a well publicized attempt to play the all-wise corporate parent still may end up paying an author a good profit and it may demonstrate that even conglomerates don't win them all. If they win very many, however, the consumer may lose, and if frequent pressures are applied successfully to mass media, Heaven help the reading and viewing public.

11. The Impact of Pressure Groups: Real and Synthetic

Only the unsophisticated or the self-serving critics of the media would claim that print and broadcast ever transmit or ever have, all the news just as it happened, as if they were mammoth pipelines of reality or mirrors for the whole, wide world. Something always is left out, sometimes including things that should not have been. In part, this grows out of the nature of the communications process; it is physically impossible to circumscribe the entirety of any event on the printed page or in a broadcast. In part, it is due to the corporate and human frailties of those that disseminate the news. Finally, if the public is to appraise media performance accurately, readers and viewers must understand which are the real and which the synthetic forces trying to influence how events are portrayed.

Among those who want media to tell readers, listeners, and viewers less than the full story may be government officials (as discussed in previous chapters), businessmen in a local community, community boosters who don't want anything to upset the status quo, special interest groups that will profit from publicity, militants of both left and right who want to advance their causes, or, in a few cases, the general public itself. Practically everyone whose name appears in print or is mentioned over the air, on occasions, will be tempted to mold the news to his own fashion. The urge, apparently, is all but irresistible. A newsman's assignment is to counter such efforts.

A long-time favorite stereotype has an advertiser rushing into a newspaper publisher's office and shouting, "If you print that story, I'll yank out all my ads." Dramatic enough, it just isn't very accurate any more. That may have been the way it was once upon a time but this approach isn't used often enough now to be the central scene in contemporary motion pictures or television dramas. Why?

First, because in limited-voice communities (as most are today) it is the publishers and their staffs who can call the tunes for advertisers, not the other way around. With few other places to go, advertisers need to attract customers through all available media for their own survival and both they and the communications managers know this.

Second, because as media became Big Business, the advertisers didn't have to tell publishers or even their senior executives the facts of economic life that they already have learned. In most communities, a representative of the local Chamber of Commerce pointing out that a news item could be bad for business carries more influence than any advertiser's threat to stop buying space. (Of course, if advertisers gang up on a publication or station, it rapidly can become a different kind of a situation.)

Third, because it is decidedly the wrong approach, being crude, blunt, and definitely challenging, to try on individuals, most of whom at least fancy they perform in the "public interest," whether they are in broadcasting or print. This is an age for subtlety if one is to have any hope of gaining such favors.

Finally, because some of the more flagrant suppressions and revisions of the news take place at the staff level, where reporters and editors, for instance, want to protect their monetary interests in such things as free trips, holiday presents, cash payments—or even some journalism prizes and plaques.

One can not truthfully say that advertising pressure is dead and buried but it certainly isn't sufficiently a bogey to merit *all* (or even most) of the blame for what sins media exhibit in the 1970's. However, it is successful just often enough so that journalists can put aside any thoughts of halos as part of their standard working uniforms. Well publicized case histories include that of a publisher who told an advertiser where he could go and ended up eventually with both a clear conscience and more money in the bank. For instance, this has happened in Portland, Ore., and in Pittsburgh. In other instances, the local advertiser had the final decisive word.

When the *Wall Street Journal* obtained complete information about General Motors' new line of 1965 automobile models and was preparing to print it ahead of other papers, the corporation threatened to withdraw its advertisements. Bernard Kilgore, the late publisher, told his colleagues to print the news anyway although he was aware that General Motors' advertising budget was the largest in the United States. For a while, the *Wall Street Journal* did lose substantial revenues but the decision, according to Ben H. Bagdikian, knowledgeable writer on media developments, may well have been "a crucial point in the growth of the Journal's prestige." The paper now has more than a million daily circulation and ranks second only to the New York *Daily News* in copies sold. Bagdikian also said most publishers were not shrewd enough to look that far ahead and to realize the eventual rewards for exhibiting such courage.

On the other hand, all four of the Chicago dailies declined to print full-page advertisements submitted by the Amalgamated Clothing Workers of America in explanation of why its members were picketing Marshall Field & Company for selling men's and boys' wear imported from abroad. Marshall Field is one of Chicago's largest retail store advertisers. *Advertising Age,* Madison Avenue's trade journal, also reported that the *Detroit Free Press* rejected an eight-page insert for a Chicago firm selling soft goods because, as a representative of the Detroit daily was quoted as saying, its policy "forbids any copy which might compete with their retailers." The advertising weekly had this reaction:

> In both cases, there is a strong implication that the decision not to run the ads was influenced by the fact that a major department store advertiser in each of the cities involved might not like them. . . . On occasion we have ourselves refused to publish advertising which we had believed to be untruthful or in bad taste or otherwise undesirable. But we think it is of the utmost importance that all media employ this right with extreme care. . . . Like most rights, it imposes on the user a duty, and all media should be mindful of this duty when exercising their rights.

William A. Emerson, editor on the defunct *Saturday Evening Post,* told the 1970 meeting of the American Society of Newspaper Editors that the viewpoint expressed in one *Post* editorial was estimated to have cost the magazine $13,000,000 in lost advertisements. He contended that the advertisers' pressures put on the *Post* were among the causes for its failing.

When Massachusetts' Supreme Judicial Court ruled that a creditor could be sued for undue harassment—a landmark extension of consumer rights, the *Boston Globe* referred to the "disputed retail bill" and the *Boston Herald-Traveler* said the case involved "a store." The loser now faced a $100,000 legal action for harassment by alleged late-evening telephone calls to the mother of a bankrupt man who owed $500 and by threats that her own credit had been revoked. What neither paper printed was that the concern was Jordan Marsh Co., which calls itself the largest department store in New England. Attorney for the mother, Joseph Stashio, claimed that the ruling should have been front-page news because it was "new law" instead of being printed well inside, and that the dailies didn't mention the store's name "because they get a lot of advertising from Jordan Marsh."

When Stanford University students released in 1970 a year-long study of air pollution in the San Francisco Bay area with company-by-company descriptions, fourteen of the seventeen newspapers that printed a story on the report—including the two San Francisco dailies—deleted references to local identifications.

A Consumers Union spokesman claimed that the press' traditional reluctance to serve informational needs of consumers tended to create the current problems in that area. Not naming consumers in a news story, he said, was shirking a basic responsibility to readers. And he might have added listeners, too. After a television station taped out names of toys demonstrated on a program about hazards of playthings, Consumers Union now refuses to grant interviews with newsmen unless names will be used.

During the 1960's, media generally ignored claims of the alleged hazards of General Motors' Corvair. Statements from Ralph Nader, the consumer advocate, and actions by government agencies mention products and concerns and now media are less reluctant to edit out the specifics than they were a decade ago. Fear of libel action is sometimes mentioned as justification for not mentioning but consumer group representatives reply that self-censorship from fear of alienating heavy advertisers is, in their opinion, more to blame.

The late William Allen White, Kansas editor who gained the title of "sage of Emporia" because of his astute observations, pointed out more than thirty years ago that a publisher's or top editor's pull toward the Establishment—and thus an inclination to go along with any push to maintain the status quo—arose from friends who "unconsciously color his opinion." He added:

> If he lives with them on any kind of social terms in the City club or the Country club or the Yacht club or the Racquet club, he must more or less merge his views into the common views of the other capitalists. The publisher is not bought like a chattel. Indeed he often is able to buy those who are suspected of buying him. But he takes the color of his social environment. . . .
>
> So it often happens, alas too often, that a newspaper publisher, reflecting this unconscious class arrogance of the consciously rich, thinks he is printing news when he is doctoring it innocently enough. He thinks he is purveying the truth when much that he offers seems poison to hundreds of thousands of his readers who don't move in his social and economic stratosphere.

What White said about the predominantly print era of his time applies equally well to today's multi-media. For instance, Joseph T. Klapper, director of social research for the Columbia Broadcasting System and frequent commentator on media, remarked that while "the conscious and manifest purpose" of a broadcast sponsor was "primarily, and almost wholly, to sell his soap," he would rally in the face of direct attack upon the existing social and economic system. Further, he admitted that there was not "any large conscious Gestalt designed to perpetuate a social system."

When reporters do uncover embarrassing facts that do get published, further inquiries may be halted because they run into even more sensitive segments of the social scene. During 1966, the *Chicago Tribune* assigned George Bliss, a 1962 Pulitzer Prize winning reporter, to investigate trucking licenses in the state and he found instances where vehicles used solely in intrastate commerce were obtaining cheaper out-of-state registrations instead of the relatively higher Illinois fees. The paper thought enough of the exposé to run a front-page advertisement in *Editor & Publisher* (July 23, 1966) to claim, "Illegal out-of-state truck licenses were costing Illinois millions in lost taxes . . . until the Chicago Tribune exposed the racket."

Some months later, in January 1967, fire destroyed McCormick Place, a lakefront exhibition and convention hall named in memory of the late Col. Robert R. McCormick, who for decades had guided the *Tribune*. In its effort to have the hall rebuilt, the paper sought to line up the financial and political support needed. *Tribune* editor W. D. Maxwell met exhibition hall officials and with Paul Powell, secretary of state for Illinois. The state official had influence with some Illinois legislators who could vote state funds to finance the rebuilding. Powell's office also had jurisdiction over truck licensing. According to newspapermen, Bliss was working on a story that might have embarrassed the secretary of state's office when the fire broke out and he was told to lay off.

The *Wall Street Journal* (July 25, 1967) commented:

> Was a deal made, the Tribune agreeing to stifle its investigation in exchange for whatever help Mr. Powell could give in gathering support for the rebuilding of McCormick Place? . . . Another possibility: That there was no definite quid pro quo, only a decision by the Tribune to avoid offending a politician whose help might prove valuable.
>
> Editor Maxwell says he made no deal with Mr. Powell and scoffs at the idea that the official has enough political pull to make such an agreement worthwhile.

Somewhat the same pattern apparently was followed during an investigation at the *Boston Herald*. A four-man "Research Bureau" was set up to conduct inquiries into corruption, crime, and social injustice directly under the publisher, George E. Akerson. One of the Bureau's early investigations turned to a complicated stock transaction in the Universal Marion Corporation. Both the Securities and Exchange Commission and the U.S. Attorney in New York City were investigating. The reporters had barely begun digging when Publisher Akerson wanted to know why they were investigating the affairs of Joseph Linsey, Boston businessman and philanthropist, explaining that he was a "stockholder" in the corporation publishing the *Herald* and *Traveler*. A little time later another corporate officer called them off that investigation entirely. One of the four reporters was let go and the other three quit in protest within a few weeks. Jim Savage, one of the bureau members, explained after departing, "We resigned because it's clear the paper isn't interested in serving the public." Other Boston papers weren't interested in the news at the time either as none reported the comings and goings at the

Herald, and even though the *Boston Globe* received two syndicated columns by Drew Pearson and Jack Anderson on the incident, it did not publish them.

How local coverage of an event may vary widely from that given in other sections of the country when community tranquility is believed to be at stake was illustrated in coverage of the 1967 Winston-Salem, N.C., racial disturbances. While a United Press International dispatch referred to the death of a black (which apparently triggered the disturbances) "after he was blackjacked by a white policeman," the local *Journal,* with the city already at high tension, phrased it "in connection with unrest created by the recent death of James Eller, Negro, who died after injuries believed sustained when he resisted arrest and was hit by Patrolman E. E. Owens." The *Journal* also carefully avoided words that might inflame any part of the public or increase community fears. Instead of "mobs," the *Journal* called them "roving gangs." Although the *Charlotte Observer* quoted the Winston-Salem mayor as saying that for about an hour shortly after midnight, "It looked as if we were going up in smoke," this statement was left out of the *Journal* reports.

Honors often come after displays of journalistic courage but they may have their price. When the Pulitzer prizes were distributed in 1958, one of the rare double awards in the competition's history went to John Netherland Heiskell's *Arkansas Gazette* for public service and to Harry S. Ashmore for editorial writing. Yet despite the honors that piled up, Heiskell's editorial position earned him a loss of more than $2,000,000 in circulation and advertising revenues as the community showed its initial resentment of the publication's policy for integration of the previously all-white Central High School in Little Rock. Some Southern editors, one may be sure, were not willing to lose anything like such sums for the sake of an editorial position and so they followed the prevailing community standards and attitudes, regardless of what they personally believed.

In other sections, too, an unpopular editorial position, such as endorsement of a minority viewpoint or a nonconformist political candidate, has brought economic reprisals to newspaper publishers and editors. For instance, in Troy, Ohio, Thomas Pew, editor of the *News* with its circulation of 10,000, criticized practices of some of the town's larger businesses but he said that although he had faced various temporary advertising boycotts, "they don't last too long."

In a few cases, a publication has had to change owners to salvage its revenues. A paper too far out of line with local mores may be a hero to outsiders but it faces reactions at home which none but the morally strong and the financially secure can survive. After his editorial stand in favor of a civil rights question brought an advertisers' boycott and threats of violence to his family, Ro Gardner, publisher of the *Hickman* (Ky.) *Courier* for sixteen years, sold his paper in March 1970 "for a fair price" to a competitor. He spent a year handling public relations for a West Virginia hospital and then bought the *Lake Elsinore* (Calif.) *Valley Sun*. When he received the 1971 Elijah P. Lovejoy Award for Courage in Journalism at Southern Illinois University, he commented, "I won't settle down to some sedentary editorial policy, but I'll be more selective about which fights I'll get into, and I'll know how to handle them better."

Weather forecasts would seem to be fairly routine items and not likely to be subject to contamination by pressure groups. Not true. At least two documented cases show that dailies in Boston and Sacramento, Calif., have performed monumental editing efforts to draw shopping crowds and thus to help downtown merchants.

For instance, when a blizzard struck two weeks before Easter in 1956, several Hub papers elected not to carry news of the approaching March snowstorms. After the snow had fallen, the Boston papers tried, through pictures and headlines, to convey the impression that main business streets were cleared, which was not the case. Four days later, while city authorities were allowing parking only near the bigger stores, the *Boston Globe* headline read, "Snow Cleanup Continues; Travel Normal." A U.S. Weather Bureau prediction of possible new snowfall and "chance of showers" appeared in the front-page weather ear as "Fair, not quite so mild." The following day, with a weather ear predicting snow, the eight-column banner read, "Boston All Clear, Snow Fighters Rest—City Open for Business as Usual."

In 1958, a *Traveler* headline said, "Snow to Taper Off This Afternoon," despite a weather prediction to the contrary. And on Good Friday, 1959, with the weather bureau issuing a "heavy snow" warning for Saturday, the Friday evening *Globe*'s double-line banner across page one said:

> Go Get your Easter Bonnet;
> Fair and Warmer Easter

The *Sacramento Bee* never prints anything stronger than "Unseasonably warm," even, as one critic said, "when you can fry an egg on the pavement." Could it be that unfavorable weather would keep the prospective customers home and hurt local business?

A generation ago the Chicago dailies—with considerable assistance from the local health department—kept under wraps the news that an epidemic of amebic dysentery had been discovered in one of the Loop hotels and had apparently been responsible for the death of Texas Guinan, well-known entertainer who was in the city for the Century of Progress exposition. After the news got out, there was some speculation on the economic effect of losing potential visitors had there been earlier publicity and some of the estimates claimed that hundreds of thousands of dollars, at least, were involved.

Careful readers and listeners not infrequently can detect when a publication or station is overly cooperative with some group, such as a special advertiser. Often among these diverse groups are professional sports teams, real estate agents, or shopping center owners and merchants —all extensive and frequent advertisers in their local community media. A curious observer may compare the names in the advertisements with those in "news" items. Especially, one should watch for the "grand formal opening" of a nearby shopping center with its assortment of chain stores of different varieties, each of which has an advertisement and very, very often an accompanying story with puffery about its merchandise, facilities, or officials. Roundups of industrial and commercial activities in the area provide opportunities for special sections of ads as well as pseudo-news items. Some magazines, even including a few of the most widely circulated in the nation, offer what appear to be feature articles in the publication's regular format, though in fine print at the top of the page is the giveaway word, "Advertisement." Of course, a cautious or suspicious reader would see this but how many thousands pass it by undetected?

In his book *The Fading American Newspaper* (Doubleday, 1960), the late Carl E. Lindstrom, who was both an editor and a college journalism teacher, wrote about "revenue-related reading matter," which he described as "everything that would not be in the paper if there were not some advertising revenue, actual or hoped for, connected with it." Documentation for any formal arrangement of this sort is hard to find.

According to Eugene Cervi, owner, publisher, and editor of *Cervi's Rocky Mountain Journal* in Denver, the following memorandum came into his possession through the mails and he presented it at a U.S. Senate subcommittee hearing in 1967. It was from Bob Carrington, business news director of the *Denver Post,* to one of his superiors and read in part:

Regarding "editorial" commitment on advertising schedules for Villa Italia Shopping Center and Joslins Store:

I am open to review on figures, based on Hatcher's [*Post*'s retail advertising manager] stated commitment of 25 per cent free space ration to advertising, but believe this is reasonably accurate.

Villa will have about (says Hatcher) 40 actual pages of ads in about 45 pages of space, 25 per cent of that is 10 pages or 1,820 column inches.

We have since Feb. 2 (date Von Frellick [shopping center builder] demanded to go this route) published in various sections of the Post 26 column inches of copy and pictures directly related to Villa Italia, through March 7.

Coverage beyond Monday (three days of grand opening, a Wednesday night preview for socialites, dignitaries, Italian ambassador, which we can't ignore and must cover with pix and stories) won't come close to the total commitment, but probably would put it over the half-way mark. If we did a picture page each day of the opening, Thursday, Friday, and Saturday, we would be providing another 546 column inches and thus be beginning to get close to the commitment figure, at least three-fourths of the way. There will be other stories as folos to the opening that we can't ignore and that would push it relatively close to the magic number.

I believe we have up to March 8 done a fine job for them in terms of publicizing the shop center, and to think of doing or having done more would be deciding to repeat it all because there is a limit in the amount of subject material.

Regarding the Joslins firm, the memo reported that it had received a total of 573 inches or "a little more than half the magic figure." Then it added the following about anticipated difficulties:

Frankly, I don't see much more that can be said about them short of repetition. We have had copy, well-prepared, on the company's new image, high fashion, first-class stores, fresh approach to merchandising, and features on some of the departments they're planning which set them apart from other stores in the industry. The next thing would be only to do a feature piece on each department and I don't like that concept because it could be said about most stores in industry and is told in the word, department. A profile on the president would be readable, but somewhat repetitious of the image story.

When asked about the arrangements and comments in the memo, W. H. Hornby, *Post* managing editor, replied:

The *Post* definitely does not have any such policy as implied in the clipping you mentioned. The conversations involved a proposed special advertising section, which I find in the end did not materialize.

As is our custom and that of most major newspapers, if an advertiser wants a special section and provides his own editorial material, it is clearly labeled as advertising matter. If we provide editorial material for such a section, we have full control over what pictures and stories we use. Apparently in this case someone had told an inquiring advertiser that such material, if provided by us, could certainly be no more than a quarter of the content because that was all we had time or staff to provide. Somehow that got transmitted in a space policy.

The *Post* does not have, never had, and never will have a policy by which any advertiser is promised any particular quantity or quality of editorial material based on proffered linage.

Hornby said the memo from the business editor was in reply to a request for "what coverage had already been given the legitimate business news event in question" and "what if any commitments had been made by the ad department because it would have been against our policy to so commit." He said no such commitments had been made.

Newspapermen, especially, have a tremendous reluctance to turn their investigative talents against a rival in their own community. On occasion, they will try to overthrow the power structure in the police department, city hall, or some state agency and, if they have Washington correspondents, they may turn them loose on a U.S. bureau, especially if they did not give editorial endorsement to the party in power. As the *Wall Street Journal* once said, "hardly a working journalist could deny that one of the gravest weaknesses in coverage exhibited by the American press is its coverage of itself."

Sunday papers that devote whole sections to sports and financial-business news fail to have even a small department devoted to covering the print media. Comments on the derelictions of potential competitors in the print media are rare; there almost seems to be agreement (although I am sure nothing is consciously worked out) not to turn news sleuths loose. *Time* and *Newsweek* find communications—print and broadcast—worth studying and both have special sections. Some years ago when I asked Lester Markel, then Sunday editor of *The New York Times,* why his paper did not have such a department, he replied that the daily items covered the field sufficiently. Apparently he thought *The Times'* Sunday readers were not interested in the subject.

Newsmen's activities are largely underreported except in the trade press but two cases during the past generation did receive extensive coverage: one involving Jake Lingle of the *Chicago Tribune* in the Al Capone era and the other, Harry Karafin of the *Philadelphia Inquirer* in the 1960's. Lingle's gangster connections were revealed publicly only after he had been shot down by gunmen from a rival group in revenge and Karafin's activities, which included shakedowns under the threat of unfavorable items appearing in the *Inquirer,* were exposed by *Philadelphia Magazine.* Karafin, who had worked for the paper for almost thirty years, much of that time as its chief investigative reporter, was fired by the *Inquirer,* and eventually convicted on several dozen bills of indictment. He was accused of extorting vast sums from individuals and corporations under threat of exposure. A month after Karafin had been discharged, the paper's Sunday edition printed a ten-column article under the following headline:

With Sadness and Regret
Inquirer Traces
The Sordid Story
Of One 'Reporter'

The article admitted that Karafin had not been asked for a full explanation until he started legal action to prevent publication of a forthcoming *Philadelphia Magazine* exposé. The implication, at least as some Philadelphia newsmen explained it, was that Karafin might have kept working save for the magazine's actions.

When newsmen go counter to their publishers' directives, they have, in a few reported cases, been fired from their jobs. For instance, Floyd Knox, city editor of the *Waterbury* (Conn.) *Republican,* ran a list of Vietnam casualties from that circulation area on the front page during

Vietnam Moratorium Day in 1969 despite his publisher's request not to do so. He was discharged for this and other earlier independent actions of this sort, it was said. Ted Hall, managing editor of the Passaic-Clifton (N.J.) *Herald News* defied his publisher's orders and persisted with an investigation of the prosecution of two local slayings, one of them involving charges against the son of another newspaper publisher in a nearby suburb. For his efforts, he was let go. A boss has the right to fire for cause in our society but in these two cases some of the commentators wondered if the actions arose primarily out of concern with the best interests of the publications' readers.

Possible conflicts of interest are a constant threat to newsroom objectivity and one does not have to be playing for big financial payoffs as were Lingle and Karafin. Responsible journalists are well aware of the hazards. Offerings come in all sizes from a free drink at some lobbyist's party to outright acceptance of cash or checks. Others might include an offer for a free trip to a war zone in an Air Force jet with room and food in officers' quarters during the stay, an all-expenses-paid tour by an automobile manufacturer to see new models, an invitation from an overseas hotel corporation to visit a new installation, or a visit to the local professional baseball team at spring training camp. The objective each time is to generate favorable coverage that otherwise would not take place.

A minor league furore developed in late 1968 when *Women's Wear Daily* quoted Miss Eleanor Lambert as saying, "I own every fashion editor in America. I can deliver them." Miss Lambert, who helped manage the advance showings for the New York fashion industry, promptly denied that she had ever used such language as "own" and "deliver." After World War II when American designers and dress manufacturers wanted to build up their clientele, they turned to Miss Lambert for a way to interest fashion writers around the country in covering New York City's openings to display new designs. She suggested that they pay expenses for writers to come East and a number of publications accepted for their staff members. However, when she tried to set the ground rules for release of copy about the new clothes, she ran into trouble. Some of the "rebels" who were not having their expenses paid would not sign agreements to hold up their stories until Miss Lambert and the fashion houses said it was all right to print. Such out-of-town dailies as the *Detroit News, Kansas City Star,* and *Milwaukee Journal* refused to embargo what they thought were stories for immediate release. They had accepted no train or plane-fare tickets so they were free to do as they pleased. The whole setup of holding up news on fashion trends collapsed within a few years, but it would hardly be surprising if some writers, including fashion writers, didn't feel indebted to those who pick up their tabs.

The "hard line" or "Mr. Clean policy" that more and more media directors are adopting is to pay for what any staff member needs to get. How this worked successfully on one paper for more than a decade was described by Robert J. Haiman, managing editor of the *St. Petersburg Times,* in *APME Guidelines* (Associated Press, 1969) with the idea that even more papers might want to try it. He explained:

All Christmas gifts of all kinds are returned with a note signed by the editor explaining our policy and asking that no future gifts be sent. Within just a year or two, the packages of cheese, caviar, pens, paper dresses, etc., have dribbled off to nothing. The mail room has orders to deliver all such packages to the editor's office regardless of to whom they are addressed. Since we don't let staffers get personal mail at the office, we can assume that any package coming to the paper is coming to the staffer in his professional status.

We accept no free tickets of any kind. This includes everything from the circus which comes through town each year to the local minor league ball game to the local tourist attractions. It's against policy for a staffer to get in any place with an admission charge on his press card and all such places in Florida have letters from ME saying so. When the sports editor takes his three kids to a minor league ball game on the editor's night off, he buys four tickets like every other father. The only exception we allow is that the sports reporter assigned to cover a ballgame does not pay his way in and a reviewer assigned to a movie, play, ballet, concert does not pay. We scrutinized this carefully and see no conflict in accepting a ticket for the working reviewer writing that night.

We go on no junkets of any kind. The travel writer accepts no free plane tickets, meal tickets or complimentary rooms. If an airline is providing a free ride to inaugurate a new flight, we send them a check for the round-trip tourist fare if we go—which is almost never.

When we sent a man to Viet Nam to cover the war, we turned down the Pentagon's free press flight offer and flew Pan-Am. When we sent a man along with the gubernatorial candidates, the press planes were provided by the candidates. We sent them a check for the fares which would have been normally charged by scheduled carriers for the same mileage.

If we are going to a $100 a plate fundraising steak dinner for a politico and the reporter is going to eat, we send a check for whatever the restaurant or caterer normally charges for that steak dinner.

We accept no merchandise for "testing and evaluation." If the fashion editor wants a paper dress, we buy it. If the food editor wants a rib roast, we buy it. If the golf writer wants to test some balls, we buy them. . . .

No one on the staff accepts anything from anyone for anything. No one on the staff owns anything or does anything which can gain him anything because of his job. And we pay our own way or don't go.

Haiman said the regulations applied to the paper's owner, too, who held no stock other than some mutual funds for long-term security. The *Times'* portfolios for the staff pension plan and profit-sharing funds include no local stocks or any others which it is thought might pose a potential conflict.

Some editors, especially after the Karafin exposé and conviction, have asked staff members to list sources of their outside income and at least a couple told their employees to drop part-time jobs that they held. One New Jersey daily requested a reporter to give up a $50-a-month out-of-office job he had writing releases for the local Red Cross which he then submitted to his own publication for possible use. But when media owners and managers do this, they have at least a moral obligation to pay their staff members enough so they do not have to "moonlight" on other jobs. Some are unwilling or unable to do that.

One chance to receive additional money is to compete for the prizes that various organizations offer for media coverage. Some are primarily to improve performance; some are little more than subtle and legalized bribery. Each reporter must decide which is which—partly as a matter of his conscience, partly as his bosses direct.

Editor & Publisher, the print journalists' trade publication, lists more than 125 prizes (and there probably are even more) available annually to newspapermen for various articles that they wrote during the previous year. On its face, giving of prizes would seem to be recognizing excellence of performance but, according to an article in the *Columbia Journalism Review* (Spring, 1970), it may also be "a subtle, sometimes difficult-to-pinpoint public relations technique" designed to obtain favorable comments. To what extent may a newsman have an idea (possibly barely consciously) that if he reports an event such and such a way, he just might win a prize and, if he does win, what of his future objectivity when he reports again on this subject? As a long-time observer of the science news reporting scene among the mass media, I have heard reporters remark, "He wrote that series on . . . because he thought a single story, no matter how well done, didn't have a chance to win the prize." That meant more news space about that topic—partly because of the prize competition.

For more than two decades, the Cigar Institute of America has offered press photographers cash awards annually for news pictures of people smoking cigars that got into print. The top award in 1969 of $1,500 was won by a *Miami News* employee, and a colleague took the $750 second prize. Two *New York Times* cameramen won $50 prizes in the contest. Sylvan Meyer, *Miami News* editor, found out that one of the two from his publication was purposely posed and he has passed the word that there are to be no more cigar pictures in the future.

According to a survey of 128 newsmen, almost equally divided between reporters and their editors, reported in the *Columbia Journalism Review* article, any of them would accept "in good conscience" an award from a newspaper or journalism group such as the local press club or Sigma Delta Chi, national professional organization, or from an educational institution such as the Pulitzer prizes from Columbia University or the George Polk Awards from Long Island University. Almost two-thirds of the respondents said they could take an award from such health groups financed by public contributions as the American Heart Association, the Arthritis Foundation, or the National Kidney Foundation. Almost as many answered in the affirmative for recognition from the American Bar Association, American Dental Association, or the American Medical Association. Only one in four answered "Yes" for awards from groups such as the American Trucking Association, the J. C. Penney Company (in association with the University of Missouri) for women's page and fashion reporting, or Trans World Airlines for travel articles.

Slightly more than two-thirds (68 percent) believed that such awards, overall, contributed to "better journalism." Thirty-one percent answered "No," the remaining 1 percent didn't know.

Asked if they knew of any cases in which a reporter's objectivity had been impaired by his winning an award, 9 percent said "Yes" and 91 percent replied "No." This meant, at least for this group, that one out of eleven felt some writer they knew had become less than fully devoted to the public because he had won a prize from some special interest group or association. A quarter of the respondents said they knew of cases where reporters had written stories in the hope of winning an award. Seventy-two percent—almost three out of four, with a larger margin among editors than reporters—believed newsmen should not accept cash prizes from groups whose activities they regularly cover, such as airline contests for travel writers and the AMA for medical reporters.

Gene Goltz, who won the 1965 Pulitzer Prize for an exposé in the *Houston Post,* commented, "I have found and seen time and again where it is very, very difficult to write biting truths about any group whose largesse you have been receiving in any way. . . . I'm sure the PR men in those organizations know this. And I'm sure that is one of the prime reasons for such contests."

Other newsmen argued that they knew few reporters who could be bought for the "lousy" amount of money offered in awards, although several carry $2,500 cash plus a plaque or certificate. Certainly no newsman worth his salary would be influenced by a few free cocktails, luncheons, or dinners. While there is an old adage, "Every man has his price," it would be as high in newsrooms as with other professionals.

Broadcasting has its prizes, too, but the ones most publicized are the Emmy Awards of the Academy of Television Arts and Sciences and the George Foster Peabody Awards administered by the University of Georgia. Since some of the professional associations and volunteer health organizations give prizes to broadcasters as well as reporters for print, many of the same problems face those who direct television and radio programing. The returns in publicity from broadcasting are larger because the audiences are far bigger for network shows than for any publication. Entertainment, however, ranks ahead of news in the minds of many broadcasters and most of the public; thus the competition for prizes in excellence for drama is more ardent than that in newscasts and documentaries.

With both print and broadcast, the key problem is for a prize winner to remain able to criticize the organization from which he won an award, be it plaque, cash, trophy, or free trip. And even when he feels free to do that, he must convince his colleagues and those smart readers and listeners who know about the award that he hasn't been contaminated in some way.

Readers and listeners, as well as newsmen, must retain some skepticism—yes, maybe even cynicism—about news from an authority, especially if the term is inside figurative quotation marks. Even when the news comes from a supposedly responsible and reliable source, reporters (and news consumers, too) should check the information against the "other side" as soon as possible. Conventional journalistic procedures call for such reporting but when the news is absent, as it sometimes is for valid reason of the impossibility of reaching the "other side," the public should hold up its ultimate verdict. For instance, if the story involves a statement from Democrats during a political campaign, a corporation during a strike or walkout, then there should be comments from the Republicans and from the union.

Hazards of unquestioning acceptance of a supposedly responsible news item were shown a couple of weeks after the Supreme Court decision allowing *The New York Times* and *Washington Post* to publish the rest of their series on the Pentagon Papers. William F. Buckley, Jr.'s *National Review* appeared with this headline:

The Missing Memoranda
1962-1966

THE
SECRET PAPERS
They Didn't Publish

The Makers of the Indochina War:

Strategy and counter-strategy from highly classified documents not published by the New York Times *and the* Washington Post, *leaked to* NATIONAL REVIEW

Most of the news media took these "documents" at face value and stories about the new "secrets" appeared on front pages of the nation's dailies and were featured in television and radio newscasts. The government's Voice of America broadcast the story overseas. When questioned by newsmen, some individuals quoted in the memoranda and papers could not recall whether they had composed them or not; a couple denounced them as inaccurate. At a news conference the following day, Buckley, who earlier had been unavailable to the press, admitted the whole business originated in his staff's imaginations. He said he had wanted to show that "forged documents would be widely accepted as genuine provided their content was inherently plausible." His media rivals were embarrassed, indignant, unforgiving. At least a dozen newspapers canceled his syndicated column.

Another example related to an announcement in early 1968 by the commissioner of the Office of the Blind in the Pennsylvania State Welfare Department that six college students had been blinded by the sun while under the influence of the drug LSD. Dr. Norman Yoder, who had been blinded in a childhood accident and had been a respected state official for more than a decade, told a representative of the U.S. Department of Health, Education and Welfare about the six blinded students and that federal official requested and received a written report of the incident from Dr. Yoder. This report got into the hands of a press association reporter in Washington and the news was out. Since it came from a conventional and official source for news and, conveniently, supported prevailing attitudes, no one checked further, for the time being. Gov. Raymond P. Shafer of Pennsylvania accepted the story as true, on the basis of Dr. Yoder's reputation and position, but requested the state's records. When the documents did not back up Dr. Yoder's claims, the whole incident was found to be a hoax.

The moral was pointed out by the *Columbia Journalism Review* (Summer, 1968):

> The Yoder case demonstrates how data that supports an organizational position gains ready acceptance within that organization. It is easy to believe in "facts" that appear to support whatever stand has already been taken. Since it was generally accepted that LSD is bad for you, Yoder's story bolstered the prevailing prejudice. This is one of the simplest and most clear-cut examples of how news is shaped at the source and then draped with credibility by the organization that releases it. If Dr. Yoder had claimed that six blind students had their sight restored by using LSD, undoubtedly everyone would have insisted on interviewing the students before accepting the account.

Hazards of accepting official versions of events without independent confirmation—if possible—and minus strict attribution to the news source attracted national attention when state troopers recaptured the New York State Correctional Facility at Attica in September 1971. Reporters, denied admission behind prison walls during the assault on the cell blocks, were informed by officials that nine hostages, blindfolded and bound, had their throats slashed by inmates as troopers moved in. Reports to that effect went around the world, with only a few pointing out that media were simply quoting the authorities. The next day a medical examiner announced that his autopsies found no signs of serious knife slashes at the throats of any of the hostages' bodies; all had died from gunshot wounds. Officials admitted that prisoners had no guns to use during the recapture of the cells. In the aftermath of self-evaluations, one news editor said the events and their reporting had raised a question of "how the press can protect itself and the public against hasty, faulty, confused and misleading explanations by officials who are usually on the scene first with their side of the story." He added that an important question remained, even with adequate attribution.

Pressures may come from segments of the reading, listening, and viewing audience, too. Church groups, militant groups of both left and right, and the conventional attitudes that the general public holds—all may influence the way a publication or station performs. At its best, this represents response to the audience; at worst, it may be buckling under to the threats of boycotts, nonsupport, and inattention. This is often a tough line to draw but it should always be done—though it isn't in some cases. And it should be done with a sense of responsibility and not by the easy way out of surrendering to majority opinion, because even that may be faithless to the overall public good. It is upon these media decisions that large portions of the public make up their minds about how fair and accurate and honest the media are. The newsman and his bosses have to do far more than gather and distribute the news and then comment upon it. They need to decide to what pressures they will yield and always seek to evaluate which are real—and for the "public interest"—and which are phoney and specious.

David Ginsburg, former aide to the National Advisory Commission on Civil Disorders, told a Pittsburgh conference on media and minorities:

The problem is made harder by the fact that accusations of bias against the media are often based on the bias of the audience itself.

What you and I might agree is neutral and objective, Strom Thurmond and a Black Panther might both believe is biased and lacking in credibility—for very different reasons.

To paraphrase a common saying, "May God protect the working journalist!" Quite truthfully, in the contemporary setup, he needs any and all the help he can get.

12. The Right to Privacy Versus Publicity for Profit

American concern with and interest in public figures and organizations mounted increasingly as the country moved into the 1970's. More than ever before citizens are aware of a "credibility gap" between the image that is presented of many of their officials, their institutions, and their ideologies and what readers, listeners, and viewers consider to be reality.

Two forces are pulling in opposite directions. The concept of using publicity to increase profit, prestige, or power often is pitted against the prerogatives for privacy or, as it frequently is called, the "right to be let alone." The first filters information to achieve a desired and pre-conceived effect; the second grows out of increasing media intrusions into an individual's actions and thoughts. During the past decade, the courts have authorized publicity about people and organizations in the arena of public discussion so that now libel action can hardly be successfully in-stituted against officials or even individuals involved in matters of general interest.

In rejecting the argument that a private individual enjoyed more pro-tection of his reputation than a public figure, Justice William J. Brennan,

Jr., spoke for the U.S. Supreme Court majority in *Rosenbloom v. Metromedia, Inc.* (1971) when he wrote:

> We honor the commitment to robust debate on public issues, which is embodied in the First Amendment, by extending constitutional protection to all discussion and communication involving matters of public or general concern, without regard to whether the persons involved are famous or anonymous.

With some touch of irony, the Supreme Court upheld the press' right to intrude upon an individual's "right to be let alone" on the basis of constitutional guarantees, while the government's legal machinery was being attacked for abridging citizens' Bill of Rights protection against preventive detention, no-knock search without warrants, wiretapping, and sweep-arrests off the streets during peace demonstrations.

During the legal shiftings of the 1960's, the courts first held that a "public official" was generally fair game for criticisms and comments—if the information media maintained "minimal responsibility" in their professional performances so as not to display malice. Then, in a case concerning Dr. Linus Pauling, "public figures" joined "public officials" as possible targets. Finally, in *Time, Inc. v. Hill* (1967), individuals connected with a "public issue" lost much of their privacy, regardless of whether they had sought the publicity or not.

Professors Donald M. Gillmor of the University of Minnesota and Jerome A. Barron of George Washington University, two knowledgeable legal observers, summarized what had happened during the decade as follows in *Mass Communication Law* (West Publishing Co., 1969):

> Making it more difficult for public figures to respond to newspaper criticism in the form of libel suits may at least theoretically serve to sufficiently embolden the press to conduct that vigorous critique of public officials which is considered one of the primary justifications for freedom of the press. But what societal interests are served by making it difficult for individuals who are the fortuitous victims of tragedy to secure recompense from a press which may exploit or falsify their tragedy?

All of this was happening while jurors were becoming more willing to award multimillion dollar punitive damages for libels. Thus the former pressure of paying out money for harming an individual's reputation—even without any malice—was removed and now a moral sense of responsibility was the chief deterrent for overly shoddy and unprofessional misconduct.

With most of the population living in rural areas when the Founding Fathers wrote the U.S. Constitution, little, if any, attention was paid to privacy invasions during discussions of possible legal embargoes. During the excesses of the "yellow journalism" of the final decades of the nineteenth century, however, lawyers took increasing interest. Two young Boston attorneys, Samuel D. Warren and Louis D. Brandeis, who later became a U.S. Supreme Court justice, wrote an article for the *Harvard Law Review* (December, 1890) that focused on the implications of the so-called new journalism and attempted to develop legal foundations for the "right to be let alone." A key paragraph from the article reads:

> The press is overstepping in every direction the obvious bounds of propriety and of decency. Gossip is no longer the resource of the idle and of the vicious, but has become a trade, which is pursued with industry as well as effrontery. To satisfy a prurient taste the details of sexual relations are spread broadcast in the columns of the daily papers. To occupy the indolent, column upon column is filled with idle gossip, which can only be procured by intrusion upon the domestic circle. The intensity and complexity of life, attendant upon advancing civilization, have rendered necessary some retreat from the world, and man, under the refining influence of culture, has become more sensitive to publicity, so that solitude and privacy have become more essential to the individual; but modern enterprise and invention have, through invasions upon his privacy, subjected him to mental pain and distress, far greater than could be inflicted by mere bodily injury.

A landmark case arose in 1902 when a teen-ager, Miss Abigail M. Roberson, had her photograph reproduced—without her consent—on the outside of boxes, 25,000 in all, under the headline, "Flour of the Family." Her parents sued for $15,000 but the judges who heard the case held, in effect, that although they had great sympathy for Miss Roberson's mental anguish, they could not open up possibilities for future recoveries which might extend far beyond the "Flour" case. "The legislative body could very well interfere and arbitrarily provide that no one should be permitted for his own selfish purpose to use the picture or the name of another for advertising purposes without his consent," the majority opinion said. Editorial writers were outraged, and because of the resulting furore, the New York legislature the next year did pass a privacy law, the first in the nation. Eventually other states enacted privacy protections.

Thus invasion of privacy took its place as a sort of younger brother (or sister, in honor of the unsuccessful plaintiff) to the long-time right of recovering libel damages when an individual's reputation had been damaged through dissemination of untruths about him.

Threats of libel litigation had hung over American journalists since the colonial period with one of the better known early cases involving John Peter Zenger and his *New York Weekly Journal.* Defenses, all qualified under certain conditions, included truth—provable in court—fair comment, and privilege, which is the accurate reporting of actual comments from public legislatures or courts of record. Such was the long sweep of the historical approach but, during the 1960's, legal interpretation of libel and privacy began to run tandem and, in some cases, follow identical routes in the courts.

The case that initiated the recent shift in judicial positions was a series of libel actions against *The New York Times* for a full-page advertisement, printed March 29, 1960, requesting contributions to support the Southern student civil rights movement and for legal defense of Dr. Martin Luther King, Jr. Because of claimed inaccurate statements, L. B. Sullivan, one of three elected commissioners in Montgomery, Ala., and other city and state officials sued *The Times* for libel damages. In the Alabama courts, Sullivan was awarded $500,000 damages and his suit was the first to reach the U.S. Supreme Court on appeal. By the time that court acted, eleven other libel actions were pending by local and state officials against *The Times* seeking $5,600,000 and five other suits against the Columbia Broadcasting System seeking $1,700,000.

Attorneys for *The Times* admitted that there were inaccuracies in the advertisement. For instance, college students cited in the ad as singing "My Country 'Tis of Thee" had in fact sung the national anthem. But they argued that the state courts had abridged the freedom of the press by, in effect, dispensing with proof of injury to the complaining official through assumption of malice as well as falsity. Sullivan's lawyers argued, "The Constitution has never required that states afford newspapers the privilege of leveling false and defamatory 'facts' at persons simply because they hold public office."

Before the Supreme Court's opinions were handed down, a majority of the states required that fair comment defenses could be used successfully only when the statements were true. Thus *New York Times Co. v. Sullivan* (1964) became a truly monumental action for informational media that wanted to comment on officials' public action. Very shortly further questions arose as to what limits, if any, were to be applied. What about former officers? What about candidates running for election to public positions? And, more controversial, what about public but non-official figures involved with public issues?

The U.S. Supreme Court justices came down hard in defense of *The New York Times'* position, as witness these portions from the majority opinion:

The present advertisement, as an expression of grievance and protest on one of the major public issues of our time, would seem clearly to qualify for the constitutional protection. The question is whether it forfeits that protection by the falsity of some of its factual statements and by its alleged defamation of respondent. . . .

A rule compelling the critic of official conduct to guarantee the truth of all his factual assertions—and to do so on pain of libel judgments virtually unlimited in amount—leads to a comparable "self-censorship." . . .

Raising as it does the possibility that a good-faith critic of government will be penalized for his criticism, the proposition relied on by the Alabama courts strikes at the very center of the constitutionally protected area of free expression. We hold that such a proposition may not constitutionally be utilized to establish that an otherwise impersonal attack on governmental operations was a libel of an official responsible for those operations.

Justice Hugo L. Black, with Justice William O. Douglas concurring, went even beyond the findings of the majority opinion. He said in part:

The half-million-dollar verdict does give dramatic proof, however, that state libel laws threaten the very existence of an American press virile enough to publish unpopular views on public affairs and bold enough to criticize the conduct of public officials. . . . Moreover, this technique for harassing and punishing a free press—now that it has been shown to be possible—is by no means limited to cases with racial overtones; it can be used in other fields where public feelings may make local as well as out-of-state newspapers easy prey for libel verdict seekers.

In my opinion the Federal Constitution has dealt with this

deadly danger to the press in the only way possible without leaving the free press open to destruction—by granting the press an absolute immunity for criticism of the way public officials do their public duty. . . . Stopgap measures like those the Court adopts are in my judgment not enough. . . .

We would, I think, more faithfully interpret the First Amendment by holding that at the very least it leaves the people and the press free to criticize officials and discuss public affairs with impunity. . . . This Nation, I suspect, can live in peace without libel suits based on public discussions of public affairs and public officials. But I doubt that a country can live in freedom where its people can be made to suffer physically or financially for criticizing their government, its actions, or its officials. . . . An unconditional right to say what one pleases about public affairs is what I consider to be the minimum guarantee of the First Amendment.

I regret that the Court has stopped short of this holding indispensable to preserve our free press from destruction.

Shortly after the *Times*-Sullivan "rule" had been delineated by the U.S. Supreme Court, a U.S. Court of Appeals upheld a dismissal of libel action against the New York *Daily News* by Dr. Linus Pauling, Nobel Prize-winning chemist and active pacifist who claimed that the paper had intimated that he leaned toward the Communist Party line. The appeals court opinion (1964) held, in part:

A candidate for public office would seem an inevitable candidate for extension [of the Supreme Court's *Times* case "rule"]; if a newspaper cannot constitutionally be held for defamation when it states without malice, but cannot prove, that an incumbent seeking re-election has accepted a bribe, it seems hard to justify holding it liable for further stating that the bribe was offered by his opponent. Once that extension was made, the participant in public debate on an issue of grave public concern would be next in line; thus, as applied to the case in hand, if a newspaper could not be held for printing Dr. Pauling's charges that a member of the Atomic Energy Commission had "made dishonest, untrue and misleading statements to mislead the American people" and that a United States Senator is "the greatest enemy . . . the United States had," as the New York Times case decides, one may wonder whether there would be sound basis for forcing it to risk a jury's determination that it was only engaging in fair criticism rather than misstating facts if it printed, falsely but without malice, that in saying all this Dr. Pauling was following the Communist line. The "profound national commitment to the principle that debate on public issues should be uninhibited, robust, and wide-open," now applied to confer immunity on "vehement, caustic, and sometimes unpleasantly sharp attacks on government and public officials," may some day be found to demand still further erosion of the protection heretofore given by the law of defamation.

That "further erosion" was not long in coming but not quite in the format that had been anticipated.

For nineteen hours during mid-September, 1952, James Hill, his wife, and five children made the nation's front pages when they were held as hostages in their suburban Philadelphia home by three escaped convicts. The family was released unharmed and Hill in a news conference immediately afterward stressed that the convicts had not mistreated the family or been violent during the time they held the seven captives. The Hills moved to Connecticut and otherwise tried to evade additional publicity. In the spring of 1953, a novel entitled *The Desperate Hours* was published and told of a family of four held captive by three escaped convicts but who experienced violence with the father and son beaten by their captors. The novel was adapted to a play and *Life* published a picture article on the Broadway thriller staged at the Hills' former suburban home near Philadelphia. The headline read, "True Crime Inspires Tense Play" and the subtitle was, "The ordeal of a family trapped by convicts gives Broadway a new thriller, 'The Desperate Hours.' " Hill sued for invasion of privacy, which he and his family had tried to protect by moving and by refusing to grant interviews in Connecticut. The jury awarded him $50,000 compensatory and $25,000 punitive damages. On appeal, the Appellate Division of the New York courts ordered a second trial, where Hill was awarded $30,000 compensatory damages without any punitive damages. Time, Inc., appealed. During presentations before the U.S. Supreme Court, Hill's lawyer, Richard M. Nixon, argued that if the *Life* appeal were upheld, "every scandal sheet in the country" would gain the license to lie about individuals for purposes of trade and profit. The justices were seriously fractionalized in their decisions.

For the majority, Justice Brennan set aside the New York Court of

Appeals ruling but allowed a retrial under new guidelines. He seemed to value press freedom more than an individual's right to privacy. He wrote in part:

> Exposure of the self to others in varying degrees is a concomitant of life in a civilized community. The risk of this exposure is an essential incident in a society which places a primary value on freedom of speech and of press. . . . Erroneous statement is no less inevitable in such case than in the case of comment upon public affairs, and in both, if innocent or merely negligent, ". . . it must be protected if the freedoms of expression are to have the 'breathing space' that they 'need . . . to survive.' . . ." We create grave risk of serious impairment of the indispensable service of a free press in a free society if we saddle the press with the impossible burden of verifying to a certainty the facts associated in news articles with a person's name, picture or portrait, particularly as related to non-defamatory matter. Even negligence would be a most elusive standard, especially when the content of the speech itself affords no warning of prospective harm to another through falsity. A negligence test would place on the press the intolerable burden of guessing how a jury might assess the reasonableness of steps taken by it to verify the accuracy of every reference to a name, picture or portrait.
>
> In this context, sanctions against either innocent or negligent misstatement would present a grave hazard of discouraging the press from exercising the constitutional guarantees. Those guarantees are not for the benefit of the press so much as for the benefit of all of us. A broadly defined freedom of the press assures the maintenance of our political system and an open society. Fear of large verdicts in damage suits for innocent or mere negligent misstatement, even fear of the expense involved in their defense, must inevitably cause publishers to "steer far wider of the unlawful zone."

Justice Black, with Justice Douglas concurring, added this pointed warning:

> One does not have to be a prophet to foresee that judgments like the one we here reverse can frighten and punish the press so much that publishers will cease trying to report news in a lively and readable fashion as long as there is—and there always will be—doubt as to the complete accuracy of the newsworthy facts. Such a con-

summation hardly seems consistent with the clearly expressed purpose of the Founders to guarantee the press a favored spot in our free society.

Justice John Marshall Harlan, who concurred in part and dissented in part, commented in his opinion on the Hill case:

> The "freedom of the press" guaranteed by the First Amendment, and as reflected in the Fourteenth, cannot be thought to insulate all press conduct from review and responsibility for harm inflicted. The majority would allow sanctions against such conduct only when it is morally culpable. I insist that it can also be reached when it creates a severe risk of irremediable harm to individuals involuntarily exposed to it and powerless to protect themselves against it. . . .
>
> A constitutional doctrine which relieves the press of even this minimal responsibility in cases of this sort seems to me unnecessary and ultimately harmful to the permanent good health of the press itself. If the *New York Times* case has ushered in such a trend it will prove in its long-range impact to have done a disservice to the true values encompassed in the freedoms of speech and press.

Time, Inc., and the Hill family agreed to an out-of-court settlement rather than go through another trial.

In a review of these developments, Prof. Harry Klaven, a student of legal trends, concluded that "the logic of *New York Times* and *Hill* taken together grants the press some measure of constitutional protections for anything the press thinks is a matter of public interest." That wasn't quite accurate, it soon became apparent. If the media failed to exercise even the "minimal responsibility" of journalistic conduct, what recourse then was there for anyone harmed? That obvious question was not long in coming before the justices and the very point of "responsibility for harm inflicted" loomed large in another 1967 decision. That legal action involved the *Saturday Evening Post* and Wally Butts of the University of Georgia athletics staff.

The March 23, 1963, issue of the *Saturday Evening Post* printed an article entitled, "The Story of a College Football Fix," which reported on a supposed telephone conversation between Butts, then Georgia athletic director, and Paul Bryant, head football coach at the University of Alabama. The story claimed that the two had been overheard planning to "fix" a football contest between the two schools. Source for the allegations was George Burnett, an insurance salesman who, it developed, had been placed on probation in connection with bad check charges. Burnett said that he had inadvertently been cut in to the Butts-Bryant phone line while making a call of his own and that he had taken notes on the conversation he overheard. Later Butts resigned.

Butts sued the Curtis Publishing Company for $5,000,000 in compensatory damages and another $5,000,000 in punitive damages. Although the *Post*'s attorneys tried to establish the truth of its allegations, expert witnesses for Butts contrasted Burnett's notes with actual films of the game itself and concluded that the two did not mesh. The trial jury awarded Butts $60,000 in general damages and $3,000,000 in punitive damages. It was one of the largest libel awards in American legal history. Since *The New York Times* "rule" was enunciated by the U.S. Supreme Court shortly after the jury's verdict, Curtis appealed to the highest court.

Speaking for the majority of a divided court, Justice Harlan sharply criticized the journalistic practices used by the *Post* writer and editors. He held that a "public figure" who is not a public official should be able to recover "for a defamatory falsehood whose substance makes substantial danger to reputation apparent, on a showing of highly unreasonable conduct constituting an extreme departure from the standards of investigation and reporting ordinarily adhered to by responsible publishers." Justice Harlan felt that the *Post*'s actions fitted into this category. He went into specifics as follows:

> The evidence showed that the Butts story was in no sense "hot news" and the editors of the magazine recognized the need for a thorough investigation of the serious charges. Elementary precautions were, nevertheless, ignored. The Saturday Evening Post knew that Burnett had been placed on probation in connection with bad check charges, but proceeded to publish the story on the basis of his affidavit without substantial independent support. Burnett's notes were not even viewed by any of the magazine's personnel prior to publication. John Carmichael who was supposed to have been with Burnett when the phone call was overheard was not interviewed. No attempt was made to screen the films of the game to see if Burnett's information was accurate, and no attempt was made to find out whether Alabama had adjusted its plans after the alleged divulgence of information.
>
> The Post writer assigned to the story was not a football expert

and no attempt was made to check the story with someone knowledgeable in the sport. At trial such experts indicated that the information in the Burnett notes was either such that it would be evident to any opposing coach from game films regularly exchanged or valueless. Those assisting the Post writer in his investigation were already deeply involved in another libel action, based on a different article, brought against Curtis Publishing Co. by the Alabama coach and unlikely to be the source of a complete and objective investigation. The Saturday Evening Post was anxious to change its image by instituting a policy of "sophisticated muckraking," and the pressure to produce a successful exposé might have induced a stretching of standards. In short, the evidence is ample to support a finding of highly unreasonable conduct constituting an extreme departure from the standards of investigation and reporting ordinarily adhered to by responsible publishers.

Eventually Butts settled the case with payment by Curtis of $460,000 in damages.

On the same day that the Supreme Court ruled against the Curtis Publishing Company, it supported the Associated Press, which was being sued for libel by former General Edwin Walker for the news agency's reporting of his actions during the turbulent entry of James Meredith into the University of Mississippi. Walker had won a $500,000 judgment against the AP for alleged misstatements in stories from a newsman on campus that were distributed at the time of the disturbances. Pointing out that in contrast with the Butts article, the news item concerning Walker was "news which required immediate dissemination," the majority opinion commented:

> The Associated Press received the information from a correspondent who was present at the scene of the events and gave every indication of being trustworthy and competent. His dispatches in this instance, with one minor exception, were internally consistent and would not have seemed unreasonable to one familiar with General Walker's prior publicized statements on the underlying controversy. Considering the necessity for rapid dissemination, nothing in this series of events gives the slightest hint of a severe departure from accepted publishing standards. We therefore conclude that General Walker should not be entitled to damages from the Associated Press.

Thus, during the 1960's, the Court's attitudes moved away from the twin threats to media of (1) possible libel action with its responsibility of having to establish in court the truth of what was printed or said over the air, and (2) possible privacy invasion suits for disseminating information about those who did not seek publicity for possible gain. At the end of the decade, the press had far greater freedom than previously. However, the justices wisely held that there were some limitations, especially if the information media did not follow, as one decision put it, "the standards of investigation and reporting ordinarily adhered to by responsible publishers." The Court also might well have added "news broadcasters" to the phraseology. For the 1970's, responsible publishers and broadcasters had little to fear from irresponsible libel actions if they could come into the courts with hands no more than slightly smudged. However, the scandalmongers and other irresponsible operators could very well have to pay the legal penalties for their misconducts. Refinements of the innovative decisions of the 1960's left some room for future court decisions to shift over details but the main course seemed to be fairly firmly charted. The legal trends were running against any individual who wanted privacy at all costs, but so were the times with greater and greater concentrations of population in crowded urban centers and the push toward increased togetherness—whether Americans desired it or not. The "right to be let alone" was becoming a somewhat Victorian concept, which is exactly when it arose—during the 1890's.

Some invasions of privacy never reach the courts and are direct confrontations in which the media publish what they find regardless of the consequences on the grounds of the public's "right to know." While most commentators lauded the paper for its investigative reporting, some few objected when *The New York Times* on Oct. 31, 1965, featured a front-page story that Daniel Burros, New York Ku Klux Klan leader and spokesman, had grown up as a Jewish youngster in Queens, including a traditional bar mitzvah. Behind that news item was ten days of intense research by McCandlish Phillips, whose byline was on the article, and at least four other reporters.

On the sixth day, Phillips talked with Burros in a luncheonette about his background, including the marriage of his parents in a Jewish ceremony in the Bronx.

"Are you going to print that?" Burros asked and Phillips said yes, it was public record on file in the Bronx Supreme Court House. Burros threatened to kill the newsman unless he promised not to publicize "the deepest secret of his life." Phillips would only promise that he wouldn't print it until he had talked to Burros one more time and he gave Burros his telephone number so he could call him that evening.

Burros warned, "If you publish that, I'll come and get you and I'll kill you. I don't care what happens to me. I'll be ruined. This is all I've got to live for."

Burros did call *The Times'* office several times and talked to Phillips, asking on the last call on Friday if Phillips could trade the news about Burros' Jewish origins for another item. Phillips explained he could not make a trade.

"I know I can't stop that story," Burros replied. "But I'm going to go out in a blaze of glory." He added that he would put on a show in *The Times* building although he knew he would "catch some lead."

Security guards and police were alerted and Phillips was assigned personal bodyguard.

Burros saw *The Times* story on Sunday while visiting in Reading, Pa. After a wild tantrum, he shot himself fatally in the chest and head. Arthur Gelb of *The Times* told Phillips of the shooting. The reporter described his reactions later in *Times Talk* (November 1965):

> I felt sad. I knew that Dan Burros had been caught in a net of evil that had pulled him down to death at 28. I said, "What I think we've seen here, Arthur, is the God of Israel acting in judgment!"

While privacy was contracting as the courts and reporters stressed media's right to inquire, to uncover details, and to probe for particulars, increasing attention was being paid to public relations, which provided such information most willingly, and how it was affecting our society. For instance, one frequently bitter critic of the contemporary scene, Prof. Amitai Etzioni of Columbia University's sociology department, wrote in the *Wall Street Journal* (Jan. 21, 1971):

> The curse of this age of mass communication is that politicians' tendency to deal in images instead of issues, with the politics of the situation rather than the situation. Political leaders, who get almost as many kudos for announcing a program as for implementing it, rapidly learn the short cut of replacing worn-out slogans with new ones, huffing and puffing while the government machinery remains mired. Before we can seriously begin to handle our grave problems, we must learn to face them, training ourselves as citizens to discount speeches, declarations and plans, and to look at actual achievements and the financial and human costs involved.

He was commenting on politicians but he might just as accurately have been discussing college presidents, detergent manufacturers, election reformers, or defenders of the capitalistic system, to mention just a few possibilities.

During the second half of the twentieth century, no sophisticated individual or organization would dream of introducing a new commercial product, conducting a political campaign, or promoting a sex goddess' newest motion picture without investigating—and using—the appropriate public relations possibilities. One of the best sellers of the late 1960's was Joe McGinniss' *The Selling of the President 1968,* its sales demonstrating the general interest in how public "image-making" and political performance may be interwoven. In many contests for media attention, the battle often becomes that between rival agencies promoting their competing clients. To be objective, however, I should point out that a number of advocates for a cleaner environment, greater consumerism, and educational restructuring have consulted PR firms or have prepared their own do-it-yourself publicity, often with great effectiveness. Public relations has become a widely used tool in modern communication.

While exact statistics are almost impossible to obtain, it is estimated that more than one hundred thousand men and women are engaged in this loosely described practice of public relations and the number may well double before the end of the 1970's. Appeals to the various publics that they seek to serve only emphasize the different techniques and philosophies that may be utilized. Roughly, however, the field breaks down into (1) financial or business work which may try to "sell" a product, a corporation, or a union; (2) governmental, which releases what officials and agencies are doing (often also serving a current officeholder and his program); and (3) institutional, such as that to promote and publicize voluntary health, educational, and similar organizations.

While definitions of public relations are voluminous and varied, they are not eminently helpful for a news consumer who wants to learn how its practices concern him but they may have at least tangential value.

For instance, *Time* (July 7, 1967) wrote that the "image merchants" had been described as variedly as inventors of gimmicks, old-fashioned pitchmen, press agents with pretensions, or new creatures with Big Brotherly skills. The news magazine claimed:

> In fact, the good public relations man is more than a press-agent—
> though not even the best is ever wholly free from flackery—and

considerably less than Big Brother. . . . But it is also a legitimate and essential trade, necessitated by the complexity of modern life and the workings of an open society. It is growing today, says Harvard Government Professor Seymour Martin Lipset, because "there is ever more direct communication between power and people."

Edward L. Bernays, who in 1970 was chosen among the five outstanding American PR professionals of the century, described a public relations counsel as a "societal technician who is fitted by training and experience to evaluate the maladjustments and adjustments between his client and the publics upon whom the client is dependent for his socially sound activity." Economics writer Robert Heilbroner wrote, "Public relations is Dale Carnegie writ large." Professor Emeritus Mark Van Doren of Columbia University bluntly commented, "Public relations is the curse of our times. It could be a sign of a very deep disease." Ernest van den Haag, sociologist with the New School for Social Research, pointed out, "Public relations can seduce, but it cannot rape." In addition, it has been called an art, business, corporate conscience, humanizing influence, pattern, process, profession, science, system, and trade. With such a diffusive target, criticism of public relations never could be very far off the mark.

Those who fault corporate or government public relations practitioners explain that they are, after all, little more than paid employees of their clients, regardless of whether they are on the payroll or are hired for fees as consultants. In all cases, it is the client's money, and the client —unless he is superhuman—wants to put his best foot forward. This is one description of public relations and it is not far afield. Why do good, as a saying goes, and *not* get credit for it? But if demands upon the practitioners become excessive, they have the right—and some of them have exercised it—to refuse to handle an account of which they do not approve. Sometimes, it was a conflict over what techniques to use; other times, it was bluntly a matter of conscience and principles.

The Public Relations Society of America, professional organization with approximately 7,000 members, has tried to improve the PR image and the quality of performance. In recent years, it has paid special attention to membership accreditation, a Code of Professional Standards, and increased concern with college training programs which will prepare future practitioners. The Code makes the conventional bows to "a general duty of fair dealing towards . . . the general public," conduct "in accord with the general welfare," and "the affirmative duty of adhering to generally accepted standards of accuracy, truth and good taste." (The American Society of Newspaper Editors has many of the same polite ideas in its code but its officers or members have never, never censured anybody in the group.) A more powerful force than the Code, many feel, is the improved social climate. It just does not pay off in dollars, in the long run, if there is rampant fakery because "Truth will out" is more than just a classroom axiom.

How do public relations people see themselves? Not surprisingly, as tremendously helpful to those who employ them in a troubled world that is becoming increasingly complex. Here is what the *Public Relations Journal* reported in its twenty-fifth anniversary issue (October 1970):

> However clouded the general outlook, the prospect for public relations is bright indeed. From the continuing fragmentation of society, the tightening of tensions within it, and the widening of what Henry Ford calls "the revolution of expectations" public relations problems will merge to plague every institution from the ivied towers to the corner grocery. And the people in charge will not find these problems easy to cope with—they will need knowledgeable help in devising policies and acceptable performance, and in building bridges to the critics. Public relations will become increasingly an art of confrontation and negotiation while continuing to counsel and communicate. Effective communication, becoming more complex than ever, will be concerned more with affected segments than with the general public, and will rely more on tailored devices than on general media. Hopefully, the practice of public relations will expand to meet the needs and benefit from the opportunities. To be expected are continuing professional development, more exacting accreditation requirements, and possibly some method of designating varying degrees of proficiency. Licensing may be in the cards. New specialities will emerge without diminishing the need for the generalist who coordinates the efforts and holds the confidence of management. The adversity of the times "is not without its comforts and hopes" for public relations, and particularly for the talented and energetic.

Not unexpectedly, this editorial like most other professional pronouncements stresses the public relations problems of corporations and institutions rather than questions for a truly informed public in a democratic society. This difference in focus probably accounts for many of the varying or even conflicting attitudes of newsmen and public relations practitioners.

The interests of a news source, including those represented in a public news release, rarely coincide with the demands of the general news consumers. Almost anyone who gives out news has his own personal, professional, ideological, or corporate viewpoint; that is, his own message with his own axes to grind. This applies whether that news source is president of the United States, head of a huge corporation, president of an Ivy League university, union official, nuclear physicist, promoter for a new rock music group—or their public relations spokesman. Whoever he is, the news source is going to prefer that the story be told in such-and-such a way. On the other hand, a typical newsman is writing and interpreting the facts as he sees and hears them with the interests of the general public in mind. The difficulties, of course, may be compounded when the reporter is biased or under some kind of special directives from his superiors. However, at least some problems would exist even if a reporter adopted the mores of the environment in which he operates and, as closely as humanly possible, tried to become a perfect transmitter of reality.

The emphasis on "image" rather than reality is no child of this century. Students of public relations cite such catch phrases from Ancient Rome as "S.P.Q.R."—The Senate and the Roman People—and the highly effective pamphleteering of the American Founding Fathers such as Samuel Adams, Benjamin Franklin, Thomas Jefferson, Alexander Hamilton, and that prolific producer, Thomas Paine. Adams used the Boston Tea Party to take advantage of what today would be known as a "staged event." The Declaration of Independence itself declared it was written out of "a decent respect to the opinions of mankind," a theme not unlike some recent statements of campus militants, including the Weathermen. General George Washington ordered all corporals to read to their squads Paine's ringing appeal on "the times that try men's souls" just before the successful attack on Trenton. And a widely-used college textbook comments, "Franklin's consummate skill in public relations has been seldom matched."

Some of the contemporary concern with imagery arose from Professor Daniel J. Boorstin's 1962 book *The Image: A Guide to Pseudo-Events in America* (Atheneum Publishers and Harper Colophon Books). The University of Chicago professor wrote, "I do not know what 'reality' really is. But somehow I do know an illusion when I see one."

And he then proceeded to explain in detail how news gathering had moved, often, to news making through skillful utilization of pseudo-events, which, he said, came about because somebody had planned, planted, or incited them; how the true hero had been supplanted by the celebrity or "the human pseudo-event"; and how the American Dream had been converted into American illusions which provide a self-deceiving magic of pseudo-prestige. Along with Marshall McLuhan's concerns with the medium, the message, and the visually-oriented, television generation, Boorstin's book was among the seminal concepts in recent communications philosophy.

For much of the three-quarters of a century that modern public relations practitioners have been on the scene, an outright condescension existed toward them from the frequently lower-paid newsmen, particularly of the print media. Almost reluctantly, reporters with a sense for reality have conceded in recent years that many fields of public activities just could not be covered—certainly not reported as effectively—if it were not for the aid of public relations men or public information specialists.

Robert U. Brown, publisher of *Editor & Publisher* and traditionally a spokesman for the newspaper industry, reflected this tribute-with-a-jab attitude in the following comments from a weekly column (Jan. 16, 1971):

> Most Washington correspondents will agree that any reasonably thorough and accurate news coverage of the multitudinous government activities in Washington would be impossible without government press agents, public relations men or information officers. They run the gamut of course, from those who try conscientiously to help reporters to those who try to do anything else but that.
>
> It is equally well known that government press agentry and information activities tend to feed upon themselves and proliferate into non-essential boon doggles.

As Brown indicated, one of the difficulties with current public relations is its own quest for identity—or possibly, the search for its own public relations "image." A large part of this trouble arose because, like others in American industry, public relations men and their practices grew up as they sought to solve problems. In that process, they undertook all kinds of assignments; some to promote a product or idea, some to enlighten the public about a new treatment for a common disease;

some to provide information not easily available to newsmen who wanted greater details to give their readers, viewers, and listeners. Jobs for a public relations man might range from getting a slightly phoney but amusing feature item on newspaper front pages or on the air to providing expertise on which university campus research projects should be publicized in a fund-raising campaign. The thrust may be direct or as subtle as the classic PR campaign to promote sales of bacon through promoting nutritional advice in favor of bigger breakfasts for Americans. (The theory—and it worked—was that if people ate larger breakfasts, sales of bacon, as a major breakfast component, would rise in proportion.)

According to one version of professional folklore, an amateur needed little more than a credit card, a mimeograph machine, and possibly a subscription to *The New York Times* before he started calling himself a public relations counselor. There might once have been some slight truth to this but today's most highly paid PR counselors with their salaries of more than $100,000 annually require considerable in-depth research and lengthy meetings with a committee of specialists before they recommend what policy a client should pursue. Successful ones are themselves big business and may advise such diverse individuals as Svetlana Alliluyeva, Richard Nixon, Eugene McCarthy, Ronald Reagan, Frank Sinatra, and Thomas Watson and such varied institutions as the Iron and Steel Institute, National Coffee Association, New York University, and Proctor & Gamble.

Despite financial successes, PR practitioners, in some cases, have become whipping boys. They were blamed for failures although sometimes the practitioners were called in only when things started to go wrong. Other times, the blame was not misplaced because they had tried to make a fast buck—as happens in almost any trade, industry, or profession.

As recently as 1969, according to court records, one financial public relations firm neglected to mention in a news release for a client that had just purchased a gypsum mine that the new property was twenty miles from the nearest railroad and thus the concern was in no position to profitably mine its new acquisition. When questioned, the public relations man said that he did not mention the lack of railroad facilities near the gypsum mine because his agency had only three hours to prepare the release and that the staff "didn't have time to include everything."

After hearings in 1970, the Securities and Exchange Commission obtained an injunction to enjoin the industrial concern from making false statements about itself, with or without any public relations guidance.

Many of the better known case histories of the transgressions of public information specialists have been reported from government. This is not unusual since the party out of power almost always has someone in the Civil Service who is willing to leak what he thinks is the misconduct of his partisan associates. The Vietnam war in two administrations, at least, has developed its own credibility gap, as pointed out in detail earlier, and approximately two-thirds of the Americans polled in public opinion surveys reported that they did not believe that either Presidents Lyndon B. Johnson or Richard M. Nixon had disclosed the full details of our fighting there. This is an intriguing result because the Department of Defense, Air Force, Army, and Navy public relations and information activities totaled an estimated $44,000,000 in 1969, $39,600,000 in 1970, and $37,600,000 in 1971.

Senator J. William Fulbright, chairman of the Foreign Relations Committee, said in the *Congressional Record* that "the admitted total for military spending on public relations activities is but the very small tip of a very large iceberg." He sought to impose "a $20,000,000 ceiling" on the public relations and public information activities of the Pentagon but he lost. Possibly this was because President Nixon on Nov. 6, 1970, asked all government agencies to cooperate with the budget chief "to bring about a curtailment of self-serving and wasteful public relations activities" since, as he said, some practices that he had observed during his administration's early years in office represented "a questionable use of the taxpayer's money for the purpose of promoting and soliciting support for various agency activities." At least one suspicious media commentator asserted it would be worth watching to see if any savings actually were made over several years.

The Associated Press in 1967 estimated that the U.S. executive branch of the government spent approximately $400,000,000 on public information; two years later Profs. William L. Rivers and Wilbur Schramm of Stanford University said that "federal expenditures on telling and showing the taxpayers" cost more than double the news-gathering budgets of the two major American wire services, the three television networks and the ten largest U.S. daily newspapers.

The public needs some of this information; for instance the National Weather Service predicts sunshine, rain, or snow; the Census Bureau supplies the best statistics on how many of us there are, what we do, where we live, and much other material; and the Bureau of Labor Statistics releases figures on the cost of living, which in turn are geared into many negotiated wage contracts. But part of it cannot escape classification as almost pure propaganda.

Just how does "image making" work?

Erlend A. Kennan and Edmund H. Harvey, Jr., in *Mission to the Moon: A Critical Examination of NASA and the Space Program* (Morrow, 1969), claimed that the space agency public relations personnel, with assists from media, had sought to turn the early astronauts into "larger-than-life scientist-athletes, Buck Rogers, Jack Armstrong, and the Hardy Boys rolled into one" when they were little more than "overglamorized pilots." Thus the public got its heroes, reporters got good news copy, and NASA, at least in the early years, got massive federal funding. Yet public interest declined in space voyages after the 1969 "moon walk"—unless some new spectacular was added. This all demonstrated that even when newsmen were willing, when public information was easily available, and when all engines of the communications machinery were "go," to use the space age jargon, the emotions and enthusiasm of the media audience could remain at low level.

Edwin Diamond, long an observer and commentator on the space program, described it this way in the Fall 1969 issue of the *Columbia Journalism Review*:

> NASA must push space spectaculars to win friends, influence Congressmen, and keep the budget appropriations coming in. This public relations factor, as much as abstract doctrines about Freedom of Information and the American Public's Right to Know, accounts for NASA's laudable open-skies policy.

Newsmen covering the first landing of men on the moon in July 1969 generally reported that news coverage arrangements at Cape Kennedy and at Houston were good. For instance, Ed Pipp of the *Detroit News* and a former president of the Aviation/Space Writers Association said, "I'm one of their [NASA's] strongest critics. I'm always giving them hell. But this time I think those guys deserve a lot of accolades." Some of the reporters felt that part of the smooth NASA media operations were due to the pressures that they had put on the space agency during earlier flights, and part to the special efforts of NASA's top brass and information officers to provide especially good service for a voyage that was headed for the history books.

Some of the cynics among the 3,000-plus individuals with NASA accreditations for the Apollo 11 flight commented, "Sure things are going well—but that's because the mission is going okay. Let something go wrong and see how fast or well NASA will inform the public." However, when the Apollo 13 mission did not go well, the agency's public information machinery came through with at least a passing grade.

Possibly NASA had learned by the tragic experience when three astronauts died in a January 1967 Apollo fire at Cape Kennedy. After releasing piecemeal information—"presumably to soften the nation's shock," some observers said later—NASA disclosed that all three crew members had been killed. This, however, came to reporters a full two hours after the blaze was first detected. The agency's information people said they had waited to notify the astronauts' next of kin.

How successful public relations procedures can be in raising funds for a voluntary health agency is illustrated by the early history of the National Foundation for Infantile Paralysis (now The National Foundation). The annual campaigns, generously supported by the U.S. public, became a classic case history of "a highly successful pattern to raise money and interest people in the conquest of diseases that afflict mankind," as they were described by one of the most knowledgeable commentators on public relations, Prof. Scott M. Cutlip of the University of Wisconsin.

Seeking treatments that would help him overcome the infantile paralysis which he suffered in August 1921, Franklin D. Roosevelt became interested in a resort hotel at Warm Springs, Ga., seventy-five miles southwest of Atlanta. On April 29, 1926, the future president signed an arrangement to purchase the entire property. Basil (Doc) O'Connor, FDR's law partner, who was drafted later to become the Foundation head, said that he thought Roosevelt was "crazy to want that big goddam four-story firetrap with the squirrels running in and out of the holes in the roof." As FDR became first New York State governor and then president, O'Connor sought various ways to rescue the nearly bankrupt Warm Springs project. In 1933, Carl Byoir, a highly successful public relations man, became interested in the program and set up a professional fund-raising activity—the President's Birthday Ball parties, to be held Jan. 30, 1934. With only two months to promote the parties, Byoir succeeded in swamping the country's press and radio with publicity. Wiley Post, who had flown around the globe, piloted him across the nation to organize local committees. Howard Chandler Christy painted a poster to promote the event. And, possibly most important as it turned out, Walter

Winchell, columnist and broadcaster, concluded one of his appeals, "I remain Mrs. Winchell's bad little boy, Walter, who urges all of you to attend the various dances held in honor of the President on his birthday, January 30th. Because if you buy a ticket to dance, then some little child who can't even walk may be able to dance some day." Byoir's publicists adopted the slogan, "Dance so that a child may walk." Press estimates at the time said that some 6,000 events were held in approximately 3,600 communities. A happy president, on May 9, 1934, received a yard-long, eighteen-inch-wide parchment check for $1,003,030.08. During the ceremony, FDR turned to Byoir and said, "Carl, I'll bet you a good tie that you can't top this figure next year." So the President's Birthday parties became an annual fund-raising event. Byoir won his tie when the total raised for 1935 amounted to $1,071,000. Despite the continuing financial successes, however, criticism arose and the need for another approach toward fund raising grew obvious.

On Sept. 22, 1937, from Hyde Park, President Roosevelt announced establishment of the National Foundation for Infantile Paralysis as a permanent, independent organization and named O'Connor as head of the Foundation. A new appeal to "the mind, heart, and pocketbook of the United States" came from this revised setup—the annual March of Dimes. Eddie Cantor, radio comedian, suggested at a committee meeting in Hollywood that sought to recruit stars for the 1938 Birthday celebrations, "We could ask the people to send their dimes directly to the President at the White House. We could call it the March of Dimes." The idea was brought to O'Connor in New York and eventually checked with the President, who responded, "Go ahead." Thus the March of Dimes was launched. Tom Wrigley, Elmira, N.Y., newspaperman and veteran Hearst employee who had turned to publicity work, was named director of the Foundation's publicity. Another former Hearst employee, Dorothy Ducas (Mrs. James B. Herzog in private life) took charge of women's activities and was to play a dynamic role in polio public relations until 1960. The first March of Dimes raised a total of $268,000 in money sent to the White House; the Foundation's first campaign received $1,823,045.46. These funds and subsequent money from other drives were used for care of those crippled by polio, research for prevention, and general information about the disease for the public. Campaign activities disseminated polio information along with the emotional appeals for helping the crippled children. As writer Richard Carter said of the early March of Dimes programs, "The new foundation possessed medical credentials that the old birthday-ball group had lacked."

As a result of the 1952 peak polio outbreak and another near-record two years later, the Foundation undertook two 1954 campaigns: the regular January one which raised $54,000,000 and a supplementary drive during the summer which brought an additional $12,000,000 for a record-breaking total of some $66,000,000 collected by a volunteer health agency within twelve months. The research grants paid off handsomely with development of vaccines by Dr. Jonas Salk and Dr. Albert Sabin, who used two different approaches to immunization. Activities then had to mobilize popular support for field tests and eventually mass innoculations as well as raise funds. Success of these programs can be measured by the virtual elimination of polio as a health danger to young Americans when they follow the advice disseminated by the Foundation. Development of the two vaccines led the National Foundation to select its new and more appropriate name as it reoriented its objectives toward the prevention and treatment of birth defects. Americans did not open their pocketbooks for the new appeal to the extent that they had during the 1950's for eradication of polio but the National Foundation remains one of the country's leading fund-raising voluntary health groups.

According to statistics compiled on American philanthropy, the top ten national health agencies raised approximately $2,500,000,000 during 1970. Figures from the American Association of Fund-Raising Councils, Inc., showed the leaders in amounts raised during fiscal year 1970 as follows:

Agency	Amount
American Cancer Society, Inc.	$65,246,696
American Heart Association, Inc.	44,172,504
National Tuberculosis & Respiratory Disease Assn.	39,955,264
The National Foundation	24,743,286
National Easter Seal Society for Crippled Children and Adults	24,504,537
National Association for Retarded Children	20,500,000 (est.)
Planned Parenthood Federation of America	17,000,000 (est.)
United Cerebral Palsy Assn., Inc.	13,700,000
National Association for Mental Health, Inc.	10,691,000
Muscular Dystrophy Associations of America, Inc.	10,171,146

For those who demand a dollars and cents aspect before making a judgment, these figures on successful appeals to Americans' pocketbooks by the voluntary health agencies provide about the most impressive measure around on how effective public relations and mass informational efforts can be.

Sophisticated students of communications claim that the truly damaging ingredient for all three areas of business, governmental, and institutional public relations is a lazy, incompetent, or hurried newsman who does not take the time and effort to uncover information that may not have been handed out in the news release. Both practitioners and newsmen agree that few facts can long be hidden from a reporter who uses probing questions, has the time really to investigate, and possesses the inclination to locate background data that aren't immediately available but that must be uncovered and publicized to flesh out the news. Some critics have said that public relations puts something over on the media—and indirectly on the public—only when newsmen are derelict in their own responsibilities. Most of the time there is no sinister effort to hide information, anyway. A puff story on a budding starlet from Hollywood may appear on front pages and in newscasts—if there is an unusual twist that tickles the funny bone or provides human interest appeal. The newsmen's rationale is, "Why not? Who is hurt? And besides, it is a good story!" But when news coverage turns to serious items that have a real social impact, responsible newsmen raise quite different questions— those that unearth what is needed for a meaningful appreciation of the event and the idea. Thus, when there is criticism of public relations one should look for possibilities of some correspondents' not-always-obvious inefficiency or laziness as well as for dirty tricks by PR operators. The working press does not freely admit this all the time—but it is true.

During the 1970's, as social turbulence increases (which it surely will), the need for a corporate and social conscience will become greater and greater; as this happens, talented PR practitioners should move increasingly to the fore. As *Time* (July 7, 1967) said:

> To the extent that p.r. men respect the intelligence of the public, the public will respect them, as helpers in the increasingly difficult struggle to unravel the complex situations and cryptic messages of modern life.

This attitude combined with an alert and intelligent media performance will provide social pluses in the processes of creating an informed public and enlightened opinion. As medical discoveries proliferate, public relations can help create public understanding and promote use of new treatments and medications, many of which arise from the operations of nonprofit health organizations supported by public contributions. In an ideal situation, then, about all that remains to becloud the situation are the biases and prejudices of the public itself, which are matters of increasing concern for psychologists and educators. But one should never forget that this is not an ideal world and the pull of profits, power, and prestige from publicity and "image" will be with us for a long time. If most people are aware of the deviations from reality and truth, the damages will be minimized, and in this informed environment publicity undoubtedly will have a value.

13. Who's to Keep the Media's Conscience?

With all the oft-cited pressures on the media, who is to insure that the press does its job? Can reporters, editors, producers, publishers, and station owners patrol and police their own efforts? In short, who will keep the media's conscience?

As all communications come under mounting charges of bias and prejudice, of serving other than commonly accepted ideas and ideals, and of supposedly flawed and inaccurate performances, the fact looms increasingly large that competent observers (including intelligent, nonprofessional members of their audiences) may have to study and even to monitor the activities and then to ascertain who is right and who is wrong in the baffling welter of controversy over press actions or lack of them.

Many readers, listeners, and viewers feel that newsmen should not —possibly cannot—undertake this assignment of self-evaluation with real effectiveness. Most print and broadcast journalists naturally have a deep involvement in their work and to expect them to be impartial would be asking for Solomon-like fairness. If mediamen were all angels, this might work, but some practitioners would not thus qualify. But I, for one (and I am sure I am not alone), would be reluctant to surrender the rights to censor and to suppress *my* reading matter or *my* broadcast programs to politicians, to lawyers and judges, or to any other special group.

Again, then, who is to keep the media on a proper track, assuming that "proper" can be meaningfully defined? What we may have to do is to borrow from some recent experimental press councils set up in smaller U.S. communities and from foreign countries' media supervision. Such an independent, impartial agency might be a media review board or one individual operating either as an ombudsman, such as in Sweden, a "resident critic," as now on the *Washington Post,* or a "readers' referee" as in Minneapolis. Charged with observing and evaluating what the press does and then issuing a report, such a group or person would use the methods of effective communications and, with some luck, there would be future improvements. This machinery would depend solely on the power of publicity, rather than any form of compulsion or penalty. It would not be a governmental commission with official powers. It would not be some other professional body trying to impose its own standards on the press.

Quite a few pluses are going for such an arrangement. For instance:

★ By providing an institutionalized channel for considering the wide range of attacks on the press, a media review board or, possibly, an ombudsman would sort out the crackpot comments and the self-seeking propagandistic criticisms so that credible observations and objections would receive serious attention and be fed into the informational system. This would provide newsmen and the general public with the necessary data to evaluate criticisms and, if necessary, to act upon them.

★ By establishing minimum standards for reporting, editing, and dissemination of news, such machinery could protect media from being tarred by the irresponsible actions of their own less reliable members and could guard the people from repetitions of such defects in the future —if publishers and station owners listened. General acceptance of such an operation would insure that attention would be paid to the findings.

★ By repeatedly stressing the need for a free and responsible media, these new agencies would serve a useful educational function in telling readers, listeners, and viewers that they are the real losers when the media bow to outside pressures and serve not them but some special interest, be it governmental, political, industrial, or individual.

★ By spreading truth, rather than current myths and fantasies, such an arrangement would improve the general level of press credibility. With a truly informed people, it would become increasingly difficult for the government to evade the First Amendment guarantees. Just what lengths a U.S. government official may strive to reach is illustrated by a 1971 order from Governor John M. Haydon, Jr., of American Samoa to deport the editor of a newspaper there which had been critical of the islands' administration.

Establishment of some kind of media review agency would bypass objections that some American editors and publishers have to organizing a group of their journalistic peers to monitor others in the field. Who, some of these objectors ask, is So-and-so that he should tell me how to run my newspaper or broadcasting station? Furthermore, these individuals argue, this smacks of violating the First Amendment guarantees (at least, for print). Nevertheless, some journalists probably would have to be members of any reviewing group to provide the know-how for sophisticated evaluations of what was taking place, why it was done, and of potential alternatives.

Such a media review board or ombudsman could borrow from the experiences of systems established in several Scandinavian countries and the United Kingdom. Also it could draw on recent experiments in this country so that it would not have to be an innovation untried in the United States.

Oldest of the press council prototypes is that in Sweden, dating from 1916. With a high ranking jurist as chairman of the board—or court of honor, as the Swedes call it—to hear complaints by individuals who feel they have been maltreated by the press, other members include representatives of the National Press Club, the Swedish newspaper publishers association, and the journalists trade union. In November 1969, two public members were added as well as a press ombudsman, a free-wheeling individual, drawn from the ranks of the Swedish judiciary, who has the power to defend the public interest by bringing complaints on his own initiative. Previously, complaints were filed only when somebody felt a paper had treated him in a manner which, without being criminal, "militates against the dictates of honour or is of a nature which for other reasons should not remain unchallenged with a view to the reputation of the press."

A short "code of conduct" adopted by the National Press Club provides that, within the legal freedom of the press provisions, there must be "rules to prevent the publication of incorrect reports and reports harmful because they are incomplete, and also for the protection of the individual from needless suffering."

Final board action consists of a statement on whether the paper's behavior had or had not been in keeping with "good newspaper practice," together with reasons for the decision. Tradition built up during the decades of operation requires the paper involved to print the board's statement without any comments of its own. Thus, an injured party has his day in the court of public opinion. If fair-minded men and women reach a "decision" against the medium, it would seem to indicate that the complaining party certainly has some merits to his case. The statement also is distributed to the entire press for possible publication. Decisions are not based on hard and rigid rules but on what the board or court of honor members believe is qualified opinion in each particular case.

Somewhat comparable courts of honor have been set up in Switzerland, where the system was launched in 1938, and in Denmark.

Americans have heard most about the British Press Council, which grew out of a formal inquiry by a royal commission into media activities after the House of Commons adopted a motion in 1946 to further "the free expression of opinion through the press and the greatest practicable accuracy in the presentation of news." Although a bulky document was handed to Parliament in June 1949, Britain's press proprietors resisted the proposal to establish a "General Council of the Press consisting of at least twenty-five members representing proprietors, editors, and other journalists and having lay members amounting to about 20 per cent of the total, including the chairman." It required another threatening move by the House of Commons to force the first "General Council of the Press" meeting in 1953. Activities became largely a debating society with endless and aimless discussions. Ten years later, the House of Commons approved another royal commission report and in mid-1963 a renovated Press Council with Lord Devlin as chairman began work. It had no enforcement power and used only the power of publicity to seek its goals. But it has become, as one American writer said, "the model for affording the reading public at least a fair hearing." And after the rejuvenated Press Council had had a chance to make a record, six out of seven British newsmen in a 1969 survey approved its activities.

Besides an independent chairman, the British Press Council includes five lay members plus twenty additional representatives of such press organizations as The Newspaper Publishers Association Ltd., The Newspaper Society, The Scottish Daily Newspaper Society, Scottish Newspaper Proprietors Association, Periodical Publishers Association, The Guild of British Newspaper Editors, National Union of Journalists, and The Institute of Journalists. Thus it represents owners, editors, unionized workers, and general public, although each group does not have an equal proportion of the membership.

Because of common interests and approaches in the two cultures, the experience of the British Press Council provides a backdrop for how a somewhat similar agency might work in the United States. H. Phillip Levy, a barrister who headed the legal department for the London *Daily Mirror,* examined the more than four hundred cases that came before the British council during its first thirteen and a half years of existence and found that more than half of the complaints were rejected. A special committee screened out the most frivolous complaints. In his book *The Press Council; History, Procedure and Cases* (St. Martin, 1968), Levy reported the top categories for cases upheld by council members were in the following order of descending percentage (number of cases involved is in parentheses):

Eavesdropping, 100.0% (3)
Reporting court proceedings, 83.3% (12)
Reporting the schools, 80.0% (10)
Sensationalism and distortion, 63.6% (11)
Persons who should not be named, such as minors and adults who legal authorities had requested not be identified in news items, 61.9% (21)
Breaking of embargoes with complaints from other newspapers, 60.0% (5)
Lack of (or inadequate) corrections and apologies, 54.5% (33)
News from hospitals or doctors, 50.0% (14)

On the other hand, the types of cases that were rejected most frequently, in descending order, included:

Confidential occasions, 100.0% (4)
Confidential documents, 83.3% (12)
Treatment of sex, 75.0% (4)
Unfair comments, 73.0% (26)
Politics and political parties, 63.6% (11)
Bad taste, 61.5% (26)
Refusal to print or editing of letters to editor, 61.2% (49)
Intrusions or invasions of privacy, 57.1% (35)

Although more complaints were rejected than upheld in the overall total, council members supported the complainants in more than half of the cases filed in each of the cited categories in the first listing. Further, on the basis of this study, council members felt the press erred most frequently—in actual number of complaints upheld—in regard to failure to make proper corrections or apologies for journalistic errors and in the identification of individuals in the news even after legal authorities had requested that such persons not be named. Specific cases in which the British Council censured the press included publishing a photograph of a reformed criminal, identifying a female victim of rape, naming a convicted murderer's wife who had adopted another name and moved to a different community, and reproducing the marriage certificate of a man sentenced as a spy which gave the name and address of his wife and her father.

The largest group of complainants (after about one out of five who were not identified) involved officers or board members of a local government—town, borough, county, or urban district authority. This category amounted to about one-eighth of the total. However, only one complaint out of sixteen arose from a political candidate or party.

Even before the first British proposal for a press council had been handed to Parliament, Americans were thinking about some way to monitor media performance. In 1947, the Commission on Freedom of the Press (sometimes called the Hutchins Commission because it was headed by the then chancellor of the University of Chicago) made general suggestions without going into the details of establishing a review board system. Instead, the Commission in its report *A Free and Responsible Press* (University of Chicago Press, 1947), proposed that "the members of the press engage in vigorous mutual criticism" and recommended "the establishment of a new and independent agency to appraise and report annually upon the performance of the press." In addition to inquiries into exclusions of minority groups from "reasonable access to the channels of communication," the Commission report advocated, "investigation of instances of press lying, with particular reference to persistent misrepresentation of the data required for judging public issues." An interesting and useful concept but Commission members did not specify just how the goals were to be achieved.

Twenty-two years later, *Mass Media and Violence,* a report to the National Commission on the Causes and Prevention of Violence (also known as the Eisenhower Commission because its chairman was the brother of the late President), cited "a need for greater interaction between the news media and the community and for responsible criticism of media performance." The National Commission task force advocated that this be done by internal as well as external reviewing agencies. Its report expanded on these as follows:

(1) News organizations should establish and publicize the existence of grievance machinery or internal appeal boards to hear the complaints of persons who feel that their viewpoint has been unfairly excluded from the press or that the press coverage of an event in which they were involved is inaccurate. Such a program has worked well at the *Louisville Courier-Journal.*

(2) News organizations should encourage local press councils to provide a continuing exchange of views between the news media personnel and representative members of the community.

Thus, the notion of evaluating media performances has been bruited about for at least a generation in this country. Between 1947 and the release of the Eisenhower Commission's report, some experiments had been held in local press councils in U.S. communities (most of them smaller size). These councils were set up during the 1960's by the Mellett Fund for a Free and Responsible Press, which was instituted under the will of Lowell Mellett, one-time Washington, D.C., editor, to "stimulate responsibility in the press while maintaining freedom." The Fund provided financing for demonstration councils, first in four smaller cities and then in Seattle and in St. Louis. Results were mixed but they were impressive enough in Bend, Ore., and in Sparta, Ill., where publishers of the *Bulletin,* a daily, and the *News-Plaindealer,* the Sparta weekly, liked the informal monthly sessions of frank comments, and in Seattle, for many newsmen to advocate extension of the experimentation. Henry McLeod, managing editor of the *Seattle Times,* called the council's effort there "immensely useful" and Ben H. Bagdikian, president of the Mellett Fund and now with the *Washington Post,* commented, "I do believe that the existence of the Seattle council has avoided serious trouble for that city."

A typical procedure for these U.S. demonstration press councils was to gather monthly in a private dining room of a local restaurant with the publisher (and possibly members of his staff) and the citizens who served as panelists. These laymen have been described as "regular readers who were not afraid to speak up," by Prof. William B. Blankenburg, now of the University of Wisconsin, who served as secretary to the Bend group and another at Redwood, Calif., during the late 1960's. Representative of other setups, council members at Bend included a circuit court judge, a surgeon, a truck driver, a social worker, a laboratory technician, two lumber executives, a piano teacher, and a Ford dealer. While all admitted that it was not a perfect cross-section of the rural community of approximately 13,000, the Bend council comprised much of the spectrum of local viewpoints.

Primarily, the nine laymen told the publisher about the informational needs of the community as they saw them rather than evaluated performance. That was not surprising since, at the beginning, the laymen lacked expertise to make complicated judgments. As Blankenburg said in *Columbia Journalism Review* (Spring, 1969), "The first, and easily overlooked, chore of a press council is to educate itself in the mechanics and traditions of journalism." Also, despite occasional news stories and a request for readers to write to the council, none did more than approach members in person with their reactions and observations. Not a single letter was received. When council members suggested that the Bend publisher assign a photographer to take night publicity pictures, he retorted that his staffer worked fifty hours a week during the daytime and he refused to send him out at night. The council seemed satisfied.

Summing up his observations, Blankenburg wrote:

> In retrospect it seems clear that a press council can have effect because of its sheer presence. A hidden value in press councils is their ability to require busy journalists to reflect on their work.
>
> Likewise, council members acquire an appreciation of the journalistic craft, its opportunities and limitations. . . . Each council rated its newspaper more highly at the end than at the beginning, and members were able to make more discriminating evaluations.

Possibly, more significant than the foreign experiences or the experimental U.S. press councils are several fairly recent efforts to introduce the ombudsman idea on nationally renowned dailies in Louisville, Washington, D.C., and St. Petersburg, Fla. The earliest of these grew out of a magazine article, "What's Wrong with American Newspapers?" for *The New York Times Sunday Magazine* (June 11, 1967), in which A. H. Raskin proposed that U.S. dailies establish "their own Department of Internal Criticism to check on the fairness and accuracy of their coverage and comment." He pointed out that such a department head should have enough independence to serve as "an Ombudsman for the readers" and enough authority "to get something done about valid complaints and to propose methods for more effective performance of all the paper's services to the community, particularly the patrol it keeps on the frontiers of thought and action." The traditional "letters to the editor" columns, Raskin said, were not enough for a paper that "boasts of itself as the community's window on the world."

One intrigued reader of that article was Norman E. Isaacs, longtime editor of the *Louisville Courier-Journal* and *Louisville Times* and prominent figure in various journalism organizations for years. On June 19, Isaacs announced to his staffs that John Herchenroeder was assuming ombudsman functions for the Louisville papers. During his first year, Herchenroeder processed approximately 400 complaints, the following year, approximately 500—plus, as he explained, "a very few compliments." From Sept. 1, 1969, to Sept. 1, 1970, he handled 1,624 telephoned complaints or suggestions from readers and 514 from those who wrote the ombudsman. In addition, he processed a number of circulation department complaints that came his way.

At Louisville, the ombudsman goes directly to the reporter or editor involved and gets complete information on each instance. He submits case-by-case reports to the associate publisher, executive editor, managing editors of *Courier-Journal* and *Times,* and the public service director.

Commenting on his several years of experience, Herchenroeder wrote:

> In some cases, the newspaper clarified the news story, in others we admitted we made an error and said we were sorry. The Ombudsman also learned that "internal criticism" was a most difficult and touchy part of the job.
>
> Some complaints also came in that were directed to the circulation and advertising departments. . . . for the first time we have a continuing flow of information about reader reaction, a sort of Early Warning System.

On the *Washington Post,* starting in September 1970, Richard Harwood, with the title of assistant managing editor, became involved exclusively as the daily's "resident critic." A reporter or editor for more than two decades, Harwood saw his job as more than just an ombudsman or in-house representative of the readership and so criticized the news product regularly for the *Post*'s publisher, editors, and the staff. For example, a loud complaint from the Department of Justice brought a front-page apology to Attorney General John Mitchell who had been misquoted in a news item. In addition, Harwood kept up a stream of private memoranda to Mrs. Katharine Graham, publisher, and her associates. He said:

> My job is mainly monitoring the paper for fairness, balance and perspective. If I see something wrong, and they agree with it, they put out a memo and fix it.

Unlike the arrangement at Louisville, Harwood claimed that he may anticipate complaints. During the first year, he contributed discussions of "problems and controversies in news coverage" for publication and thus the enlightenment of *Post* readers. One explained practices at the "Presidential backgrounder" briefings of the Nixon Administration and another, after the November 1970 congressional elections, discussed "Columnists on the Meanings, if Any, of Elections." Harwood's barbed remarks on the contradictory postmortems reportedly outraged some of the syndicated writers for the *Post*. Remarked one veteran who was not one of the targets, "For some unknown reason, newspapermen despise having mistakes corrected in print. The mere fact of confirming error just sends them up the wall." Commenting on a trial that received columns of news space and an acquittal rating only a few lines, Harwood's memo commented, "We are great on indictments and short on acquittals." Executive Editor Ben Bradlee of the *Post* approved the project and commented, "Just because it's hard doesn't mean we shouldn't do it."

On the *St. Petersburg Times* and *Evening Independent,* Del Marth was named "The People's Voice" in November 1970, and during his early months on the job he received as many as ten letters and forty phone calls daily. His telephone does not go through any switchboard operator or secretary; he answers it himself. Marth reported that readers felt that "I'm one of them even though they know I sit behind a desk at The Times Publishing Company." When there is sufficient material, he writes a column giving readers' comments and sometimes his replies. He explained his goal as "to achieve maximum accuracy and fair play in our newspapers for the benefit of all our readers." He said he felt he was effective because he had absolute authority to say and write what he believed was necessary.

The St. Petersburg operation grew out of a speech by Nelson Poynter, board chairman of the Times Publishing Company, during which he said:

> Editor and reader need a hot line to build mutual confidence which will make the press a more effective instrument for building a more responsive government and society.

Too often, however, media operations have been business-as-usual. As a result a tinder pile of frustration, resentment, and anger among the mass audience has increased rapidly. Vice-President Spiro T. Agnew's criticism of both broadcasting and print ignited what already had been smoldering for some years.

Thus it was little wonder that Norman E. Isaacs wrote as follows in the *Columbia Journalism Review* (Fall, 1970):

> If the polls are correct—and I do not challenge them—journalism can not continue to sweep the idea [of some sort of monitoring] under the rug. One fairly recent Gallup Poll reported that only 37 per cent of the public feels newspapers deal fairly on political and social issues. Some 45 per cent think newspapers unfair. Listed as not sure were 18 per cent. It is significant that the more highly educated the person questioned, the stronger the feeling that newspapers were unfair. . . .
>
> I considered and still consider the Agnew attacks a form of intimidation of the press. Though his more recent approaches stress "sensible authority," it is not inconceivable that a drive for "sensible authority" could be stretched to the creation of an overview agency by government ostensibly to preserve and protect the First Amendment freedoms. Far better, I hold, for the press to create its own protection. . . .
>
> We needed to be rebuilding faith in the American press; the shrugging off of inaccuracy and slanting in news columns was the most dangerous course we could follow. An ethics or grievance committee—or, if you will, a press council—seemed to be an effective way to deal with the situation.

Fears, some legitimate and some seemingly fantastic, have been expressed about the proposals to form press councils in this country. There is no question that an effective operation would restrict an editor's freedom of action if only by making him more responsible for inaccuracies and slanting in the news he printed—and thus impelling him to do a better job. But that really is not the key objection, obviously, although some publishers and some editors seem to regard the First Amendment guarantees as granting to them rights to any kind of activity short of outright murder. Not very far in the background of such monitoring considerations are (1) the possibility of licensing newsmen and (2) the successful application of community pressure to cow editors into submitting to majority opinions.

Dr. W. Walter Menninger, psychiatrist and member of the National Commission on the Causes and Prevention of Violence, nullified much of that group's support for local press councils when he went to the National Press Club in Washington early in 1970 and called for journalists to meet the same practices as doctors, lawyers, and educators: ". . . laws for licensure and certification assure the public that the practitioner has fulfilled minimum standards, met certain requirements for training and demonstrated competence in the profession." The prospect of regulating the profession in this way—of saying who could be a journalist and under what circumstances—raised totalitarian nightmares. Even Dr. Menninger in a later speech in his home town of Topeka, Kan., conceded that he might have chosen "the wrong word to emphasize a concern about professional standards in journalism" and that, given the First Amendment, there undoubtedly would be "many legal, constitutional, and procedural problems that would make certification or licensure of journalists by law well nigh impossible."

Certainly any licensing of journalists in the United States would have to be instigated over the limp bodies of many working newsmen and their bosses. One Midwestern editor commented:

American publishers approach the issue of self-sanitation as the reluctant bride faces her wedding night. The publishers want to be loved but they fear the process of pregnancy.

What may be accepted for doctors, lawyers, and educators does not automatically translate into good practice for newsmen. Journalists who work more in the fields of ideas and creativity—on occasion—should not be put in straitjackets.

Another objection to monitoring and evaluation centers around the idea that an editor of either print or broadcasting should have the chance and the courage to buck the majority of his own community. If there is no place at all for courage, even if only rarely utilized, then most editors might as well be replaced by computers programed to scan public opinion polls and utilize the results for playback in editorials, cartoons, opinion columns—and, where the greatest damage may be done in creating a democratic and informed public reaction, in the news coverage and its positioning.

J. Russell Wiggins, former executive editor of the *Washington Post* who quit his job to represent this country briefly at the United Nations, was concerned about the reinforcing effect that such local press councils would have in tightening the Establishment's hold, already not insignificant, on the local mass media. Such mechanisms, he properly pointed out, could easily become "channels through which the very worst special-interest groups would bring pressures to suppress or withhold news." These groups could make "the collective opinion of the community irresistible at the very moment when that opinion was the most misguided and most in need of contradiction and restraint." One has only to recall the actions of most German newspapermen and broadcasters under the lash of the Hitler regime to realize that editorial bravery can be a rare commodity, in scarcest supply when needed most. Institutionalization of criticism might stifle such independence as remains and, as Isaacs put it, "most middle-sized and smaller newspapers are already, to some degree, prisoners of 'the establishment.' "

Already the philosophy that the First Amendment guarantees should be restricted and reinterpreted is in the arena of public discussion. Under this proposal, the communications complex would be converted into something like a public utility, such as telephone service or a community's sewage system. Most prominent of its advocates during the 1960's was Prof. Jerome A. Barron, who wrote a frequently cited presentation for the *Harvard Law Review* in 1967. He argued that media monopolization in the twentieth century and other contemporary trends demanded that an affirmative responsibility be imposed under the First Amendment if the "marketplace" theory was to operate in the present economic and communications environment. He wrote, in part:

> What is required is an interpretation of the first amendment which focuses on the idea that restraining the hand of government is quite useless in assuring free speech if a restraint on access is effectively secured by private groups. A constitutional prohibition against governmental restrictions on expression is effective only if the Constitution ensures an adequate opportunity for discussion. Since this opportunity exists only in the mass media, the interests of those who control the means of communication must be accommodated with the interests of those who seek a forum in which to express their point of view. . . .
>
> If the mass media are essentially business enterprises and their commercial nature makes it difficult to give a full and effective hearing to a wide spectrum of opinion, a theory of the first amendment is unrealistic if it prevents courts or legislatures from requiring the media to do that which, for commercial reasons, they would be otherwise unlikely to do. . . .

The changing nature of communications process has made it imperative that the law show concern for the public interest in effective utilization of media for the expression of diverse points of view. Confrontation of ideas, a topic of eloquent affection in contemporary decisions, demands some recognition of a right to be heard as a constitutional principle. It is the writer's position that it is open to the courts to fashion a remedy for a right of access, at least in the most arbitrary cases, independently of legislation. If such an innovation is judicially resisted, I suggest that our constitutional law authorizes a carefully framed right of access statute which would forbid an arbitrary denial of space, hence securing an effective forum for the expression of divergent opinions.

With the development of private restraints on free expression, the idea of a free marketplace where ideas can compete on their merits has become just as unrealistic in the twentieth century as the economic theory of perfect competition. The world in which an essentially rationalist philosophy of the first amendment was born has vanished and what was rationalism is now romance.

Prof. Barron's arguments generally are opposed by media managers, both print and broadcast, but his idea may provide a rationale for imposing new ways on the dissemination of news, opinions, and ideas. Already the Federal Communications Commission has expanded its "fairness doctrine" to mandate airing of differing, rebuttal viewpoints over the airways. And minority groups, especially the blacks during the early 1970's, have been successful in moderating long-standing station policies (some of which definitely were racist) when they mobilized aggressively to complain at license hearings. Potential loss of authorizations worth multimillion dollars has proved a powerful prod to force ideological modifications toward better "marketplace" programing. The FCC's power to approve or to reject license applications presents an opportunity for evaluation of broadcasters' operations. For instance, the Commission does judge how well a station has lived up to its own promises to serve its home community, as outlined in its original application, and poor marks in this category have caused many anxious moments for those whose actions have not conformed to their pledges. The National Association of Broadcasters, too, has used a code for performance to govern station operations to a far greater degree than editors and publishers ever have done with any of the professional print credos.

The concept of an independent, outside monitoring and evaluating agency has implications for broadcasting and print that would be more palatable than imposition of any sort of A. T. & T. regulations by what might become the news division of a state or federal public service commission. A truly impartial evaluating agency, such as a media review board, would have far more pluses than minuses in comparison with public utility regulations, at least for the professionals and probably for the public as well.

Neither the motivations for journalistic procedures nor the procedures of such a media review board can be cleanly outlined like a series of rates for the regulated prices of natural gas or electricity. Too many subjective values are involved for such massive and exacting classifications. However, there is no reason why editorial judgments should not be studied and, yes, even evaluated. The media are not above criticism—and improvement—and if this is done intelligently, rather than emotionally and self-servingly, they and the public should both gain. In the fall of 1971, the first state review board, or press council, was established for Minnesota and, if the anticipated pluses actually take place, this may well be a model for other such efforts.

Some media evaluations already are being done although the resulting findings are not widely disseminated outside professional circles. If they were, the information might help reduce the antagonisms toward the press. Among the publications which are doing this are the *Columbia Journalism Review,* which celebrated its tenth birthday in 1971; the *Chicago Journalism Review,* a professional fallout after the Chicago Democratic convention coverage; comparable publications in other sections of the country; *Nieman Reports,* put out by the journalism fellows of Harvard University; the almost in-house studies of the *Associated Press Managing Editors,* an independently incorporated organization of representatives from members of the press association; occasional articles in Association for Education in Journalism publications such as *Journalism Quarterly* and *Journalism Monographs;* and infrequent federal and state inquiries into some special aspect of the communications operations.

However, there exists no wide channel for redress open to individuals or organizations that believe they have a substantial grievance against the media for alleged sloppy, incompetent, or vicious actions. Of course, a suit for libel is possible but, as pointed out in Chapter Twelve, during the 1960's this doorway was closed to keyhole size so that a court victory for an injured party now follows only the most flagrant form of journalistic malpractice.

If an ombudsman, with real independence and unintimidated, operates for the media, then anyone believing he has been injured may appeal to him. But, as noted earlier, only a few papers and no major broadcasters have established this procedure. If they had done so, then the need for another channel would be far lessened.

Media review boards could fill this gap. An individual with an objection against one or several of the media and who had tried unsuccessfully to solve his own problem could take his complaint to the review board, stating as many of the specifics as possible. Moreover, it should not be required that he hire an attorney and proceed as if this were a court case. An investigator from a media review board would try to find out all the relevant facts; probably he would (1) talk to the complainant for even further information, (2) obtain copies of the pages or pictures or, in the case of radio and television, tapes of the broadcast, (3) interview representatives of the publication or broadcast station, and, if necessary, (4) ascertain additional information from the probable news source or other informed witnesses. Most frivolous and inconsequential complaints should be filtered out before getting far in this four-stage inquiry.

If a valid case thus appeared to have been documented, then the investigator could suggest (this word "suggest" is mighty important because it never should be an order to media) to the print or broadcasting representative that an injustice seemed to have been done and that possibly the publication or station would want to correct the wrong with a retraction or apology. If this effort failed, then the media review board would set the time and place for a formal hearing with notices to both sides so that a full-dress discussion could be held. After these sessions, a finding or "decision" would be released to all the news channels and agencies and eventually to the general public. What the media did with these findings or facts or "decisions" would, of course, depend on their own operations and their own consciences.

If newsmen did not want to cooperate, the proceeding could move forward as *in absentia* trials are held in some foreign countries. This has a slight smack of antidemocracy, but then this machinery is outside the courts and even the legal system. It depends, as said previously, on that cardinal point of the media themselves: the power of publicity to change things after the people know the facts. Under such circumstances, probably, the publication or station concerned would not publicize the findings but many of the professional journals would, probably reprinting considerable excerpts from them. Certainly this "raw material" on media performance would have far greater usefulness than some of the highly subjective flotsam and jetsam that drift across the contemporary communications scene as supposed criticism. Thus the media could count on a better-informed general audience the next time around.

Should some type of compensation for damages be allowed? Probably not. If an individual wanted to recover with a cash settlement for alleged losses to his business, his reputation, or even his honor, let him proceed exclusively through the court system. There are laws and judges for just those kinds of cases. Why not use them—if money is the principal goal sought? Probably most Americans, if given the chance, would simply want to "see justice done" and would not try to establish a cash value for injured honor or reputation. Even the largely nominal and "symbolic" fines imposed by some of the foreign press councils could well be eliminated from any U.S. counterparts. Actual financial losses resulting from a news item might be something else again and it should be the function of the courts rather than the media review board system to determine damages. At least, that has been the trend overseas.

How would one go about organizing a system of media review boards for all the United States? Should there be a wide range of local operations, expanding into many communities—and especially into the larger metropolitan areas—as the ˙Mellett Fund has been able to do in a very few towns? Or should Americans fit into the common tendency and set up a national superagency or nongovernmental conglomerate group in Washington or New York City to handle the misconducts of the country's communications system in all its parts?

As an initial tentative experiment, I would propose that boards be established on a series of levels, starting at the local scene:

(1) A local board for each area to handle those errors and mistakes that concern only a limited audience and have only, at most, regional distribution. These would be much like nonstaff ombudsmen or the Mellett-funded local press councils. Probably like these, they initially would feed back community opinion and thinking more than evaluate performance. Much of the initial efforts probably would have to depend on the cooperation and financial backing of responsible local media.

(2) A regional or state middle layer of review boards to treat those matters that were spread well beyond a single city or community.

(3) Some type of national organization for the most flagrant and widespread cases. A nationwide agency of some sort would appear desirable because some cases would have impact across the country. For instance, how would several dozen or more local media review boards handle

a news item from Washington, D.C., which allegedly injured some individual and which was printed as a press association dispatch on most front pages of the nation and broadcast from most radio and television stations? Or the misconduct might be against a minority segment or a whole national group. For local boards to conduct repetitive inquiries would be wasteful, at best; self-defeating and confusing, at worst. However, inauguration of the national phase might well wait a couple of years until the merit of the review board idea has been proven first on the local, and then the regional, level.

If and when the three-level review boards were in operation, I would not propose that hearings, like cases in the U.S. courts, be appealable to a higher jurisdiction so that all the key cases would be heard eventually by the national review board. Let the complainant pick his level and, if justified, make him stay with it. These review boards should not be confused with the legal machinery; they are, in a way, the nonviolent equivalent of the old-fashioned system of dueling in that they are designed to satisfy one's honor and reputation, not to enrich one's pocketbook. A finding in an individual's or organization's favor by a local board would be vindication in the eyes of neighbors and acquaintances as much as a national finding.

Even a local media council decision may have far-reaching effects. For instance, the Honolulu Community-Media Council, which brings together a group of laymen with print and broadcast representatives, examined the use of such phrases as "Communist forces," "enemy," and "Reds" in news stories from Southeast Asia when more appropriate and accurate terms might have been "National Liberation Front," "Democratic Republic of Vietnam," "North Vietnamese," and "mainland China." A report from a "committee on euphemisms" in 1971 commented:

> We are particularly concerned with the use of such terms as "Communist" and "enemy" which are too easily employed to refer to a wide variety of people and organizations in Indochina. These terms should be avoided as much as possible in favor of more descriptive terms which accurately designate the people and organizations to which they refer.

The council adopted the committee report unanimously and it was disseminated widely. Roger Tatarian, editor and vice-president of United Press International, which had been mentioned because of its greater use of "Communist" in preference to "North Vietnamese," cited the Honolulu council findings in a newsletter sent to UPI clients and employees. He wrote that "specifics are preferable to generalities and should be used wherever possible." Thus the Honolulu council's action became a basis for an international news service's policy revision.

All media review boards must keep their inquiries away from editorials and commentary. Any publication's or broadcasting station's right to state its subjective comments and opinions should not be called into accountability by such a group. Media review boards' attention should center on the accuracy and validity of news reporting and on questions of ethics and responsible journalism, such as those involving calloused intrusions of privacy, for example, and not be concerned with whether editorials square neatly with local community mores. However, such exemption from inquiry of publications' and stations' editorial position does not imply that they will receive a free ride if they deny others a chance to express their viewpoints. In other words, letters to the editor columns and rebuttal guest editorials can not forever be closed to any sizable segment of a community. Obviously, this poses formidable problems for opinionated proprietors of media—but with a little diplomacy and skill in human relations a blatant case of suppression could be handled, I would suspect, without transgression of the conventional concept of freedom of the press. I would only hope that these would not be the first cases to come before members of a media review board; they could use experiences in the more conventional straight news field before they tangled in this region of opinion and commentary.

Membership of the media review boards poses a whole series of sticky problems.

Essential to any efficient and effective procedure is the requirement of enough journalists to supply technical information on how the media operate. Entirely civilian groups commenting on the press in the past have lost much of their thrust because they just did not know how news was gathered and disseminated. While too many newsmen on a board could bias decisions against complainants who have valid cases but presented them in such a way as to arouse journalistic chauvinism and defense mechanisms, too few newsmen could result in insufficient attention being paid to deadline pressures and other professional and mechanical circumstances, thus divorcing the whole operation from reality and thereby diluting its impact. Possibly individuals recently retired from print or broadcast assignments could supply both a background of know-how and an objectivity somewhat greater than working newsmen involved directly in cases like those under consideration. Again, communities with schools and departments of journalism and communications might tap these resources for board members.

Community leaders, always in demand for launching new projects, could provide the program with at least initial supportive recognition from the Establishment. Obviously, this would be a minus in some sections of the country and among some parts of the populace. To compensate for this, articulate (but probably, if the scheme is to obtain general support, not too abrasive) representatives of non-Establishment viewpoints as well as of any sizable minority groups in a community would have to be included. Obviously, again, it is easier to suggest this than to get such a cross-section to serve.

Recent chairmen in the relatively successful press councils of Britain and the Scandinavian countries have been intelligent laymen as far as media experiences were concerned. And, apparently, they have learned the requisite details about techniques in rapid style. It should be possible to follow the same approach in the United States. Yet some individuals with in-depth knowledge need to serve, even if not as board chairmen, in order to educate the other members.

Failing their outright support and membership participation, at least a guarantee of no violent opposition or sabotage will be necessary from the media managers. They and their associates have the power to block and thwart well-intentioned efforts that others may initiate and try to carry forward—unless, of course, the review system is enacted into law, which could well conflict with First Amendment guarantees. In any case, the whole concept of media review boards, as outlined here, rigorously tries to avoid even the slightest semblance of a powerful governmental bureau with enforcement and punitive authority. To attempt to ram findings of facts and "decisions" down throats of disapproving writers, editors, and broadcasters would negate most of the essential purposes of an impartial, informed board for considering alleged wrongs and, if they turned out to be that, for providing some nonmonetary redress for those hurt. It is a matter of fair play and decency, not promulgating findings by fiat and authority.

Where will the spark for establishing these boards come from? That is a vital question and no easy answer is at hand.

The foundations, which have fueled so many innovative programs since World War II, have displayed, at least until recently, a distinct reluctance to affront publishers, editors, and broadcast executives. This is not without cause. After Sigma Delta Chi, professional journalism society, approved the idea for evaluating the 1956 presidential election coverage, interested foundations made their financing contingent on the approval and cooperation of the nation's newspaper publishers and editors. That group voted overwhelmingly—and vehemently on the part of some representatives—in the negative. The project withered and no wide-range, national study of that sort has ever been conducted. Change, however, is much in the air. Within the next several years, the people who control foundation allocations might be willing to earmark substantial funding for experimental media review boards. (Probably a requirement would be that the term "press council" not be mentioned in any proposal requests or in plans submitted to print or broadcast executives for comments. Such a phrase brings the same reaction as mentioning "socialized medicine" to almost any group of U.S. medical men.)

By participating honestly and actively in the review system, the media would gain substantial advantages in the marketplace of public opinion since much of the current resentment against them arises from the frustrated and angry feelings that one's chances of winning a battle with the press are even less than in the proverbial fight with City Hall. With some modest successes, the media review boards should damp down such sentiments to a substantial degree.

At least, that was the result of Houstoun Waring's several feedback procedures at the *Littleton* (Colorado) *Independent,* semiweekly of a Denver suburban community. In 1946, Waring, then the editor, established an Editorial Advisory Board, which six years later became an annual Critics Dinner. In November 1967, a Community Press Council was set up. Just before its fourth birthday, Waring wrote me:

"Our own Littleton Press Council, which offers criticism three times a year, has prevented any credibility gap here. I think our public image is the best in 83 years."

One argument that should have far greater impact with newsmen in the 1970's than before Vice-President Agnew and others began their current attacks on media is that such review boards might help to educate the general public about the procedures and techniques of print and broadcasting operations. This, alone, would be a tremendous benefit because it could provide what might be called "adult education" for the opinion leaders of each community in which such boards existed.

As Professor J. Edward Gerald, University of Minnesota journalism teacher, wisely explained, an effective media review board or press council would be "a two-phased educational institution," which benefited both public and journalists. To many individuals, including some public officials, it would represent a way of obtaining a public hearing of grievances.

For journalists' benefit, it would force aggrieved individuals to think—possibly for the first time—about the importance of the media and to accept freedom of the press as a principle at once superior to private convenience and indispensable to political freedom.

Criticism and contentiousness from high government circles have alerted the more sensitive and perceptive media managers that they may have to act themselves to avoid regulations and restraints being imposed upon them from outside. It may be that print and broadcast professional organizations and even some individuals and affluent publications and stations—or networks—will agree that it would be far better for them (and for the public which are their audiences) to act now with some freedom of choice on how an evaluating or monitoring system is established than to have one imposed by the government, which undoubtedly would be the worst of all possible solutions. The media would even do well to consider underwriting the initial costs of setting up the system. Such expenditures might be the insurance premiums against governmental actions in which they would have a great deal to lose: probably the true essence of freedom of the press.

When the media do a good job, let them get full credit where all can see—as they would, with the open and full reporting of media review board findings. And when they do a poor job, under a review system they will merely receive public attention comparable to that editorial writers and other commentators have given politicians, private citizens, corporations, and social groups for several centuries.

The credibility gap between the media and their audiences should narrow when (1) the public realizes that newsmen do care about accuracy and fairness and that something can be done when individuals or groups suffer undue harm and (2) readers, listeners, and viewers develop more sophistication about how news is processed. When a majority of the population appreciates that most of those with media are men of good will and good intentions (although they do not always attain their goals), the appeals of the demagogues and others who whip the press for their own selfish reasons should diminish. This, in turn, would enable the media to get on with the business of reporting the news, the bad as well as the good, without fearing the frequent fate of the bearer of ill tidings. Just conceivably, with this improved popular understanding, the news of what is wrong with the world will have greater impact than ever before and more serious efforts will be made to solve the problems described.

For Further Reading

The *Columbia Journalism Review,* issued six times a year now by the Graduate School of Journalism, Columbia University (700 Journalism Building, Columbia University, New York, N.Y. 10027), provides a running account of media developments. It is in its second decade of publication.

In addition to such trade publications as *Advertising Age, Broadcasting Magazine,* and *Editor & Publisher,* a wide range of local and regional reviews, including the *Chicago Journalism Review* and *[MORE]* in New York City, have grown up since 1968. *Nieman Reports* from Harvard University; *IPI Report,* put out by the International Press Institute in Zurich, Switzerland; and such publications of the Association for Education in Journalism as *Journalism Educator, Journalism Monographs,* and *Journalism Quarterly*—all print material of interest to the curious layman from time to time.

The annual *Alfred I. duPont-Columbia University Survey of Broadcast Journalism* takes what it calls "a penetrating and impartial look" at what that medium is doing for television and radio reporting.

Those who want to read the full texts of key decisions in communication-law cases are referred to two widely used textbooks: Donald M. Gillmor and Jerome A. Barron, *Mass Communication Law: Cases and Comment* (West Publishing Co., St. Paul, Minn., 1969) and Harold L. Nelson and Dwight L. Teeter, Jr., *Law of Mass Communications* (The Foundation Press, Mineola, N.Y., 1969).

Index

ABA, *see* American Bar Association

Academy of Television Arts and Sciences, 186

advertisers' influence upon media, 170-190

Advertising Age, 172, 239

Agnew, Spiro T., 5, 8, 23-24, 26-29, 49, 58-59, 66, 139-140, 227

Akerson, George E. 175

Akron Beacon Journal, 110

Alsop, Joseph, 151

American Association of Fund-Raising Councils, 214

American Bar Association, 15-17

American Broadcasting Company, 88, 107-108, 167-168

American Dilemna, An, 95

American Newspaper Publishers Association, 93

American Society of Newspaper Editors, 13, 29, 206

Amsterdam, Anthony, 31

Anderson, Jack, 176

Annenberg, Walter H, 94-95, 143, 166-167

Anti-Defamation League of B'nai B'rith, survey by, 114

Anything but the Truth, 83

APME Guidelines, 183-184

Arkansas Gazette, 176

Arnett, Peter, 19

Ashmore, Harry S., 176

Associated Press, 19, 73, 89-90, 113, 121, 146-149, 159, 168, 201, 210

Associated Press Managing Editors, 5, 107, 109, 112, 231

Association for Education in Journalism, 231, 239

Atlanta Constitution, 139

awards, for media coverage (*see also* Emmy Award; George Foster Peabody Award; George Polk Award; Pulitzer Prize), 184-187

Bache, Benjamin Franklin, 8

Bagdikian, Ben H., 4, 160-161, 172, 223

Baltimore Sun, 139-140

Barnds, William J., 20-21

Barron, Jerome A., 192, 229-230, 239

Batchelor, Charles, 135
Bates, Ted, Company, 70
Bell, James F., 15
Bennett, James Gordon, Sr., 9
Bernays, Edward L., 205
Bickel, Professor Alexander M., 34
Bigart, Homer, 19
Bingham, Barry, Jr., 54
Black, Hugo L., 37-38, 50, 151, 195-196, 198
Blackmun, Harry A., 40
Black Panthers, 6, 30-31, 80
Blakeslee, Alton, 90
Blankenburg, William B., 223-224
Bliss, George, 174-175
Boorstin, Daniel J., 207-208
Boston Globe, 32, 173, 176-177
Boston Herald, 175-176
Boston Herald-Traveler, 173
Boston Herald-Traveler Corporation, 62-64
Boston Traveler, 177
Bradlee, Ben, 226
Brandeis, Louis D., 193
Brennan, William J., 37-38, 191-192, 197-198
Broadcasting Magazine, 239
Brown, Robert U., 208
Browne, Malcolm W., 19
Bryant, Paul, 199-201
Buckley, William F., Jr., 151, 187
Buggs, John, 104-105
Bunker, Ellsworth, 83
Burch, Dean, 29, 65
Burger, Warren E., 32, 34, 39-40, 59-60
Burlington (Vt.) *Free Press,* 5
Burnett, George, 200-201
Burros, Daniel, 202-203
Butts, Wally, 199-201
Byoir, Carl, 212

Caldwell, Earl, 6, 30-31
Calley, William L., Jr., 84
Canterbury, Robert H., 92-93

Carmichael, John, 200
Carpenter, Mrs. Elizabeth, 86
Carrington, Bob, 179
Carter, Richard, 213
CATV, *see* community antenna television systems
CBS-TV News, 21, 26-27, 116
Cervi, Eugene, 155, 178-179
Charlotte (N.C.) *Observer,* 176
Chicago conspiracy trial, 95-96, 128
Chicago Daily News, 83
Chicago Journalism Review, 231, 239
Chicago Sun-Times, 32
Chicago Tribune, 29, 48, 94, 151, 174-175, 181
Chicago Tribune Company, 165-166
Childs, Marquis, 54
Christian, George, 83
Christian Science Monitor, 32, 158, 160
Christy, Howard Chandler, 212
Clark, Ramsey, 55
Clark, Tom, 16, 76
Cleveland Plain Dealer, 56, 120, 150
Cobbett, William, 8
Columbia Broadcasting System, 6, 23, 30-31, 105, 127-128, 131, 167, 174, 194
Columbia Journalism Review, 3, 4, 29, 87, 89, 114, 121, 168, 185, 188, 211, 224, 227, 239
Commission on the Causes and Prevention of Violence, 95
Commission on Freedom of the Press, 222
Communication Act of 1934, 60, 68
Communications Satellite Corporation (Comsat), 69
community antenna television systems (CATV), 69
Comsat, *see* Communications Satellite Corporation
Congress, 3, 5, 6, 23, 31, 37-39, 41, 43, 53, 58, 60, 73-74, 163
Conot, Robert, 104

Courier-Journal, 54
Cowles Communications, 144
Cuban missile crisis, 44, 82
Curry, Jesse E., 132-133
Curtis Publishing Company, 200-201
Cutlip, Scott M., 212

Daniels, Derick, 145
Davis, Elmer, 11, 102
decline in number of dailies, 157-160
DelCorso, Sylvester L., 92-93
Dellinger, David, 96
Democratic convention, 1968 (see also Walker Report), 22-23, 80, 128-129, 138-139
Democratic party, 10, 22-23, 30, 96
Dennis et al. v. United States, 51-53
Denver Post, 179
Des Moines Register, 151
Des Moines Tribune, 151
Desperate Hours, The, 197
Detroit Free Press, 92, 110, 114, 145, 172
Detroit News, 182, 211
Diamond, Edwin, 211
Dickinson, William B., 107
Dispatch News Service, 21
"Doomsday Flight, The," 73
Douglas, William O., 33, 38, 52, 195-196, 198
Dow Jones and Company, 142-145
Ducas, Dorothy, 213
Dulles, John Foster, 44, 73
Dun & Bradstreet, Inc., 143
duPont, Alfred I.–Columbia University Survey of Broadcast Journalism, 26, 69, 108, 117, 145, 152, 239

Editor & Publisher, 125, 131, 144, 158, 174, 184, 208, 239
Editor & Publisher International Yearbook, 157
Eisenhower, Dwight D., 14, 81-82, 86, 131, 139

Elijah P. Lovejoy Award, 177
Eller, James, 176
Emerson, William A., 172-173
Emmy Award, 31, 116, 186
Estes, Billie Sol, 75-77
Etzioni, Amitas, 203
extortion, by newsmen, 181

Fading American Newspaper, The, 178
Failing News Bill, see News Preservation Act
Fairfax, Jean, 48
"fairness doctrine," 66-67
Federal Aviation Administration, 73
Federal Bureau of Investigation, 30, 93, 132
Federal Communications Commission, 27, 29, 46, 58, 60-61, 63, 65-69, 74, 127-128, 143, 146, 150, 159, 161, 168, 230
Federal Trade Commission, 58, 70-71
Federated Publications, Inc., 166
Field Enterprises, 143
Files, Robert, 110-111
Filo, John Paul, 123-125
First Amendment, 2, 4, 17, 30-39, 41-42, 45, 50-54, 62, 67-68, 72-73, 192, 196, 219, 227-229, 236
Fleming, Robert H., 88
Forum Communications, 63
Frank, Reuben, 26
Frankfurter, Felix, 51-53
Free and Responsible Press, A, 222
Freedom of Information Act, 55-56
Friendly, Fred W., 27
Fritz, J. Will, 134
Frontier Broadcasting Company, 64
Funk & Wagnalls, 169

Gallagher, Wes, 89
Gallup, George, 151
Gallup Poll, 227
Gannett Co., Inc., 143-144, 164, 166

Gansberg, Marty, 115
Gardner, Ro, 177
Garst, Roswell, 131
Gelb, Arthur, 203
Genovese, Catherine, 115
Gerald, J. Edward, 237
Gillmor, Donald M., 192, 239
Ginsburg, David, 189-190
Glendon, William R., 34-35
Goltz, George, 186
Gould, Jack, 64
Graham, Mrs. Katharine, 29, 226
gratuities, 182-186
Greeley, Horace, 9
Griffith, Thomas, 101
Griswold, Erwin N., 33, 35-36
Grosjean v. American Press Company, 74
Gurfein, Murray I., 32, 34,

Hagerty, James, 82, 131
Haiman, Robert J., 183-184
Halberstam, David, 19
Hall, Ted, 182
Hannegan v. Esquire, 71
Harlan, John Marshall, 33, 40, 199-201
Harnwell, Gaylord P., 94
Harris, Louis, Poll, 43
Harvard Law Review, 61, 193, 211, 229
Harwood, Richard, 103, 225-226
Hayakawa, S. I., 125-126
Haydon, John M., Jr., 219
Hearst Headline Service, 147
Hearst, William Randolph, 9, 80, 163, 165
Heilbroner, Robert, 205
Heiskell, John Netherland, 176
Hemingway, Ernest, 112
Herchenroeder, John, 225
Hersh, Seymour M., 21, 87
Hickel, Walter, 84
Hickman (Ky.) *Courier,* 177

history of media as institution in modern society, 2-3, 8-13, 45-46, 99-100, 102, 194, 197-199
Hoffman, Julius J., 96
Holmes, Oliver Wendell, 50, 53
Honolulu Community-Media Council, 234
Honolulu Star-Bulletin, Inc., 166
Hoover, Herbert, 59
Hornby, W. H., 180
Horvitz, Harry, 150
Hosty, James Patrick, Jr., 132
House Committee on Interstate and Foreign Commerce, 22-23, 31
House of Representatives, 6
Houston Post, 186
Hughes, Charles E., 42
Humphrey, Hubert, 89, 90
Hutchins Committee, *see* Commission on Freedom of the Press

Image, The: A Guide to Pseudo-Events in America, 207-208
International Radio and Television Society, 48
International Telephone and Telegraph Corporation, 167-169
invasion of privacy, 191-216
Isaacs, Norman E., 29, 225, 227

Jackson, Andrew, 8-9
Jefferson, Thomas, 8
Jensen, Jay W., 46
Johnson, Lyndon B., 4, 19-20, 82-83, 85-86, 88, 210
Johnson, Nicholas, 61, 66
"journalism of advocacy," 101-103
Journalism Educator, 239
Journalism Monographs, 231, 239
Journalism Quarterly, 26, 231, 239
Judicial Conference of the United States, 17
Justice, Department of, 5-6, 8, 30-31, 33, 43, 56, 71, 162, 225

Kaplan, John, 14
Karafin, Harry, 181, 184
Katzenbach, Nicholas, 129
Kendall, Amos, 8-9
Kennan, Erland A., 211
Kennedy, John F. (see also Oswald, shooting of; Warren Commission), 12-15, 19, 82, 121, 131-134
    assassination of, 12-15, 121, 131-137
Kennedy, Robert F., 17-18, 89
    assassination of, 17-18
Kent State, 92-93, 110, 123, 125
Kent State: What Happened and Why, 124
Kerner Commission report, 48, 113, 126-127, 152, 189
KFBC-TV, 64
KHJ-TV, 64
Khrushchev, Nikita (see also U-2 incident), 81-82, 130-131
Kilpatrick, James J., 43
King, Cecil, 106
King, Martin Luther, 194
Klapper, Joseph T., 174
Klaven, Harry, 199
Klein, Herbert, 3
Knight, John S., 167
Knight newspaper group, 32, 93, 109, 144, 163
Knoll, Erwin, 83
Knopf, Terry Ann, 121-122
Knox, Floyd, 181-182
Kratzke, Edward F., 128

Lambert, Eleanor, 182
Law Enforcement Assistance Administration, 18
Law of Mass Communications, 239
Lawson, Winston G., 133
Lee, Ivy, 86
Lee, Robert E., 63
Levy, H. Phillip, 221
Lewis, Claude, 80
libel, 191-216

license to broadcast, 58, 60-65, 68
    renewal of, 60-65, 68
Life, 30, 71, 153, 197
Lincoln, Abraham, 9
Lindbergh, Charles A., Jr., 14
Lindstrom, Carl E., 178
Lingle, Jake, 181
Lipset, Seymour Martin, 205
Littleton (Colo.) Independent, 237
Lodge, Henry Cabot, 82-83
London Daily Mirror, 106, 221
Long, Huey, 73-74
Long Island University, 185
Los Angeles Times, 3, 32, 48, 90, 125, 151
Louisville Courier Journal, 223, 225
Louisville Times, 54, 225
Lowry, Dennis T., 26
Lukas, J. Anthony, 95, 115

McCarthy, Eugene, 89
McCarthy, Joseph, 8, 11, 102
McCone, John A., 82
McCormick, Robert R., 94, 175
McGaffin, William, 83
McGee, Frank, 81
McGill, Ralph, 139
McGinnis, Joe, 204
McLuhan, Marshall, 104, 208
Making of the President, The, 1968, 89
"managed news," 54-55, 57-77, 80-88, 94
Manson, Charles, 18
March of Dimes, 213
Markel, Lester, 181
Marshall, Thurgood, 36-38
Marth, Del, 226
Mass Communication Law: Cases and Comment, 192, 239
Mass Media and Modern Society, The, 46
Mass Media and Violence, 125, 130, 144, 146, 222-223
Maxwell, W. D., 175
Mecklin, John, 86-87

media review boards, 232-236
Mellett Fund for a Free and Responsible Press, 223, 233
Menninger, W. Walter, 228
Meredith, James, 89, 201
Metromedia, Inc., 144
Meyer, Philip E., 114
Meyer, Sylvan, 185
Miami Herald, 75-76
Miami News, 185
Michener, James, 124
Miller, Jeffrey, 124
Milwaukee Journal, 182
Minow, Newton N., 161
Missett, John Victor, 127-128
Mission in Torment, 87
Mitchell, John, 30, 32, 225-226
Mohr, Charles, 19
Mollenhoff, Clark R., 56-57
Monberg, Helene C., 56
Montgomery, L. D., 136
Moratorium demonstration, 126
Moynihan, Daniel P., 100
Multimedia, 144
multimedia ownership, 141-154, 161
My Lai, 21, 84, 87, 120
Myrdal, Gunnar, 95

Nader, Ralph, 55-56, 71, 173
    report on Freedom of Information
        Act, 55-56
Nation, The, 26
National Academy of Television Arts
    and Sciences, 31
National Advisory Commission on
    Civil Disorders, report of, *see*
    Kerner report
National Aeronautics and Space Administration (NASA), 106, 211-212
National Association of Broadcasters, 65, 230
National Broadcasting Company, 26, 30, 81, 107, 153, 167
National Commission on the Causes
    and Prevention of Violence, 228

National Educational Television, 116, 152
National Foundation, The, 212-214
National Guard, *see* Kent State
National Press Club, 228
National Review, 187
NBC News, 26
Near v. Minnesota, 42
Nelson, Harold L., 239
Newark Evening News, 167
Newark riot, 126-127
new fields of news covrage, 1-2
Newhouse, S. I., 163-164, 166
"new journalism," 98-118
New Republic, The, 84
Newsday, 151
newspaper dailies, decline in number, 157-160
Newspaper Enterprise Association, Inc., 147
newspaper ownership, 155-169
Newspaper Preservation Act of 1970, 162-163
newspapers, joint operating arrangement of, 162-163
Newsweek, 19, 30, 53, 121, 122, 181
New York *Daily News,* 29, 63, 151, 165, 172, 196
New York Herald-Tribune, 3, 105, 147
New York Times (see also *New York Times Co. v. United States;* Pentagon Papers), 2-6, 8-9, 19, 21, 27-29, 31-44, 48, 64, 84, 95-96, 106, 115, 121, 130-131, 140, 144, 149, 151-153, 160, 168, 181, 184-185, 187, 194-195, 200, 202-203, 209
New York Times Co. v. Sullivan, 195-196
New York Times Co. v. United States (*see also* Pentagon Papers), 2-3, 5, 31-43
New York Times Sunday Magazine, 224
New York Tribune, 9

New York Weekly Journal, 194
New York World Journal Tribune,
147-148
Nichols, Alice, 14
Nielsen, A. C., Company, 69
Nieman Reports, 231, 239
Nixon, Raymond B., 158-161, 164
Nixon, Richard M., 1-6, 18, 24-44,
58-59, 66, 84, 90, 94, 100, 103,
126, 197, 210, 226
Northwestern University, 127-128

obscenity, 96
O'Connor, Basil, 212-213
Office of War Information, 102
ombudsmen, 218, 224-226, 231-232
"one-party press," 10-11
Osborne, John, 84
Oswald, Lee Harvey, shooting of, 12-
15, 121, 132-137
Owens, E. E., 176

Pacifica Foundation, 68
Palmer, L. F., Jr., 152
Passaic-Clifton (N.J.) *Herald News,*
182
Pastore, John O., 64
Pauling, Linus, 192, 196-197
Payne, Darwin, 132
Peabody, George Foster, Award, 186
Pearson, Drew, 176
Pennekamp v. Florida, 75-76
Pentagon Papers (see also *New York
Times Company v. United
States*), 3, 5, 8, 19, 31-43, 50-51,
53, 82, 187
Permissible Lie, The, 169
Perry, Mert, 19
Peterson, Theodore, 46
Pew, Thomas, 176
Philadelphia Evening Bulletin, 80, 107
Philadelphia Inquirer, 94-95
Philadelphia Magazine, 181
Phillips, McCandlish, 202-203
pictorial journalism, 119-140

Pipp, Ed, 211
police, 12-13, 17, 30, 80, 129-137
Polk, George, Award, 115, 185
pornography, 68, 72
Postal Service (U.S.) restraints upon
newspapers and magazines, 71-
73
Post-Newsweek Stations, Inc., 64
Powell, Paul, 175
Powers, Francis Gary, *see* U-2 inci-
dent (1960)
Poynter, Nelson, 226
press associations, 146-153
*Press Corps and the Kennedy Assas-
sination, The,* 132
press councils:
British, 220-222
Danish, 220
Swedish, 219-220
Swiss, 220
U.S., 218, 223-224
prime-time programming, 68-69
Project Argus, 44
public relations, 204-216
*Press Council, The: History, Proce-
dure and Cases,* 221-222
Public Relations Journal, 206
Public Relations Society of America,
205-206
Pulitzer Prizes, 87, 89, 95, 115, 174,
176, 186

Quill, The, 145

Race and the News Media, 129
Radio Corporation of America, 167
Rapid Shave commercial, 70-71
Raskin, A. H., 224
Raymond, Henry J., 9
Reader's Digest, 115, 169
Reardon, Paul C., 15
Reddin, Thomas, 18
*Red Lion Broadcasting Co., Inc., v.
FCC,* 67
Redwood City (Calif.) *Tribune,* 112

Reid, Ogden R., 3
Reston, James, 4, 44, 151
Resurrection of Richard Nixon, The, 90
Republican party, 3, 10, 14, 24, 96
right to publish, 3
"Right to Know, to Withhold & to Lie, The," 20-21
Rights in Conflict (see also Democratic convention, 1968), 80, 129
Riordan, James, 96
Rivers, William L., 46, 168
Rivers of Blood, Years of Darkness, 104
RKO General Corporation, 64
Roberson, Abigail M., 193
Romney, George, 90
Roosevelt, Franklin D., 10, 83, 85, 139, 212-213
Roosevelt, Mrs. Franklin D., 81
Roosevelt, Theodore, 9
Rosenbloom v. Metromedia, Inc., 192
Rosenthal, A. M., 115
Rowan, Carl, 152
Royster, Vermont, 138-139
Ruby, Jack, 14
Rusk, Dean, 86

Sabin, Dr. Albert, 214
Sacramento Bee, 178
St. Louis Post-Dispatch, 32
St. Petersburg Evening Independent, 226
St. Petersburg Times, 124, 183-184, 226
Salant, Richard, 26, 116
Salisbury, Harrison E., 20, 131
Salk, Dr. Jonas, 214
San Francisco State College, 125-126
Saturday Evening Post, 172-173, 199-201
Saturday Review, 149, 163
Savage, Jim, 175
Schenck v. United States, 50, 53
Schmidt, Bill, 92

Schramm, Wilbur, 111, 210
Schultz, David N., 112-113
Scribner's Magazine, 141
Scripps-Howard Broadcasting, 143, 163, 166
Seattle Times, 223
"Selling of the Pentagon, The," 6, 31
Selling of the President, 1968, The, 204
Senate, V. S., 59
sensationalism in journalism, 9, 15-16, 104
Shafer, Raymond P., 188
Sheehan, Neil, 19
Sheppard, Sam, 15-16, 75
Shine, Neal, 110
Sigma Delta Chi, 27, 55, 185, 236
Sirhan, Sirhan B., 17-18
Sisco, Joseph J., 153
Small, William A., 162
Smith, Franklin B., 5
Smith, Howard K., 107-108
Stanton, Frank, 6, 23, 31
Stashio, Joseph, 173
State, Department of, 58, 72-73
Steffens, Lincoln, 141
Stein, M. L., 26
Stevenson, Adlai, 10-11
Stevenson, M. W., 134
Stewart, Potter, 2, 33-34, 36, 41, 76-77
"subpoena epidemic," 29-31
Sully, Francois, 19
Sulzberger, Arthur Ochs, 29
Supreme Court, U.S., 2-3, 5, 15-17, 31-43, 51, 53, 59-60, 67, 70-71, 74-77, 83-84, 151, 173, 187, 192-197, 201-202
Swedish National Press Club, 219-220
Sylvester, Arthur, 20
syndicates, 148-153

Tatarian, Roger, 234-235
Tate, Sharon, 18
Taylor, John L., 113-114

Teeter, Dwight L., Jr., 239
Thirty-Eight Witnesses, 115
Time, 19, 30, 101, 116, 144, 157, 181, 204, 215
Time, Inc., 167, 197, 199
Time, Inc., v. Hill, 192, 197-199
Time-Life Broadcasting, 143
Times Mirror Company, 142, 144
Tobin, Richard L., 149
Trial of Jack Ruby, The, 14
Triangle Publications, Inc., 166
Troy, Frosty, 139
Troy (Ohio) News, 176
Truman, Harry, 86
Tucson Daily Citizen, 162-163
Tucson Newspapers, Inc. (TNI), 162-163
Tucson Star, 162-163
Tulsa Tribune, 139
TV Guide, see Annenberg, Walter H.
"Two Worlds of Linda Fitzpatrick, The," 115

underground press, 109
University of Georgia, 186, 199
University of Mississippi, 201
United Press International, 19, 27, 113-114, 122, 146-150, 159, 168, 176, 234
U-2 incident, 81-82

Valley Daily News, 124
Van den Haag, Ernest, 205
Van Doren, Mark, 205
Variety, 65
Vecchio, Mary, 125
Vietnam, 5, 19-21, 24, 29, 33, 38, 80, 82, 84, 87, 90, 120-121, 210
Voice of America, 188

Wade, Henry, 133-134
Waist-High Culture, The, 101
Walker, Edwin, 201

Walker, Stanley, 105
Wall Street Journal, 138, 160, 163, 168, 172, 175, 180, 203
Waltz, Jon R., 14
Waring, Houstoun, 237
Warren Commission, 12-14, 23, 131-137
Warren, Earl, 12, 70
Warren, Samuel D., 193
Washington (D.C.) Evening Star, 64
Washington News Committee, see Associated Press Managing Editors
Washington, George, 8
Washington Post, 4-5, 8, 27-29, 32-34, 37, 42, 103, 122, 123, 151, 160, 168, 187, 218, 223, 225-226, 228
Waterbury (Conn.) Republic, 181
Watts riots, 104-105
WBBM-TV, 127-128
Weathermen, 30
Webster, Noah, 8
Western Papers, 56
WGCB, 67
WGN, 166
WHDH, 62-64
Wheeler-Lea Amendment of 1938, 70
White, Byron R., 35, 41-42
White, Theodore H., 89
White, William Allen, 174
Wiggins, J. Russell, 103, 228
Wilkins, Roy, 152
Wilson, Woodrow, 9-10
Winchell, Walter, 212-213
Witcover, Jules, 3, 90
WMAL-TV, 64
Women's Wear Daily, 182
WPIX, 63-64, 166
Wrigley, Tom, 213
WTOP, 64

Yalta Papers, 44
Yoder, Norman, 188
Yorty, Samuel, 17-18

AP

N
i

DE

01